THE PREHISTORY OF NORTH CAROLINA
An Archaeological Symposium

The Prehistory of North Carolina

An Archaeological Symposium

Contributors
**DAVID SUTTON PHELPS
H. TRAWICK WARD
BURTON L. PURRINGTON
JOFFRE L. COE**

Edited By
**MARK A. MATHIS
JEFFREY J. CROW**

NORTH CAROLINA DIVISION OF ARCHIVES AND HISTORY
Department of Cultural Resources
1983

MARK A. MATHIS is a staff archaeologist with the Archaeology Branch, Archaeology and Historic Preservation Section, North Carolina Division of Archives and History.

JEFFREY J. CROW is the administrator of the Historical Publications Section, North Carolina Division of Archives and History.

Front Cover: The Frutchey Mound (Town Creek Temple Mound), prior to excavation. Photograph by Joffre L. Coe, 1937.
Back Cover: The Frutchey Mound, reconstructed. Town Creek Indian Mound State Historic Site, Mt. Gilead, North Carolina. Photograph by Linda J. Eure, 1983.

Cover layout and artwork by Margaret B. Pierce and Mark A. Mathis

COPYRIGHT © 1983, BY THE NORTH CAROLINA DIVISION OF ARCHIVES AND HISTORY, DEPARTMENT OF CULTURAL RESOURCES.
ALL RIGHTS RESERVED.

Printed by UNIVERSITY GRAPHICS, INC.
North Carolina State University
Raleigh

NORTH CAROLINA DIVISION OF ARCHIVES AND HISTORY
Department of Cultural Resources
109 East Jones Street
Raleigh, North Carolina 27611

To the memory of
David A. McLean
Peter P. Cooper II
L. Jill Loucks

CONTENTS

List of Contributors ix
Foreword xi
Preface xiii

1. Archaeology of the North Carolina Coast and Coastal Plain: Problems and Hypotheses
DAVID SUTTON PHELPS

Introduction 1
The Coastal Plain Environment 2
History of Research in the Coastal Plain 6
    The First Generation 7
    The Period of Modern Research 8
    Impact of the Third Generation 12
Culture History: An Initial Model 15
    Spatial and Temporal Dimensions 15
    The Paleo-Indian Period 18
    The Archaic Period 22
    Emergence of the Regions 26
    The Woodland Period 27
Conclusions 49

2. A Review of Archaeology in the North Carolina Piedmont: A Study of Change
H. TRAWICK WARD

Introduction 53
The Piedmont Environment 53
Early Work in the Piedmont 57
The Current State of the Art 61
    Paleo-Indian Period 63
    Archaic Period 65
    Woodland Period 70
Problem Areas: An Overview 76
Conclusions 80

3. Ancient Mountaineers: An Overview of the Prehistoric Archaeology of North Carolina's Western Mountain Region
BURTON L. PURRINGTON

Introduction 83
The Natural Environment 88
History of Investigations 98
Cultural Sequence and Suggested Research Questions 102
    Pre-Paleo-Indian 107
    Paleo-Indian 107

Archaic Period 110
Woodland Period 131
Mississippian Period 142
Conclusions 152
Assessment of Significance in the Appalachian Summit 152
A General Research Design for the Appalachian Summit Region 158

4. Through a Glass Darkly: An Archaeological View of North Carolina's More Distant Past
JOFFRE L. COE

Introduction 161
Search for Identity 162
Foundation Building 165
Explanation and Frustration 173

References *178*
Index *195*

LIST OF CONTRIBUTORS

David Sutton Phelps, Department of Sociology, Anthropology and Economics, East Carolina University, Greenville, North Carolina 27334

H. Trawick Ward, Research Laboratories of Anthropology, University of North Carolina, Chapel Hill, North Carolina 27514

Burton L. Purrington, Center for Archaeological Research, Southwest Missouri State University, Springfield, Missouri 65802

Joffre L. Coe, Department of Anthropology, University of North Carolina, Chapel Hill, North Carolina 27514

FOREWORD

> A rock pile ceases to be a rock pile the moment a single man contemplates it, bearing within him the image of a cathedral.
>
> *Antoine de Saint-Exupery*

Any scholarly, scientific endeavor requires communication as a key to success. This is particularly true of archaeology, whose shifting currents of method and theory are espoused almost daily in journals, books, graduate theses and dissertations. As indicated by Joffre L. Coe, in succeeding pages, there is indeed a great deal already written about the prehistory of North Carolina. However, much of this information, particularly the more recent, has not been distributed on a broad scale; nor has it been aimed at the general public. Much of this data has remained in university libraries, on the bookshelves of teachers and students, or has been given ephemeral exposure in spoken presentations. While available to the public, most were known only to professional archaeologists and their students. And, there has been less than a full measure of effort given to creating a tangible synthesis of the state's past for the interested lay public.

The expert authors of this volume give the needed synthesis of their work as well as that of students and other professionals. No unified ideology or single school of thought pervades their approaches. Each author's professional training, as well as themes in the history of American archaeology, is reflected in what is said and what is emphasized. Perceptive readers may find gaps, discrepancies, and contradictions. These can be rectified only through further research and recurrent attempts to communicate and synthesize.

This volume is intended as only the first by the North Carolina Division of Archives and History to achieve two primary goals: to foster an integrated and updated knowledge of the prehistoric past; and, to expand public awareness and concern for a part of the state's past, the existence of which is threatened each day. This is a mandated, but also self-selected role which can be well-served by the archaeological programs of the Division.

Cathedrals are not built by the efforts of one person. Moreover, in archaeology, rockpiles are approached differently and the intended "cathedrals" are often as variable as the number of observers. We must hasten our efforts to protect and preserve archaeological remains and to learn about the past. We must hasten in the proper direction at the same time. The succeeding pages reflect the efforts of many to tell us more while providing that direction.

Thomas D. Burke
Chief Archaeologist
Archaeology Branch
Division of Archives and History

PREFACE

For well over a century archaeologists—amateur and professional alike—have explored the countryside searching for bits and pieces of North Carolina's distant past. Such artifacts have stirred investigators' imaginations and have given rise to many tales and theories about the people who created the artifacts, about the ways in which tools and implements were made and utilized, and about how the makers lived and died. Much of what has been told and written has represented high standards of scientific inquiry; but much has been little more than uninformed speculation. To separate fact from fiction in prehistory requires more than just a fertile imagination; it requires a knowledge of physical and cultural processes and of the relationships between material culture—artifacts—and human behavior.

Such is the role of the professional archaeologist and the purpose of archaeological research, and to these ends the essays in this volume were written. The essays published here serve at least two purposes. First, they reflect the status of archaeological studies and knowledge in North Carolina in the 1980s. Second, just as importantly, they synthesize the archaeological work conducted in North Carolina since the late nineteenth century and document the first uncertain efforts to identify, interpret, and understand North Carolina's prehistory. Consequently, this volume provides a context for understanding and interpreting the past. The essays summarize what has been done, what is being done, and what the professional archaeologists in the state currently know about the prehistoric past.

That this volume exists reflects in part the changing nature and role of archaeology in contemporary American culture. Archaeological sites are often, and rightfully so, referred to as "nonrenewable resources." Once a site has been disturbed or destroyed it cannot be replaced. The information that site may have contained—the story it had to tell about the past—is lost forever. Yet each year hundreds of sites are destroyed under the pressures of economic growth and development. With the construction of new housing developments, highways, and other land-clearing and ground-disturbing projects, the number of archaeological sites diminishes. The looting of artifacts from many of North Carolina's most important sites has also contributed to the loss of information about prehistory. The danger of continued site destruction is that a time may come when there will be no prehistoric archaeological sites left to study.

Recognition of this danger has led to the passage of many laws, rules, and regulations designed to identify and protect archaeological sites. But legislation provides protection for only a small portion of the archaeological resources. Most sites receive no professional attention prior to their destruction. The rate of site destruction is so great that every threatened site cannot be afforded equal protection or investigation. Thus, decisions must be made as to which sites are to receive attention, which are to be preserved, and which are to be excavated. These are difficult decisions, requiring that each site threatened be evaluated in terms of its historical significance and research potential.

The type of protective attention an archaeological site receives often depends upon whether or not it is eligible for inclusion in the National Register of Historic Places, administered by the U.S. Department of the Interior. An archaeological site, and particularly prehistoric sites, are considered eligible for the Register if they have yielded or have the potential to yield information deemed important to an understanding of prehistory or history. In determining a site's significance the archaeologist confronts practical problems as well as professional concerns. Not only may the archaeologist's decision directly affect the continued existence of the site, but it may entail the expenditure of substantial amounts of time and money. The decision, therefore, must be founded in a comprehensive knowledge and understanding of what makes an archaeological site important. The archaeologist must place the site within a context of what is already known about the time periods, cultures, materials, and locational situation represented by the site. Given the appropriate context, the archaeologist is better able to evaluate the potential yield of information from and relative significance of the site and in turn decide whether it is actually worth the expense of research or preservation efforts. The essays contained in this volume should prove a valuable source of information for any archaeologist faced with such decisions, for the contributors offer the foundations upon which contexts for archaeological research are built.

These four essays are expanded versions of papers presented at a symposium held on March 28, 1980, in Raleigh, North Carolina. The symposium was sponsored jointly by the North Carolina Division of Archives and History and the North Carolina Archaeological Council and was intended to be the first step in the development of a comprehensive overview of North Carolina's prehistory. In this initial step, the essays deal with broad regional perspectives. The first three essays, by David S. Phelps, H. Trawick Ward, and Burton L. Purrington, deal with the archaeology of the three major physiographic regions of the state—the Coastal Plain (Phelps), the Piedmont (Ward), and the Mountains (Purrington). While much of the information presented in the essays has been synthesized from other written works, each also contains important new information, collected and analyzed by the authors themselves. Consequently, this volume goes beyond a simple summary of past archaeological studies. It contributes new insights into North Carolina's prehistoric past, while presenting important refinements to some of the cultural sequences and artifact typologies. The volume should thus prove useful to both the amateur and the professional archaeologist.

The final paper in the volume is by Joffre L. Coe, whose career and experience in North Carolina archaeology span a period of nearly fifty years. His contributions to our understanding of North Carolina prehistory and to the field of archaeology in general are well known to both his colleagues and the interested public. In his paper Coe takes a critical and sometimes whimsical look at the history and future of archaeology in North Carolina and offers several insightful comments on the first three papers. His paper alone will stand as an important reference for anyone interested in the beginnings and development of archaeology in the state.

The Prehistory of North Carolina: An Archaeological Symposium was the brainchild of many people, although most of the credit must go to Larry E. Tise, former director of the North Carolina Division of Archives and History, and Jacqueline R. Fehon, former chief archaeologist, Archaeology Branch, Division of Archives and History. Their contributions to the state's archaeological program, not just the concept of the symposium, long will be appreciated.

In addition to the four principal participants in the symposium, introductory remarks and comments were provided by Sara W. Hodgkins, secretary of the Department of Cultural Resources; Michael Hammond, then chairman of the Governor's Archaeological Advisory Committee; and the late David A. McLean, then the chairman of the North Carolina Archaeological Council. Their participation contributed to the success of the symposium.

Arrangements for the symposium, including everything from finding slide projectors to designing announcements, were coordinated or accomplished directly by Carol S. Spears and Jacqueline R. Fehon, although many members of the Division of Archives and History staff provided able assistance.

As is frequently the case in such endeavors, editing this volume is the product of the energies of more than just the two names on the title page. Portions of the various drafts of the manuscripts were reviewed, commented on, and proofed by David A. McLean, Jacqueline R. Fehon, Thomas H. Hargrove, Thomas D. Burke, Dolores A. Hall, Patricia R. Johnson, Jan-Michael Poff, Carol S. Spears, John W. Clauser, David G. Moore, Stephen R. Claggett, Susan G. Myers, Catherine E. Bollinger, Thomas E. Scheitlin, and, of course, the authors themselves. Lucille L. Walker typed and retyped parts of the manuscripts. Margaret B. Pierce produced artwork for the cover and for portions of the text. With few exceptions, the figures in the papers were prepared by the authors. Indexing for the volume was done by Robert G. Ferris. We would also like to thank

William S. Price, Jr., director of the Division of Archives and History, for his encouragement and interest in seeing this volume published, and John J. Little, administrator of the Archaeology and Historic Preservation Section, who helped us find the money to have it printed.

Last, but by no means least, we extend our deepest appreciation to the authors—David S. Phelps, H. Trawick Ward, Burton L. Purrington, and Joffre L. Coe. It is only through their years of dedication to the study of North Carolina's prehistory that this volume is possible.

Mark A. Mathis

Jeffrey J. Crow

1

Archaeology of the North Carolina Coast and Coastal Plain: Problems and Hypotheses

David Sutton Phelps

INTRODUCTION

The North Carolina Coastal Plain has been the least known archaeological region of the state, has received less professional attention, and supported fewer projects than other regions until very recently. For that reason I have chosen to present this summary in a "traditional" format, as some of my colleagues call it, rather than to randomly select specific methodological and cultural problems from the existing literature. I make no apologies for this choice since the concept of this symposium arose, in part, from the need to determine the significance of archaeological sites, a determination that cannot be accomplished, regardless of how well preserved their context, without a basic understanding of the cultural matrix in which the sites belong. As applied here, "traditional" refers to the descriptive level of archaeological studies, or cultural-historical integration (Willey and Phillips 1962:5). By that definition it primarily addresses two of the three acknowledged objectives of contemporary archaeology (Thomas 1979:137-138), construction of a cultural chronology and reconstruction of extinct lifeways, while contributing less to the explanation of cultural processes, the third objective. Just as one cannot accurately describe muscular anatomy and the processes of movement when learning to walk, valid explanations of cultural processes must be preceded by adequate chronologies and a knowledge of culture history. While the Coastal Plain is not quite "pristine," as Thomas (1979:138) describes areas totally lacking in previous archaeological research, it is one of many regions in North America for which there has been insufficient basic data because of the paucity of sustained research.

No comprehensive chronology or culture history for the Coastal Plain has been proposed, and recent regional summaries prepared for the *Northeast* volume of the *Handbook of North American Indians* (Trigger 1978) reflect this lacuna, as only a handful of studies available at the time of preparation (1972-1974) were cited in the publication. Reasons for this lag in archaeological knowledge of the Coastal Plain become quite clear when the history of research is reviewed, but this is no solution to the problem. The major content of this paper, then, is an initial model of culture history for the region, fraught with all of the inadequacies of current data, but offered as a basis for future work. Without such a framework, future basic research will be impeded, many of the ever increasing number of environmental archaeological projects will continue to result in accumulations of noncontextual data, and no true management of cultural resources will ensue. Moreover, the significance of sites proposed for nomination to the National Register of Historic Places presumes knowledge of how each articulates within current cultural models and what benefit will accrue from a particular site's preservation or excavation. If there is no cultural framework in which the site can be validly placed, it follows that problems that might be answered can hardly be identified. A more pressing need, however, is a continuity of basic archaeological research designed to refine the cultural-historical model and answer specific problems of cultural form and process. It is this type of research that provides the cultural matrix for the random data from environmental impact projects.

The following sections of this work discuss the complex natural environment that nurtured human societies, the history of archaeological research, and the culture history of the Coastal Plain as it is currently known. Dispersed throughout these sections are the numerous existing problems of cultural interpretation, description and analysis, and the hypotheses that can be formulated within the limitations of current data.

THE COASTAL PLAIN ENVIRONMENT

The province of the North Carolina Coastal Plain, as we know it today, has a general configuration characteristic of only the last 5000 years. Many changes have taken place throughout its geologic and climatic history, some of which have left their evidence on the landscape while others have been obliterated. Changes during the late Pleistocene and Holocene geological epochs are those particularly pertinent to the currently known interval of man's existence in the region.

The present Coastal Plain province (Figure 1.1) includes two physiographic regions, the Tidewater and the Inner Coastal Plain (Stuckey 1965:6). The Suffolk Scarp, a remnant beach line of the Sangamon Interglacial sea stand some 100,000 years ago, marks the boundary between the two regions (Bellis et al. 1975: 15-16). East of the scarp is the Pamlico Terrace of marine sediments, deposited during the Sangamon Interglacial, which form the Tidewater region. West of the scarp lies the Talbot Terrace of marine sands and clays laid down on the Inner Coastal Plain during the earlier interglacial sea stand.

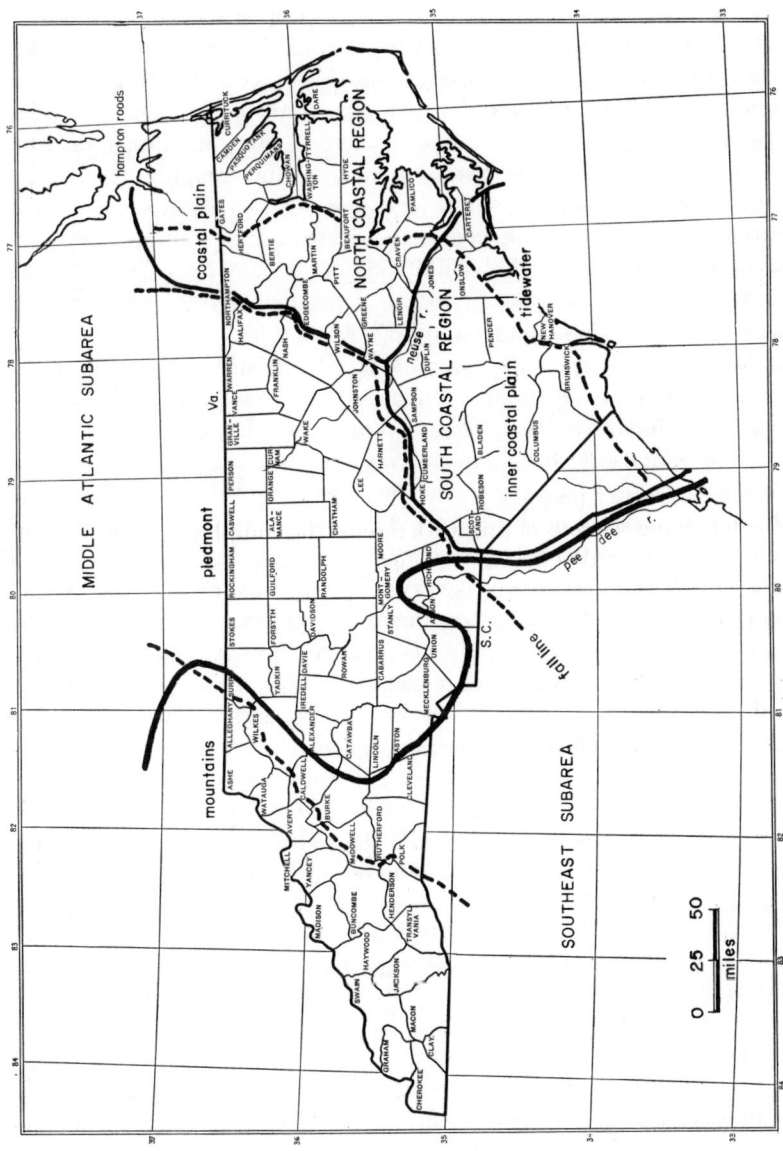

FIGURE 1.1. Physiographic and cultural divisions of the North Carolina Coastal Plain.

The Tidewater region, including one of the world's more complex coastlines, begins with a fragile line of barrier islands separating the Atlantic Ocean from the sounds of the interior. These islands, collectively called the Outer Banks, constantly change in response to the processes of wind and wave erosion, sedimentary deposition, tidal action, and changes in sea level. Inlets through the barrier islands shift continually, even in the face of attempts to stabilize them by the most advanced technology, and necessarily exist to provide discharge outlets for the numerous river systems. The surface of the barrier islands is sand, ranging in elevation from sea level to dunes over 100 feet high. Various coastal grasses and maritime forests of live oak, cedar, and other species stabilize some sections of the islands, particularly on the sound side, and provide humic soils to cover the dunes. Organic soils are deposited in the few freshwater ponds that have formed in topographic lows on the wider sections of some islands. In a few areas on the sound side of the Outer Banks and on the larger islands behind the barrier, such as Colington and Roanoke, typical oak-hickory climax forests are found. Where these have been cut over the years, secondary pine forests now dominate.

Behind the Outer Banks in the northern section of the Tidewater is the vast, shallow expanse of the sounds. The largest sounds, Albemarle and Pamlico, are the estuaries of the major river systems that dissect the Coastal Plain. Some of these river systems, such as the Chowan and its tributaries, have their headwaters in the Coastal Plain, while others rise from Piedmont (Tar, Neuse, and Cape Fear rivers) or Mountain (Roanoke River) watersheds. Marshes flank the shores of the estuarine zone, and the mainland is an area of nearly level upland sandy and loamy soils (Tant et al. 1974) interspersed with numerous swamps, shallow lakes, and bogs or pocosins. With the exception of the Cape Fear, no major rivers traverse the southern section of the Tidewater region, and thus no development of broad estuaries has occurred. Instead, the southern Tidewater region is narrow (Figure 1.1), and the small barrier islands closely parallel the mainland shore. Geological studies have shown that this difference in the northern and southern estuarine zones results from the fact that the southern coast is tectonically rising while the northern coast, from Cape Lookout northward, is subsiding (Riggs and O'Connor 1975:3).

The Inner Coastal Plain is a region of gently sloping sandy and loamy uplands dissected by the major rivers and their tributaries, which in this region have well developed, broad floodplains. Elevation increases from around 50 feet at the Tidewater boundary to heights between 300 to 700 feet along the western margin. Large swamps and pocosins are found across the Inner Coastal Plain but are more frequent in the southern section. The numerous, enigmatic oval and elliptical shallow lakes and swamps known as the "Carolina Bays" (Stuckey 1965:13) are widely scattered across the region. Oak-hickory and pine forest types dominate the uplands of the mainland section of the Tidewater and the Inner Coastal Plain while gum, cypress, pond pine, and other species are found in the stream floodplains, swamps, and pocosins.

Food resources are varied and abundant in the region, and evidence from the archaeological record is now revealing a wide exploitation of these resources by prehistoric cultures. From the coast to the fall line, the deciduous forests produced hickory nuts, acorns, and walnuts; these with the pine and swamp forests furnished abundant wood for cultural purposes and harbored varied faunal communities of mammals, reptiles, and birds. Numerous edible plants were available, and with the advent of agriculture the arable sandy loam uplands became prime crop-bearing lands. The rivers, estuaries, and ocean provided fish and shellfish in ample supply. Such an environment existed in the Coastal Plain no earlier than 6000 B.C. and represents the end result of a series of climate changes.

Pollen cores from the Dismal Swamp in the northern Coastal Plain of North Carolina and Virginia, and other locations in the southern Coastal Plain, have demonstrated a series of climate changes from the late Pleistocene to the present. As summarized by Whitehead (1972:213), a boreal pine-spruce forest type covered the Coastal Plain until about 8000 B.C. followed by a transition to a white pine-hemlock-northern hardwood (beech, maple) type. This was replaced beginning at about 6000 B.C. by the current oak-hickory climax type of the uplands and the gum-cypress communities in wet areas. Faunal communities associated with these forest types underwent similar changes from the Pleistocene into modern times.

Sea level has also changed in response to climate and other processes, from a low of about 300 feet below the present stand around 18,000 years ago during the final stage of the Wisconsin glacial. Since that time, the sea level has been rising, although fluctuations have been recorded, and still continues at a rate of 0.5 to 1.5 feet per century (Bellis et al. 1975:13). The significance of this for the archaeological record is that successive erosion and drowning of the shoreline from the late Pleistocene onward have obliterated the coastal sites of early cultural stages, and even the evidence of riverine sites in what was once the Coastal Plain is submerged beneath the estuaries. Severe erosion continues to take its toll as the sea transgresses, now affecting the late prehistoric sites as well as modern activities and construction.

The modern Coastal Plain has been modified by human cultures since the earliest occupation, but most changes have occurred in the last 300 years. Land use throughout most of the region is dominated by agriculture, a use that destroys evidence of archaeological sites slowly but continuously. In the Coastal Plain those areas that are now prime farmland, the upland sandy loams, were also the chosen locales for prehistoric agricultural activities and sites and were selected by preagricultural cultures for other reasons. Since these upland areas, long cleared of vegetation, have experienced little soil accretion and continuous disturbance from component after component, little remains in many sites except a "horizontal stratigraphy" of subsurface features. Deeply stratified sites may be encountered on river levees and bank ridges that have not been farmed, but they are rare on the higher, long utilized elevations. Other modern cultural practices, such as the "borrowing" of prehistoric shell middens for agricultural lime and road beds, have also seriously altered the cultural resource base.

It is normal in the history of man for each generation to obliterate some or all of the evidence of previous ones, and the North Carolina Coastal Plain is no exception to this process. This vast, complex natural province has supported man and his culture for at least 12,000 years, but it has seen archaeologists only occasionally during the past century.

HISTORY OF RESEARCH IN THE COASTAL PLAIN

The history of archaeological research in the North Carolina Coastal Plain is analagous to three generations of scholars, each reflecting the research goals, level of methodological sophistication and theories of its time. But unlike normal generational sequences that accrue information passed either genetically or socially, each generation of archaeological researchers seems to have taken its own direction, ignoring clues and problems posed by the preceding work. There have, of course, been exceptions to this pattern, and the slow development of archaeology in the region has been due in large measure to (1) the paucity of archaeological personnel and facilities in, or with an active interest in, the Coastal Plain; (2) the absence of research continuity; (3) the narrowly defined research designs and goals of many projects; and (4) the disproportionate amount of time spent on environmental or contract archaeology as opposed to basic cultural research in the last few years. The cumulative result of previous work leaves us in the unenviable position of attempting cultural synthesis and explanation while still accumulating data on the classificatory-descriptive level necessary for sound cultural-historical models.

The three generations of research include an initial period of precursory descriptive investigations in the late nineteenth and early twentieth centuries, a second period of academic-based archaeology beginning in the 1930s but not gaining impetus until the 1970s, and a final period initiated in 1974 with a new generation of environmental impact archaeology. The latter two generations continue contemporaneously, often taking diverse and noncomplementary directions.

The First Generation

The first generation addressed two problems, one current throughout American archaeology in the late nineteenth century, and the other a perennial local problem, still unsolved.

The first problem, that of the controversy surrounding the "Mound Builders" of eastern North America, was laid to rest by Cyrus Thomas in 1894, but not before the preceding half-century of argument had stimulated an effort to locate and study burial and platform mounds throughout the area (Willey and Sabloff 1974:43-58). Two studies addressed that problem in the South Coastal region of North Carolina. The first of these was an account of burial mounds examined by J. A. Holmes (1883) in Duplin, Sampson, Robeson, Cumberland, and southern Wake counties and a listing of other such sites reported to him but not directly observed. Holmes described the mounds as being constructed of sand mounded to a maximum height of 3 to 4 feet above the surrounding terrain and containing mass secondary burials as well as occasional primary inhumations and cremations. Occasionally, artifacts accompanied burials but were more frequently found scattered in the mound fill or in caches. Charles Peabody's (1910) report on the excavation of a similar mound near Hope Mills in Cumberland County concluded the interest in these burial mounds for the moment. Both of these reports followed the standard descriptive format of the time, without speculation on temporal placement or comparison with other such manifestations.

A third bit of research during this initial period was stimulated by a still current, unsolved problem in coastal North Carolina, the disappearance of Sir Walter Raleigh's "Lost Colony." The colonists abandoned Roanoke Island in 1587, culminating a four-year period (1584-1587) of exploration and colonization, the first such attempt by the English (Corbitt 1953; Quinn 1955). The tercentennial recognition of those events generated considerable interest and the eventual dedication of a commemorative marker at the site of Fort Raleigh, which the settlers had erected to protect the ill-fated colony (Peele 1907:283-291). A number of popular articles and scholarly papers resulted from the renewed interest, among which was one describing the location and investigation of archaeological sites possibly contemporary with or related to the Lost Colony. Talcott Williams, the author, described four sites or areas on Roanoke Island, excavated test trenches in at least one site, and speculated upon the location of the village established by Raleigh's colonists (Williams 1896:47-61). Williams was sufficiently knowledgeable to distinguish differences in the surface finishes on prehistoric ceramics and basically correlated these with stratigraphy exposed by erosion on the north end of the island. In one of his test excavations he exposed a mass burial in what he believed to be an artificial "mound" on a sand ridge near Alder Branch and described shell midden at the south end of Roanoke Island. Neither of these sites received further professional attention until the 1970s.

The Period of Modern Research

The second generation of archaeological research began after a quarter-century hiatus, with the establishment of the archaeological program at the University of North Carolina at Chapel Hill. In the mid-1930s archaeology had begun the trend toward the more sophisticated professionalism directly responsible for the current state of the art, and from the beginning a set of research goals for North Carolina was perceived by Joffre Coe, who initiated and has guided research toward those goals ever since. Coe's strategy, developed during those years, was to investigate North Carolina on a regional basis using the direct historical approach based on ethnohistoric data in order to construct sound regional sequences. Initial work began in the Piedmont and eventually resulted in the publication of a basic regional model (Coe 1962; 1964). Attention then shifted toward the mountains, but the Coastal Plain remained unattended. For purposes of the broader plan, however, a statewide survey was initiated, and site data were accumulated for all regions from the 1930s onward, so that for each region some data existed to formulate pertinent questions and to design research when funds were available for projects. Coastal Plain studies by students of Coe were initiated from the basic site data accumulated over the years. Recent archaeological programs established at the regional universities have also benefited from this data base.

Between 1944 and 1953 four publications appeared that summarized the available ethnographic and ethnohistoric data for the Coastal Plain. Swanton's summary works for the Southeast (Swanton 1946) and North America (Swanton 1952) include descriptions of the locations, culture, and linguistic affiliation of most of the Coastal Plain populations. While many of Swanton's assignments and conclusions remain doubtful, the summarized references and information did provide a platform from which the direct historical approach in archaeological studies could be launched. Of greater value and depth was Maurice Mook's (1944) detailed study of the Carolina Algonkians. Mook utilized the English accounts of the exploratory period (Corbitt 1953), because, as he said, "Other than by the use of archaeological methods it is impossible to come nearer to the aboriginal situation in precontact times in this area than by study of White's drawings and the written records of 1585-1590" (Mook 1944:182). From the historic records he delineated the area occupied by these most southerly Algonkian-speaking societies, described their cultures, compared them with their neighbors, and traced them through the period of English colonization to extinction and absorption. After noting that Speck (1916) could elicit no memory of history or custom from the acculturated remnants of the Machapunga, Mook proposed: "Archaeological excavation and the study of documentary sources remain the only methods by which ethnic history can be investigated in this important area of aboriginal America" (Mook 1944:225).

The fourth study summarized the historic documents available on the Tuscarora, the other major group in the northern Coastal Plain, from the time of the Tuscarora War (1711-1714) to their final migration to New York (Paschal 1953).

In the period following World War II, the first major archaeological projects in the Coastal Plain were initiated in conjunction with development of the Fort Raleigh National Historic site on Roanoke Island and the Cape Hatteras National Seashore. The work at Fort Raleigh, directed by J. C. Harrington of the National Park Service from 1947 to 1953, was designed to excavate and reconstruct the fort and locate any other evidence of the settlement around it (Harrington 1962). The first goal was achieved, but the second met with little success; in the process, however, Harrington did uncover some evidence of Algonkian use of the fort area after the disappearance of the English colony in 1587.

Development of the Cape Hatteras National Seashore in the 1950s resulted in an extensive archaeological survey of the Tidewater region by William Haag in 1954-1955. Supported by funding from the Office of Naval Research, the study had two goals: one was to find the Lost Colony, which was not achieved; the other was "to delve into the Indian past and reconstruct an occupation of the region from earliest times until the dispersal of Indian Culture by white men" (Haag 1958:1-2).

During a brief visit in the summer of 1954 and a full summer of research in 1955, Haag and an assistant surveyed a number of miles of coastline from the Neuse estuary northward to the Virginia border, a quite formidable undertaking in the short time allotted. The work resulted in recording and collecting the surface of 81 sites, the majority of which were on Hatteras, Roanoke, Bodie, and Colington islands, the lower Currituck peninsula, and along the shores of the Pamlico estuary. A few sites were tested without clear stratigraphic results. The survey was by no means a comprehensive study of the traditional Algonkian homeland.

Perhaps the most important contribution of the Haag study was the rudimentary chronology based on seriation of ceramics into an Early Period of sand-tempered ware just prior to A.D. 1000, a Middle Period characterized by the grit- (sand and grit) tempered, cord-marked, fabric-impressed, and net-impressed ware, and a Late Period (A.D. 1500-1585) in which shell-tempered ware with fabric-impressed and simple stamped-surface finishes were present (Haag 1958:126-133). It should be remembered that this work was conducted at a time when most archaeological chronologies were slanted toward the recent; radiocarbon dating was just beginning to emerge at that time, and its impact on the earlier relative chronologies would not be fully realized until the 1960s. For all of its limitations, Haag's study laid a groundwork for future research and has remained the oft-cited and only major study in the North Coastal region to the present time.

The next study of importance was only peripherally applicable to the Coastal Plain. In 1956 the University of North Carolina conducted a survey of the Roanoke Rapids reservoir and salvaged sites prior to construction of the Virginia Electric and Power Company facilities and dam just above the fall line of the Roanoke River. This work, summarized by Coe (1964:84-119), provided a sequence for the northeastern Piedmont from Middle Archaic times to the Protohistoric period. Radiocarbon dates for the Middle and Late Archaic periods were obtained, and a ceramic sequence for three Woodland phases (Vincent-Clements-Gaston) was developed. The Woodland sequence suffered from a time lag similar to Haag's periods but nevertheless offered stratigraphic comparative material for the inner section of the Coastal Plain.

The decade of the 1960s witnessed the publication of one hallmark study, a proposed ceramic sequence, and a reinvestigation of the burial mound problem in the southern Coastal Plain, as well as a number of miscellaneous studies.

First accomplished was South's survey of the southern coast of North Carolina and adjacent South Carolina, a project conceived to provide a broader range of material for establishing relationships between Brunswick Town State Historic Site and the surrounding area and to fill in a gap between Haag's work to the north and the Savannah River local sequence developed earlier to the south. Keying on ethnohistoric cultural differences reported for the northern (Algonkian) and southern (Siouan) coast areas, South proceeded to collect and analyze a moderate ceramic sample that did indicate differences, as well as some similarities, between the two localities. Although carried out in 1960, the formal published version of this study appeared in 1976 (South 1976), by that time slightly modified to incorporate more recent data and a more comprehensive ceramic taxonomy for the South Carolina coast. While not yet submitted to the test of firm stratigraphic relationships, the proposed sequence does provide a base for future research designs to assay its accuracy.

The hallmark study, appearing in 1964, was the masterful stratigraphic record reconstructed by Coe (1964) for the Piedmont region. While the Woodland phases of the sequences are specific to the Piedmont, the Paleo-Indian and Archaic period phases apply not only to the Coastal Plain and Mountain regions of North Carolina but to much of the eastern United States south of the Ohio Valley (cf. Funk 1978).

A brief revival of interest in burial mounds in the southern Coastal Plain occurred in the early 1960s with the excavation of the McLean mound by Howard MacCord, an amateur working under the guidance of Coe. While the study was not directly stimulated by the earlier work of Holmes and Peabody, MacCord did discuss these works briefly in his site report (MacCord 1966), speculate on the distribution and temporal placement of such sites, and construct comparative trait lists. Two other burial mound excavations (South 1966; Keel 1970), both exploratory rather than comprehensive, occurred during this time but added little more than expanded spatial distribution to the earlier study.

The "new archaeology" may have been spawned on the upper tributaries of the Chowan River by Binford's (1964a) study of the protohistoric groups who occupied the North Carolina-Virginia border area of the Coastal Plain. Relying almost entirely on previously published environmental and ethnohistoric data, the study utilized small archaeological sampling areas in the traditional territories occupied in the protohistoric period by the Meherrin, Nottoway, and Wyanoke tribes. Hypothetical cultural models were constructed on the basis of ethnohistoric descriptions and surface collections from 50 sites, a very small sample along three major rivers and their tributaries. More recent projects in the same locality report discrepancies in the data recorded by Binford (Hall 1979:69) and cast doubt on some of his interpretations (Smith 1971:24).

A final study of the 1960s decade was the site survey along the Neuse River in Lenoir and portions of adjacent counties by Crawford (1966), which provided data for the master's thesis. While somewhat useful in a local sense, the typology and seriation developed in the study will require extensive correlation with other localities.

In 1970 the available data base, cited in the preceding passages, was meager, at best; there was no regional chronological framework beyond those suggested by Haag and South on the basis of their ceramic seriations of surface collections; no sites other than Fort Raleigh and a few burial mounds in the southern Coastal Plain had sustained major professional excavation; some sites had been tested; and only a few Coastal Plain counties had more than a handful of sites recorded. Ethnohistoric studies had been accomplished, but few archaeologists had attempted to extend this knowledge backward in time. There was certainly no lack of problems to solve.

A new era of second generation research in North Carolina began with the establishment of the archaeological programs at many regional universities of the University of North Carolina system and some private schools during the 1970s. For the first time since the 1930s there was more than one professional archaeologist interested in and actively researching the state's past. In the Coastal Plain this era began in the fall of 1970 when East Carolina University employed an archaeologist and provided facilities for archaeological research; the University of North Carolina at Wilmington followed suit in 1975. From its inception the archaeology program at East Carolina University has utilized a regional research design emphasizing the direct historical approach, particularly in the northern Coastal Plain, and assigned high priority to the establishment of a regional chronology and its correlation with adjacent regional sequences. The cultural information resulting from these research activities and others since 1970 forms the basis of the cultural-historical model below, a construct necessary to useful assimilation of the third generation of research.

Impact of the Third Generation

In the late summer of 1974, East Carolina University accepted its first two contracts for environmental impact surveys, taken in the earnest belief that it was a responsibility of the practicing archaeological community. Only three years into designed research for the Coastal Plain, at a point where accumulated data were just becoming sufficient for chronological controls, basic models, and major research proposals, those types of culturally productive studies were overwhelmed and essentially shelved by what we have come to know as "environmental impact archaeology." Between 1974 and 1980, 95 percent of the archaeological research done by East Carolina University was the latter type. This is not an isolated example but rather typical of the impact of cultural resource management, the third generation.

Cultural resource management, as presently conceived, has two major thrusts: (1) the location and assessment of archaeological resources endangered by various types of construction funded or sanctioned by state and federal agencies or private construction for which a state or federal permit is required; and (2) the preservation, excavation, or salvage of sites judged sufficiently significant to be nominated to the National Register of Historic Places. A more recent and advantageous addition to the management theme, the survey and planning grant, provides for inventory and evaluation of sites and other types of studies, but these grants are seriously hampered by matching fund requirements, time limitations, and excessive administration. These are admirable goals and the legislative acts, statutes, and executive orders (North Carolina Division of Archives and History 1978) that formulated them were all of the best intent and generally acceptable to the archaeological community, but somewhere along the road the buggy quite literally has gotten before the horse. Environmental impact archaeology and its progeny, cultural resource management, are now dangerously close to becoming an end in themselves rather than the originally intended means.

This third generation of archaeology has produced a monumental accumulation of data analogous to incomplete fragments of a mosaic for which a master design was never executed. Now a post-hoc design, the statewide survey or management plan (Mathis 1979), has been constructed in order to provide a predictive model for site types and distribution. But the major problem with environmental surveys is one of limitations: project-related data from environmental impact surveys will always have specific spatial limitations; predictive models based on such samples will be biased toward the sites recorded in the project area but will not necessarily define the relationship of the project area to the broader, functionally integrated settlement patterns that produced them unless the investigator has some knowledge of the region in which the project is located.

As third-generation research has grown, the number of private sector organizations has increased. In one sense this development is a blessing which allows university archaeologists once again to direct their interests to basic research and the broader cultural problems. In another sense, however, it has intensified the problem of fragmentary information. Many private sector archaeologists, and some university-based archaeologists as well, working outside their areas of familiarity, do not have the experience necessary to classify correctly artifacts or define culture systems in the regions in which they are working. Some environmental studies in the North Carolina Coastal Plain have tried to classify specimens using the Piedmont typological model or even models from other states. Apparently, this problem is quite widespread; Hester Davis (American Anthropological Association 1981:7) has complained of a similar situation in Arkansas, making the point that archaeologists from other areas working on environmental projects there make no attempt to consult with resident personnel or familiarize themselves with problems, models, or typology. With some consistent exceptions, this has been the case in the Coastal Plain as well as in other areas of the state. It has, hoewever, been more crucial in the Coastal Plain because of the fact that the archaeological data base is severely limited by the lack of research prior to 1970, and basic requirements such as an accurate cultural-historical continuum are just beginning to emerge. This, however, is no excuse for laments about the Coastal Plain being an archaeological "terra incognita"; Haag (1958:1) could validly claim such a condition, but recent cultural resource management studies (cf. Garrow 1978:5; Garrow and Watson 1978:23) have an equal responsibility with everyone for learning and building upon what is available at any given moment, offering the project-derived data in a positive rather than a negative sense.

A list of reports available as of 1980 in the Archaeology Branch, North Carolina Division of Archives and History (Hargrove 1980), lists 340 for the 39 counties in or adjacent to the Coastal Plain; excluding approximately 40 that were not related to cultural resource management, the remaining 300 or so have produced very little significant data for archaeological purposes other than expanded knowledge of site distribution. Those reports that do have meaningful data were produced by investigators resident in the region and thus familiar with current problems and the status of knowledge or by those very few outside investigators who took the time to draw on the resident expertise for familiarity. Until such a cooperation occurs, many environmental archaeology projects will continue to produce minimal cultural information, and, in most cases, will not be able to address validly the crucial issue of National Register eligibility.

While cultural resource management studies have and will continue to produce information on site content and distribution, these data will assume maximum value only when reliable local and regional sequences, settlement and subsistence models, and concepts of cultural process and interregional relationships have been developed. Unfortunately, these latter types of broad studies are the ones usually not fundable under cultural resource management. Perhaps the most beneficial advancement of cultural resource management would result from an expansion of the concept of survey and planning grants to include a broader range of studies necessary to maintaining the state's archaeological data base. This should include expanded time frames for projects as well as a change in administrative practices and guidelines. One final factor that would aid in integration of data from environmental impact archaeology into broader academic research is some regular means of disseminating reports to the institutions normally engaged in regional studies. In conceiving the management system the main omission seems to have been a means of synthesizing the monumental outpouring of information. Since synthesis is usually accomplished on a regional basis, it would seem logical to require that every archaeological impact project provide a copy of the final report to the pertinent agency or school actively involved in studies of the particular region.

In summary, research in the Coastal Plain has proceeded from a few early descriptive works in the late nineteenth and early twentieth centuries to the first ethnohistoric studies, site surveys, and classification schemes in the period from 1945 to 1970, to the emergence of regional research designs and their initial implementation from 1971 to 1975, and to the recent years of environmental impact surveys, which have often been given some explanatory flair by imposition of cultural system models without a sound classificatory base. The current status of Coastal Plain prehistory directly reflects this developmental sequence and presents us with as many problems as answers.

CULTURE HISTORY: AN INITIAL MODEL

The cultural-historical model of Coastal Plain prehistory presented here, with suggestions of subsistence and settlement patterns, and process and change based upon it, should be viewed as a working model to be modified and structured more efficiently as new data are accumulated and assimilated. This is a crucial issue, since most cultural frameworks of this nature, once they are described and presented graphically, tend to perpetuate themselves without the necessary testing that hypothetical constructs require for validity. This status as a working model is even more important when one begins to understand that the Coastal Plain was a complex area in prehistoric times, occupied by differing linguistic and ethnic groups subject to the acculturation processes attendant upon a major culture area boundary and adapted to a wide variety of natural habitats. The historical view of a long sequence of unchanging, traditional cultures espoused in previous studies (Haag 1958:133) may be untenable in light of present information.

Spatial and Temporal Dimensions

Culture area boundaries tend to change through time, and those in North Carolina are no exception. Within North Carolina and South Carolina lies the boundary between general northeastern and southeastern cultural traditions spatially distinct from about 2000 B.C. onward. In current cultural-spatial models this boundary is variably located, depending upon whether it is defined from archaeological or ethnohistorical data. For example, Willey (1966:Figure 5.1) places the division of his Middle Atlantic and Southeast subareas of the Eastern Woodlands culture area along the North Carolina-South Carolina line in the Coastal Plain and then swings it northwestward, including the Pee Dee (Coe 1952:301-311) and Cherokee cultures of the Piedmont and Mountains within the Southeast. On the other hand, Trigger (1978:1), using historical and ethnographic records, includes only the Iroquoian- and Algonkian-speaking peoples of the northern coastal region in his Northeastern culture area, thereby leaving the remainder of North Carolina in the Southeast. The major difference between the two is the placement of the Siouan-speaking peoples of the North Carolina southern Coastal Plain and Piedmont and the Virginia Piedmont. Trigger's exclusion of these from the Northeast apparently follows earlier ethnographic division (cf. Swanton 1946) based on linguistic affiliation and distribution. While it can be argued that the southernmost Piedmont Siouan groups and perhaps those in the southern Coastal Plain were somewhat acculturated to Southeastern cultural patterns in the Late Woodland and Protohistoric periods, the degree of acculturation appears to have been no greater than that of the Carolina and Virginia Algonkians who are assigned to the Northeastern area. In this paper both the Coastal Plain and Piedmont Siouan distributions are included in the Middle Atlantic subarea, an assignment somewhat confirmed by the absence among these groups of some core traits typical of the southeastern Mississippian Tradition.

Willey's subarea boundary reflects the differences that existed during his Temple Mound periods between the archaeological manifestations of the Woodland and Mississippian traditions (Willey 1966:247-248). Recent comparative work with ceramic assemblages in the Coastal Plain of Virginia, North Carolina, and South Carolina (University of North Carolina Archaeological Consortium 1980a; 1980b) suggests that this boundary should be set along the Pee Dee River drainage, the northernmost extent of complicated stamped ceramics and other traits typical of the Mississippian Tradition. The temporal limits of the boundary thus defined (Figure 1.1) are from A.D. 800 to the varying dates of European colonial intrusion (ca. A.D. 1650-1715), the Late Woodland period in the chronological sequence suggested in this paper. For practical purposes, then, the Middle Atlantic subarea lies north of the Pee Dee River and includes the northern part of the South Carolina Coastal Plain and the entire Coastal Plain of North Carolina. There is some evidence, discussed below, that the subarea boundary was farther north, along the Neuse River, in early and Middle Woodland times and represented the northern margin of an overlap zone, an area of shared cultural traits, which extended southward to the Savannah River.

The Coastal Plain physiographic province has been divided into two cultural-spatial units, the North Coastal and South Coastal regions (Figure 1.1). This division is based upon cultural differences that appear to begin near the end of the Late Archaic and continue throughout the prehistoric continuum, culminating in differing ethnic and linguistic distributions in the ethnographic present.

The temporal dimension in the Coastal Plain is more difficult to organize with authority at the current stage of knowledge, lacking stratigraphic controls and adequate radiocarbon dates for much of the sequence. The chronological chart with its regional sequences in Figure 1.2 is an adaptation of extant frameworks modified to more clearly express cultural realities in the Coastal Plain. The major periods and subperiods follow those of Griffin (1967:177), whose terminology, Paleo-Indian-Archaic-Woodland, is more appropriate to this area than such constructs as the Burial Mound and Temple Mound periods proposed by Willey (1966:Figure 5-2).

dates	period	sub-period	regional phases	
			NORTH COASTAL	SOUTH COASTAL
			sub-regional phases	
			TIDEWATER | INNER COASTAL PL.	
1715-	HISTORIC			Waccamaw
1650-			Carolina Algonkians | Meherrin / Tuscarora	
		Late	Colington | Cashie	Oak Island
800-	WOODLAND			
A.D./B.C.		Middle	Mount Pleasant	Cape Fear
300-				
		Early	Deep Creek	New River
1000-				
2000-		Late		Stallings
3000-			Savannah River	
	ARCHAIC	Middle	Halifax | Stanly	Guilford / Morrow Mountain
5000-				
		Early	Kirk	
8000-				
	PALEO-INDIAN	Late	Palmer / Hardaway	
10,000-				
		Early	Hardaway-Dalton / Clovis	
12,000				

FIGURE 1.2. The cultural sequence of the North Carolina Coastal Plain.

The Paleo-Indian period has been adapted to a two-part division suggested by Funk (1978: Figure 12) to provide for a more finite accommodation of future data, and the dates have been adjusted to reflect current perceptions of that part of the chronology in the North Carolina Piedmont (cf. Oliver 1981a:16). Dates for the Archaic subperiods similarly reflect recent modifications of the original definition (Coe 1964) upon which the chronologies of both Willey and Griffin were based. The Late Woodland segment of the sequence (Figure 1.2) differs from that of Griffin (1967:187), who defines the "early Late Woodland" (A.D. 300-900) in terms of a decline from Hopewellian ceremonialism, in that radiocarbon dates for the Coastal Plain suggest a change from the Middle Woodland to the Late Woodland period around A.D. 800. This date also varies from current Northeastern area chronologies (Fitting 1978; Snow 1978), which place the beginning of the Late Woodland period around A.D. 1000.

The regional phases suggested for the Coastal Plain correlate in their present form with the subperiods of the Woodland period, but this gross correlation can be modified as new data accumulate in controlled stratigraphic context and as the subtle changes in the sequence can be defined. When this is possible, the phase designation can be modified to reflect change by the addition of numbers such as Deep Creek I, II, III, etc. The present cultural record of the Coastal Plain provides a view of culture change only in the larger sense of the major period and occasional indications of microchange within them.

The Paleo-Indian Period

The reported distribution of fluted projectile points in the Coastal Plain is sufficient indication of how little is known of this early prehistoric period. Many of the recorded finds of these points are from surface collections reported by amateurs (Perkinson 1971; 1973) and number approximately 16 for the entire Coastal Plain. In addition to these, fluted points have been collected from sites in Bertie, Carteret, Edgecombe, Hertford, Nash, and Pitt counties in the course of both environmental and normal research surveys and have been observed in private collections from Beaufort, Craven, and Gates counties, but the total number of sites with these projectile points is less than fifty. The formal types represented include Clovis, Cumberland, Quad, Dalton, and Hardaway, as well as variations on these typological themes, all of which are generally placed within the period 12,000-8000 B.C. A temporal sequence of the above projectile point types, seriating them by attribute changes, was proposed for the Southeast (Williams 1965:24-51), but there is little current stratigraphic or chronometric evidence for this particular sequence. The two-part Paleo-Indian sequence proposed by Funk (1978:16-19) reflects a consensus of ideas about changes within the period, but his dates for this manifestation in the Northeast (Early Paleo-Indian, 10,500-8000 B.C.; Late Paleo-Indian, 8000-6000 B.C.) are later than those generally accepted elsewhere in the East.

More recently, Gardner outlined a three-phase sequence for the Paleo-Indian period based on stratigraphy at the Thunderbird site in Virginia, although his last phase falls within the long-accepted definition of Early Archaic. Gardner's Fluted Point phase is divided into a Clovis subphase, a Middle Paleo subphase with smaller fluted points, and a final Dalton-Hardaway subphase (Gardner and Verrey 1979:15). Gardner's Middle Paleo subphase includes many of the smaller fluted points reported in North Carolina, and his Dalton-Hardaway subphase is similar to that originally described by Coe (1964:81) at the Hardaway site. Included within the latter are small points with reduced fluting and variations in shape ranging from "Dalton-like" through "Hardaway-like" to triangular forms with deeply concave bases (Gardner and Verrey 1979:15). The phenomenon thus described is the variation inherent in the transition from fluting to notching, and a considerable quantity of these points occur throughout the Coastal Plain, where they have been provisionally designated as a "Paleo-Indian Transitional" type (Phelps 1975b:124, Fig. 2). These specimens (Figure 1.3) appear to be specifically transitional between the small Hardaway and Palmer types without assuming the modal attributes of either type and may well be the regional variant of the Hardaway side-notched type as described by Coe (1964:67). Their concave bases are usually ground, extreme basal thinning is more frequent than fluting, and rudimentary notches produce a slightly "eared" effect reminiscent of the Hardaway side-notched type. A recent revision of the Piedmont sequence recognizes four developmental phases in the Paleo-Indian period projectile points: the Hardaway blade (or large Hardaway, considered a regional variant on the Clovis theme) and Hardaway-Dalton, from 12,000 to 10,000 B.C.; and the Hardaway side-notched and Palmer corner-notched, from 10,000 to 8000 B.C. (Oliver 1981a:16). This revised sequence incorporates Gardner's Fluted Point phase into its 12,000-10,000 B.C. segment and places his "Hardaway-like" forms and Phelps's "Paleo-Indian Transitional" type in the 10,000-8000 B.C. segment, which ends the Paleo-Indian period with the Palmer type. It is this chronology that forms the basis for the early (12,000-10,000 B.C.) and Late (10,000-8,000 B.C.) phases of the Paleo-Indian period in this paper.

Confirmation of the Paleo-Indian sequence in the Coastal Plain will have to await more comprehensive site distributional data and the location and excavation of stratified sites. Stratified sites do exist in the Coastal Plain, and it remains to locate them without benefit of a sophisticated predictive model. One site with a possible intact Late Paleo-Indian stratum can be used as an example; 31Pt3, discovered and tested

FIGURE 1.3. Projectile points typical of the Late Paleo-Indian period in the Coastal Plain. Length of upper left point is 3.3 centimeters.

during an environmental survey (Phelps 1977b:14) lies on an older Tar River levee, buried 1.1 meters below the surface and overlain by Early and Middle Woodland occupations. The levee has experienced no modern disturbance, other than a colonial period road, and was densely wooded when surveyed. The implication follows that older Archaic and Paleo-Indian sites with intact stratigraphy can be found in the remnant levees and terraces of major trunk streams, both adjacent to the active channel (depending on the stream system) and the floodplain. Upland areas, where most of the Paleo-Indian sites presently recorded have been found, have generally experienced a combination of extensive agricultural disturbance and sheet erosion, and since such locales do not experience any appreciable amount of soil accretion, no deep stratification has developed. Other situations, such as the fragment of a Clovis point reclaimed from a hill-top site with shallow stratigraphy at the fall line of the Tar River (Phelps 1980a:100), are typical of the disturbed nature of some multicomponent sites. In this case a Late Woodland component had apparently disturbed the Early Paleo-Indian occupation level.

Coastal Plain

With so few recorded sites, it is impossible to discuss settlement patterns in a meaningful way; the most that can be said at the moment is that fluted points typical of the early Paleo-Indian period occur at widely scattered locations in the Coastal Plain, which, at the time of their occupation, were on the Inner Coastal Plain. With the rise in sea level since 18,000 B.C., their coastal counterparts now lie beneath the ocean on the Continental Shelf, and the riverine base camps were inundated as trunk streams became estuaries (Oaks and Coch 1963:979-980; Riggs and O'Connor 1975). Data provided for fluted points collected by amateurs are too general to permit a statement regarding site type and location, but most of the fluted points in the East Carolina University collection were found in multicomponent sites with a maximum occupation frequency during the Archaic period. The low frequency of Paleo-Indian projectile points and the end, side, and oval scrapers associated with them (Coe 1964:73-79) suggest sites of small size and temporary nature and site selectivity factors similar to those of the Archaic Period. The small "transitional" and Palmer corner-notched points typical of the Late Paleo-Indian period are much more numerous and widely distributed throughout the Coastal Plain, but again their frequency per site is relatively low, and they are usually found along with the later Archaic assemblages in multicomponent sites.

Based on present knowledge, one may hypothesize that some of the sites with Paleo-Indian components located on the major streams probably served as base camps, but specimen frequency in the sites does not permit even an estimate of band size, as suggested in Mathis's (1979:27) settlement model. It is also logical to assume that the smaller sites on tributary streams served as "specialized activity," probably subsistence-oriented, sites, but nowhere in the Coastal Plain are distributional data sufficient to reconstruct the settlement pattern of even one band. Gardner's (1979) proposed settlement models for the Dismal Swamp and North Carolina offer elements, which, with some modification, lend themselves to testing in the Coastal Plain. In the Dismal Swamp model (Gardner 1979:14-15), he suggests that the Williamson site is the primary base camp and quarry for a band whose territory extended 80 or more miles to hunting camps at the western margin of the Dismal Swamp. This construct is based on finished artifacts of Williamson site chert at the hunting camps and reliance on a "central quarry" concept. Given the range of locally available materials from which the Paleo-Indian artifacts (projectile points, scrapers) found in the Coastal Plain have been produced (quartz, quartzite, slate, rhyolite, chert, jasper), the central "quarry" organization seems inappropriate and trade between territories may just as readily explain the presence of chert from particular sources. In the North Carolina model (Gardner 1979:15-16), territorial range, which is erroneously called "catchment area" (see Roper 1979a:120-121), may extend 130 miles or more from predicted quarries in the Piedmont slate belt to the eastern edge of the Coastal Plain. Gardner also notes a distinct absence of sites in the Coastal Plain, which reflects the status of site survey rather than cultural reality, and he attributes this to lack of stone resources in the region, except perhaps along major rivers such as the Roanoke. In actuality, the eastern edge of the Coastal Plain in Paleo-Indian times was 230 to 300 miles from the Piedmont, and all of the rivers with Mountain and Piedmont headwaters probably carried considerable loads of pebbles and cobbles downstream from their source. Even in the Late Woodland period the Carolina Algonkians were "mining" jasper from the old channels beneath the Outer Banks. The broad North Carolina Coastal Plain lends itself to a different settlement model than that of Piedmont and Mountain quarry sites as the "central place" in the territory.

The Paleo-Indian settlement model may well have been dictated by subsistence resource exploitation rather than lithic resources, but if settlement patterns are poorly known, the subsistence base is even less understood. The Coastal Plain environment during the Paleo-Indian period was one of broad river valleys in which the stream channels braided around numerous sandbars, freshwater marshes along the stream edges, and a boreal pine-spruce forest on the interstream uplands (Whitehead 1972:313). The carrying capacity of such an environment for human populations was certainly lower than those prevalent in more recent times, and a low density of human population would be expected. The subsistence strategy may have been generalized hunting and gathering or may have emphasized the hunting of larger animals as in the classic model (Willey 1966:37-38), although a combination of these strategies seems most plausible. Given the expected rarity of preserved food remains in Coastal Plain Paleo-Indian sites, knowledge of the subsistence strategy will probably result only by implication from a correlation of settlement patterns with past environment when these are better known.

The Archaic Period

In contrast to Paleo-Indian, Archaic period sites literally dot the Coastal Plain landscape, and our knowledge of this distribution results in large part from recent environmental impact surveys, which are primarily useful for this type of data.

As is the case with Paleo-Indian sites, stratigraphy is lacking for the Archaic sequence in the Coastal Plain. However, artifacts diagnostic of its various phases (Figure 1.2) are the same as those of the Piedmont where relatively firm stratigraphic control exists and that control enables accurate seriation of surface materials. The Archaic sequence described by Coe (1964) for Piedmont North Carolina is seen as a tradition defined by technological changes in projectile points. The tradition began in the Paleo-Indian period with the Hardaway blade as a regional variant of fluted point contemporary with the Clovis type, continued with the evolution of the Hardaway-Dalton, and passed through a transition from fluting to corner-notched points of the Palmer type in the Late Paleo-Indian period. Kirk corner-notched projectile points, generally larger and without the ground base characteristic of Palmer, usher in the Early Archaic period. This was also a time of transition in climate during which pines, hemlock, birch, and northern hardwoods, such as beech and maple, gradually replaced the earlier boreal forests and provided environments for different and more extensive faunal communities. The Kirk phase midden of the Hardaway site (Coe 1964:60) was deposited in continued use of the site over many generations, indicating a change in settlement function and patterns perhaps related to different subsistence strategies. Kirk corner-notched points are gradually replaced by the Kirk stemmed type, often with serrated blade edges, but other artifacts in the assemblage, such as end and side scrapers, blades, and drills continued to be produced in the same manner and form as they had since the Paleo-Indian period.

The Middle Archaic witnessed a transition in the indigenous tradition from the Kirk stemmed to Stanly stemmed points and the presumed introduction of polished stone, semilunar spearthrower weights of the Stanly type. Around 6000 B.C. the pine-birch-hemlock forests of the Coastal Plain were being gradually replaced by oak-hickory in the warmer and drier climate of the hypsithermal (Whitehead 1972:313), and this change signals the beginning of the modern plant and animal communities. In this changing environment new artifact types appeared: Morrow Mountain and Guilford points, which Coe (1964:122-123) believed were introduced from western sources, appear without technological precedent and apparently represent competition for resources with the indigenous culture. The Morrow Mountain and Guilford phases have been referred to as the "Western Intrusive horizon" (Phelps 1964). Halifax projectile points, isolated stratigraphically only at the Gaston site near the fall line, appear in the sequence for the first time around 4000 B.C. and suggest northern influences (Coe 1964:123) in the last moments of the Middle Archaic. Halifax points are well represented in collections from sites in the northern Coastal Plain, but their cultural context remains to be identified.

The Late Archaic was a time of return to homogeneity, and the Savannah River assemblage of this period represents the final phase of the indigenous Archaic tradition.

Projectile points typical of the three Archaic subperiods are well represented in the North Carolina Coastal Plain, but identification of the other artifacts in each phase assemblage remains a problem to be solved by stratigraphic context or single component sites.

Stratified sites certainly exist in the Coastal Plain, probably in niches similar to that suggested for Paleo-Indian sites as well as in a broader spectrum of upland stream margins where such material may be buried beneath some midden deposits from the Woodland period. Earlier Archaic sites in the Tidewater have been flooded like those of the preceding period; previous riverine base camps and coastal sites should not be expected except as re-sorted beachline deposits and dredged secondary depositions (Phelps 1977c:62), but upland sites still exist along tributary streams and adjacent to some pocosins. A major research concern for the future should be a search for intact sites of this period. This would be enhanced considerably by a comprehensive synthesis of presently known Archaic site distribution derived from the reported surveys. My impression is that a workable settlement model and prediction of stratified Archaic sites may exist within the data from various studies; what is needed is the application of the deductive process, testing, and additional survey to fill in spatial discrepancies.

The higher frequency of presumed transitional Paleo-Indian to Archaic period material may reflect increasing population during the Pleistocene-Holocene shift, but early Archaic sites are certainly indicative of a higher population and a more efficient adaptation to natural resources. Ameliorating climate and its effect upon floral and faunal communities during the Archaic period undoubtedly produced a favorable situation for population growth and resulted in a settlement pattern designed to take advantage of the variety of food and other resources in the Coastal Plain. The specific foods utilized during the Archaic period must await data from excavated sites with sufficient preservation; at the moment, the subsistence patterns may be implied from site locations in relation to potential resources within their presumed catchment areas. The known range of site locations spans every microenvironment in the Coastal Plain, from saline estuary shores to margins of major trunk streams and their entire tributary systems as well as pocosins and floodplain swamps, each with its own potential foods and other resources.

While nowhere do we have information on a settlement distribution that can be attributed to a single society, some generalizations can be offered about Archaic period settlement patterns and their diachronic changes. Two facts are obvious immediately: (1) The density of Archaic sites in the Coastal Plain is the highest of any prehistoric period, and (2) they are everywhere irrevocably related to stream accessibility. Both points can be illustrated by a number of studies of Coastal Plain watersheds, but two will suffice. Of 56 sites (approximates 50% sample) located in the Swift Creek watershed at the boundary of the Tidewater and Inner

Coastal Plain, 53 had Archaic occupations. Six of the 53 Archaic components could be classified as base camps while the remainder were small temporary sites probably used in conjunction with some specialized subsistence activity (Phelps 1976a:320). The sites were distributed equally along all the stream classes (1 through 3) within this tributary system, and the six base camps occupied stream confluence situations scattered throughout the distribution. Along 20 miles of Class 1 through 3 streams in the Thoroughfare Swamp watershed, Wayne County, 156 sites were located, closely approximating a 100% sample of this locale in the Inner Coastal Plain. Ninety-seven sites had Archaic period components, and ten of these were base camps (Phelps 1976b). Both of these watersheds are drained by lateral tributaries of the Neuse River system, and neither project area included the major trunk stream. The recorded sites thus do not reflect the total territory or environment probably utilized by Archaic period social groups in either locality, and the "base camps" observed during the studies may be seasonal rather than main bases. These studies suggest a need for investigation of a "real" territory rather than aribitrary project areas in order to understand fully settlement-subsistence relationships during each phase. The surveys cited above also tend to confirm the direct association of site locations with stream systems. The streams provided transportation access (presuming that boats had been in existence for some time), or their banks were easily followed directional paths if travel was pedestrian; they were equally important for readily available water supply and offered valley and floodplain resources varying from those on their upland margins and terraces. While the uplands between stream systems were certainly exploited, the distance between streams is never great in the Coastal Plain, and upland areas were readily accessible from the stream bank sites. It should be noted that this stream locational model applies to Woodland sites as well as those of the Archaic, and it is not modified in the Coastal Plain until historic times.

There is a gradual increase in the number of sites from Early to Middle Archaic times, with an initial increase in the Kirk phase reaching a maximum density during the Morrow Mountain phase, a phenomenon recognized in many localities (Phelps 1976b:22; Mathis 1979:99). Site density appears to remain relatively stable into the Late Archaic, but some localities show a noticeable reduction of Late Archaic site density along smaller tributary streams. This trend may reflect changes in subsistence strategies and increasing sedentariness, a harbinger of things to come.

The final phase of the Late Archaic is Savannah River (Coe 1964), long recognized as having a relatively homogeneous cultural assemblage along the Middle and South Atlantic Coastal Plain (Sears 1954) and similar to contemporary manifestations such as Susquehanna in the Northeast (Tuck 1978:37-39). Beginning around 4000 B.C., the Savannah River phase is usually characterized by a higher degree of sedentary residence resulting from expertise in subsistence adaptations, and artifacts typical of the phase, such as steatite vessels, reflect this. Decorative art in the form of incised bone pins (Fairbanks 1942) and burials with red ochre and projectile points deposited as burial goods are known from other regions—all indicators of increasing complexity in the culture. By 2500-2000 B.C. ceramic manufacture appeared in the Savannah River assemblage, and the distribution of this fiber-tempered ware traces the first outline of the Southeastern subarea. The first division of the North Carolina Coastal Plain also results from the extension of this ceramic distribution into the South Coastal region.

Emergence of the Regions

The South Coastal can be tentatively differentiated from the North Coastal region somewhere around 2000 B.C., based on dates for fiber-tempered ceramics in the Southeast (Williams 1968:329-331; Stoltman 1966). South (1976:28-29) has outlined a sequence for the South Carolina coast in which the Stallings series of fiber-tempered ware and its succeeding ware-group, Thom's Creek, occupy the formative phase of ceramic development, from about 2500 to 1000 B.C.

Fiber-tempered pottery has been known in the extreme southern part of the region at least since 1959, when it was collected from the Turner site (31Cb4), and it was first formally reported in Brunswick County in 1960 (South 1976:27) with the assumption that it was limited to the South Carolina border area. The first specimens reclaimed from sites in Greene County in 1971 by East Carolina University survey teams were quite unexpected in the Neuse drainage. Surveys (Loftfield 1979a, 1979b; Phelps 1975a, 1975b, 1976b; Wilde-Ramsing 1978) and studies of collections (M. Trinkley; personal communication) since 1975 have reported more sites, and this ware is now known from approximately 38 sites widely scattered in the Coastal Plain (Figure 1.4). The only type so far represented in the collections (Figure 1.5) is Stallings Plain (Sears and Griffin 1950), perhaps implying that the full-fledged ceramic series with its decorative types did not extend into the South Coastal region. Where sufficient information exists, the ceramics occur in sites with other typical specimens of the Late Archaic complex such as Savannah River points and their round-base variant, steatite vessel sherds and "net sinkers" of the grooved type, "winged" atlatl weights, and grooved axes. Sites with Stallings Plain sherds are concentrated from the Neuse River system southward, but three sites with this ware in the Tar River drainage (Phelps 1975a) and three others in the North Albemarle and Chowan localities have been identified. It appears that the distribution of fiber-tempered pottery north of the Neuse River is rare, representing a minor influx. Recognition of the

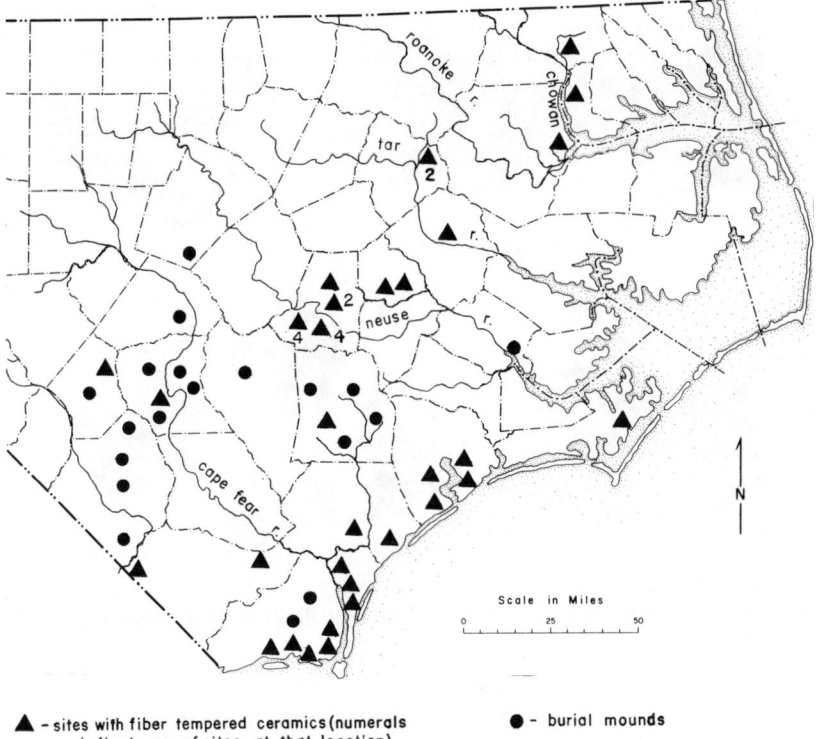

▲ - sites with fiber tempered ceramics (numerals indicate no. of sites at that location).

● - burial mounds

FIGURE 1.4. Distribution of fiber-tempered ceramics and burial mounds in the Coastal Plain.

existence of fiber-tempered pottery in the South Coastal region is recent, but the implication of this distribution is the earliest known boundary between the Southeast and Middle Atlantic subareas. In succeeding centuries the boundary moved southward, but the two regions it defined within the North Carolina Coastal Plain remained distinct and by about 1000 B.C. had developed their own characteristic traits.

The Woodland Period

The Early Woodland period is at once the most crucial for understanding exchanges between developing traditions to the north and south in the Coastal Plain because so little is known of this temporal segment.

In the classic Southeastern sequence, Stallings fiber-tempered ware was replaced by Thom's Creek (Phelps 1968; Trinkley 1980a) sand-tempered pottery around 1300 B.C. as if new technological traits in ceramic production had been introduced. While there is considerable temporal overlap of

FIGURE 1.5. Stallings Plain fiber-tempered pottery from the South (upper row) and North (bottom row) Coastal Plain. Width of sherd on upper left is 4.8 centimeters.

Stallings and Thom's Creek, and some investigators emphasize this contemporaneity (Trinkley 1980a:19), there is certainly a linear traditional relationship between the two wares. Thom's Creek, in turn, was followed by the Deptford series (Caldwell and Waring 1939), which introduced paddle stamping and replaced the other series. This ceramic sequence has been established in South Carolina and Georgia and can be seen in the South Coastal region of North Carolina as a ripple effect. The Coastal Plain section of the Pee Dee River drainage in South Carolina is probably the most northerly extent of the classic Southeastern sequence, but Thom's Creek Plain and Punctate and Deptford Linear Check Stamped, Bold Check Stamped, and Simple Stamped types are present along the Cape Fear (South 1976; Wilde-Ramsing 1978), and the Thom's Creek ware appears to extend northward nearly to the Neuse River. The three series, then, have decreasing spatial distributions from the Neuse River southward to the Pee Dee; Late Archaic Stallings ware is present in the Neuse drainage and in minor amounts north of it; Thom's Creek in the earliest part of the Early Woodland is limited to a range south of the Neuse. Deptford, in the later Early Woodland, is present only along the Cape Fear River and the northern tributaries of the Pee Dee River.

Beginning about 1500-1000 B.C. a different ceramic tradition is found along the Middle Atlantic Coast and in the Northeast. The Marcey Creek plain and cord-marked, steatite-tempered vessels with flat or rounded bases identified by Manson (1948) appear to be the earliest ceramics in the Middle Atlantic; farther north the cord-marked Vinette ware described by Ritchie (1959) is the earliest manifestation. Both of these ceramic innovations were added to regional Late Archaic coastal assemblages (Tuck 1978:39).

While the degree of influence of the Marcey Creek steatite-tempered ware in the North Carolina Coastal Plain is not yet known, only a small number of sherds having been so far reported (Phelps 1975a; South 1976; Loftfield 1979a), the spread of sand- or grit-tempered, cord-marked ceramics spans the two regions and extends southward to the Savannah River (Anderson 1975). This "Northern Tradition," in Caldwell's (1958) definition, probably spread into the North Coastal region between 1000 B.C. and 1944 + 250 B.C., the radiocarbon date for the preceramic Savannah River phase of the Gaston site (Coe 1964:97, Table 15).

Deep Creek, the phase nomenclature chosen for the Early Woodland in the North Coastal Plain, derives from the tributary of the Tar River where the ceramic complex typical of the phase was first recognized at the Parker site (Phelps 1975a). The ceramic collection from the Parker site included coarse sand-tempered, cord-marked pottery as the majority type with minor quantities of the same ware with net-impressed, fabric-impressed, and simple-stamped surfaces. Also found at the site were a few Stallings Plain fiber-tempered and Marcey Creek Plain steatite-tempered sherds (Phelps 1975a: Table 1); "small stemmed" projectile points, considered transitional from the older Savannah River type (Phelps 1975a:68), and now classified as Gypsy points (Oliver 1981a); and Roanoke large triangular points (Coe 1964:110). Deep Creek was the terminal component at the Parker site, closing an occupational sequence that spanned the previous Archaic period. Other sites with a similar sequence terminating in the Early Woodland are now known in the region, and the data from these along with mixed Woodland component sites have permitted a preliminary seriation of the Deep Creek assemblage. The presently known assemblage, in its mature form, includes the ceramic series or ware group of Deep Creek cord-marked (Figure 1.6a), Deep Creek net-impressed (Figure 1.6b), and Deep Creek fabric-impressed, only rarely accompanied by a plain type. Vessel shapes include both conoidal and, more rarely, flat base containers. The series had its origin further north in the Middle Atlantic and probably correlates with Evans (1955) Stoney Creek types in southeastern Virginia. The large Roanoke triangular points are certainly part of the assemblage, but other elements are less secure in their association. Steatite vessels may have continued in use, based on associations observed at the Thorpe site (Phelps 1980a:72-75).

A hypothetical three-phase sequence for the Early Woodland can be proposed as a model for testing when stratified sites have been identified. Deep Creek I represents the initial introduction of ceramics (steatite-tempered and the coarse sand ware) and triangular points from the north,

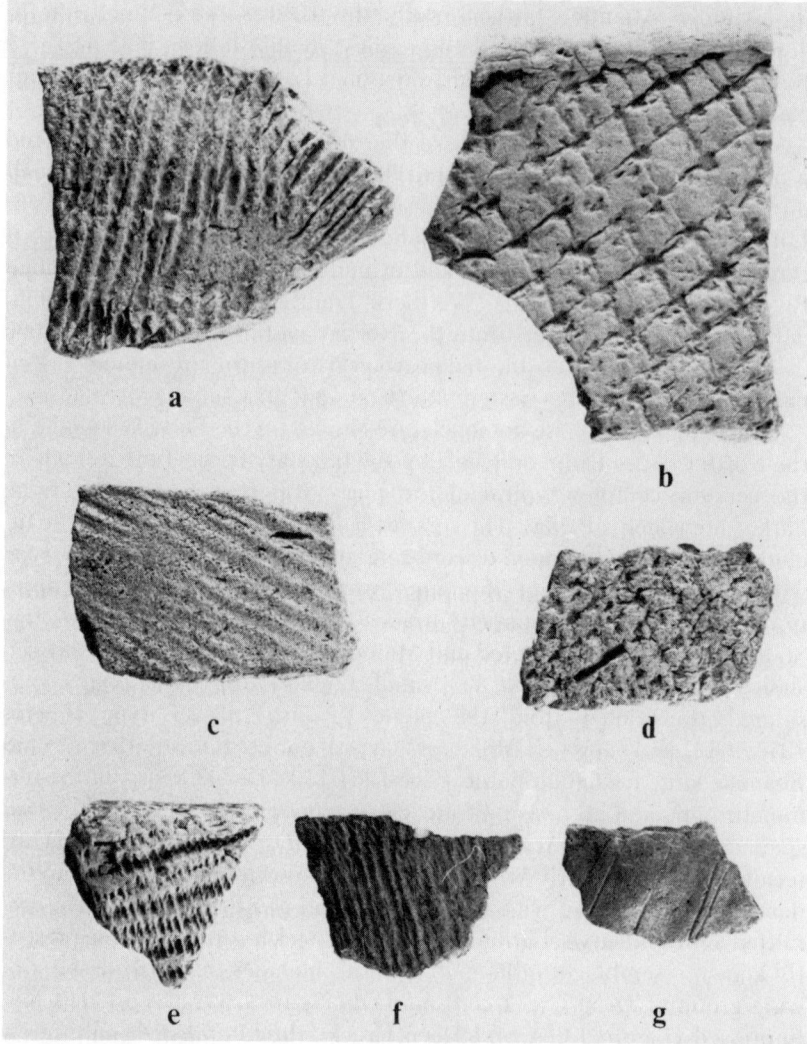

FIGURE 1.6. Deep Creek and Mount Pleasant phase ceramics. Deep Creek cord-marked (a) and net-impressed (b) occur with a simple-stamped type (c) similar to Deptford and Thom's Creek simple-stamped. Mount Pleasant types include net-impressed (d), fabric-impressed (e), cord-marked (f), and incised (g). Length of sherd in upper right (b) is 8 centimeters.

influencing a change in the Late Archaic culture in which the older stemmed points were made smaller (Gypsy type) and then finally replaced by the triangular type. Deep Creek cord-marked was the prevalent ceramic type, while net fabric-impressed just was becoming popular and simple-stamping was being introduced from the south. The origin of this simple-stamping lies somewhere within the Stallings-Thom's Creek continuum but is reinforced by the paddle-stamped type that is typical of the later Deptford phase. Both dowel-like impressions reminiscent of Stallings and Thom's Creek simple-stamping (Williams 1968:249; Phelps 1968:21) and the rectangular land and groove type of Deptford (Figure 1.6c) are present in the North Coastal region, but the former type probably belongs in the Deep Creek I phase. The northern limits of simple-stamping have yet to be determined, but this type of pottery is certainly associated with Deep Creek as far north as the Chowan River drainage (Phelps 1981a:11). Deep Creek II may have begun around 800 B.C. with an increase in the popularity of net- and fabric-impressed surface finishes on the ceramics and popularity of the Deptford simple-stamped type. This may also have been a period of experimentation with ceramics, during which the net-, fabric-, and cord-impressed ceramics discovered by Painter (1977) in Currituck County were produced. Both shell and grit tempering occur in these specimens, often in the same vessel, and that limited experimentation with shell may be related to the origin of later shell-tempered wares in the Middle Atlantic subarea. In the Deep Creek III phase simple-stamping probably waned in popularity, finally disappearing by Middle Woodland times, but cord-, fabric-, and net-impressed surfaces on ceramics continued in equal popularity to set the stage for the next period.

New River is the phase named suggested for the South Coastal region in the Early Woodland period, derived from Loftfield's (1976:149-154) proposed earliest ceramic series in the Onslow County locality. The New River series is essentially similar to that described above for the North Coastal region and is here subsumed under the Deep Creek classification in order to standardize typology across the Coastal Plain. The Deep Creek series fills a niche not provided in South's (1976) original chronology for the southeastern North Carolina coast and is contemporary with Thom's Creek and Deptford in hypothetical New River I and II phases. The South Coastal varies from the North Coastal region in the presence of these southeastern series that define the northern edge of the overlap or cultural exchange area extending from the Neuse to the Savannah. South of the Pee Dee River, net- and fabric-impressing decrease in frequency (Anderson 1975), and only cord-marking extends to the Savannah River. A small site excavated by the author on the Savannah River below the fall line is illustrative of the dual tradition. In two feet of stratified deposits, Deptford ceramics (linear check-stamped, bold check-stamped, geometric-stamped, and simple-stamped) occurred in equal frequencies with a sand-tempered, cord-marked type much like Badin cord-marked; both the "small stemmed" Gypsy points and Roanoke triangular types were also present. Cord-marking appears to have reached Georgia during the Thom's Creek phase, when it appears as a lip decoration on Thom's Creek ware (Phelps 1968:25).

Little is known about settlement distribution or subsistence in the Early Woodland of the Coastal Plain, and until the proposed phases can be authenticated, little more than hypothesizing is possible. Settlement patterns similar to the Late Archaic have been suggested (Phelps 1976a), but such statements are valid only to the extent that Early Woodland materials can be seriated from surface collections at the moment. If the Deep Creek and New River phase settlement patterns are continuations from the preceding Archaic, then subsistence strategies may well have been similar. The presumed introduction of cultigens during the Early Woodland period may have had little effect in these regions, but the question will be answered only by research designed for that purpose.

The Middle Woodland can be discussed with slightly more authority than the preceding period, but it too poses a number of unsolved problems. Phase names for the period are Mount Pleasant for the North Coastal region, derived from the locale of the Freeman site (31Hf19) on the Chowan River, and Cape Fear, taken from South's (1976) original sequence for the South Coastal region. While 300 B.C. is assumed as a beginning date for the Mount Pleasant phase, current radiocarbon dates range from around A.D. 200 to 800. Two dates, A.D. 265 ± 65 (UGa-1088) and A.D. 890 ± 80 (UGa-3849), bracket the pure Mount Pleasant component at Rush Point on Colington Island, and a date of A.D. 460 + 85 (UGa-3435) falls within the occupation of the Tillet site (Phelps 1981b: Table 5). One date (A.D. 685 ± 75, UGa-3144) from a feature at the Thorpe site (Phelps 1980a:71) near the fall line applies to the contemporary Clements phase of the northeastern Piedmont (Coe 1964).

The basic assemblage of the Mount Pleasant phase has been identified in both inland and coastal sites, among which a few have produced stratified features and radiocarbon dates, while others are single component representatives of the phase. The Mount Pleasant ceramic series (Figure 1.6d-g) is a ware tempered with sand and larger clastic inclusions (pebbles, "grit") in varying amounts with types defined by surface finishes of fabric-impressing, cord-marking and net-impressing, simple-smoothing to produce a plain type, and incising on otherwise plain surfaces (Phelps 1981b:41-42). The Hanover cord-marked and fabric-impressed clay-tempered pottery defined by South (1976:16) is frequently found in minor quantities with the Mount Pleasant series in both the Tidewater and Inner Coastal Plain, as is a fine sand-tempered ware with the same surface finishes. Whether or not there is a temporal differential in the relationship of the clay and fine sand types with the Mount Pleasant series is not known. Mockley shell-tempered ceramics with net and cord impressions (Stephenson and Ferguson 1963:103-109), typical of the Middle Woodland period from southeastern Virginia to Maryland, have been observed in only a few sites along the Chowan River, indicating that shell as a tempering medium did not become popular in the Tidewater zone of the North Coastal region until the Late Woodland period. The Mount Pleasant phase ceramic complex appears to be a traditional continuity from the early Deep Creek ware, varying from the latter in a possibly higher frequency of net-impressed surface finish, a trend toward larger clastic temper, and the addition of incised decoration. The size of tempering material varies widely, a fact noted by Haag (1958:71) in the analysis of his "Middle Period" grit-tempered ware.

Surely associated with the ceramic complex are triangular projectile points of the Roanoke type, small variety (Coe 1964:110-111). Other artifacts known to occur in Mount Pleasant assemblage context are blades (bifaces) of varying shapes, sandstone abraders, shell pendants or gorgets, polished stone gorgets, celts, and mats woven of *Juncus* (black needlerush marsh) grass.

Burial patterns for the phase include both primary inhumation and cremation. The former type is prevalent, known from sites in both the Inner Coastal Plain and the Tidewater, where flexed and semiflexed burials have been recovered from Jordan's Landing (31Br7) and Astoria (31Mt16) in the Roanoke drainage (Phelps 1977a:20), the Baum site (31Ck9) in Currituck County (Phelps 1980:6), and the Tillet site (31Dr35) on Roanoke Island. One of the flexed burials at 31Br7 contained seven small Roanoke Triangular points as grave goods, the only known instance of this to date. One primary cremation (see Figure 1.7a) is known from the Baum site (31Ck9); the individual had been wrapped in a *Juncus* grass mat, the fragments of which produced a radiocarbon date of A.D. 360 $\pm$ 65 (UGa-1085). This cremation immediately overlay an earlier flexed inhumation burial (Figure 1.7b), indicating coexistence of the two burial patterns during this phase. Cremation was a widespread practice in the Middle Woodland period, but little is known of its popularity and distribution during this phase in the North Coastal region.

Mount Pleasant phase settlement patterns indicate a change from the preceding phase. There is a noticeable decrease in the number of small sites along the smaller tributary streams in the interior and an increase in sites along the major trunk streams and estuaries and on the coast. Seasonal subsistence camps like those on Colington and Roanoke islands were primarily shellfish collecting camps, as evidenced by abundant shells, but some hunting of land fauna and fishing also were minor activities. These sites often appear large from the accumulated shell and other midden debris, but they were probably occupied at any one season by only a few extended families or some other social grouping of comparable size (Phelps 1981b: 47-53). Inland riverine sites have the same pattern but reflect adaptations to shellfish and other species of the riverine environment. Evidence of structural remains in the form of a par-

FIGURE 1.7. Mount Pleasant burial patterns include primary cremations (a) and inhumations (b), as represented here by Burial 2 and Burial 3, respectively, at the Baum site (31Ck9). The cremation of the individual in Burial 2 (a) was wrapped in a *Juncus* grass mat and directly overlay the semi-flexed individual in Burial 3. The crematory pit outline can be seen above the lower pit of Burial 3 (b).

tial wall pattern at one such camp (31Hf19) suggests a seasonal residence structure. Sedentary villages are probably the largest settlement type of the period, but none has been excavated to the extent of understanding their intrasite patterns. The shift in settlement patterns is presumed to be related to increased dependence on domesticated plants, and pollen cores from the Dismal Swamp confirm the presence of maize in the region by 2,000 years ago (Whitehead 1972:311).

The Cape Fear phase in the South Coastal region is less well known in many respects and presents some quite severe problems. The Cape Fear ceramic types described by South (1976:18) are essentially similar to the Mount Pleasant series and Haag's "grit-tempered," and both of these have been included in the Mount Pleasant definition to provide a comprehensive ceramic horizon across the Coastal Plain. The Hanover series, which South places around 200-100 B.C. (South and Widmer 1976:45), is a clay- or sherd-tempered series with a higher frequency along the immediate coast and may covary with a Mount Pleasant distribution in the interior of the Coastal Plain. Loftfield's (1976:154) Carteret types have been included in the Hanover classification on the basis of their similarity.

A distinctive cultural feature of Middle Woodland age in the South Coastal region is the rather extensive distribution of low, sand burial mounds, placed within the Cape Fear phase because of their content and occurrence elsewhere in the eastern Woodlands area in this temporal position. Little can be added to MacCord's (1966) study at this time, other than to note that he too argued strongly for a Middle Woodland date for these mounds, and a radiocarbon date (A.D. 970 ± 110) is near the terminal part of the period (MacCord 1966). The high frequency of secondary cremation, platform pipes, and other objects in the mounds, and the fact that at least some of them seem to be placed away from their contemporaneous habitation sites, points to southern influence during this period in the South Coastal region. Their known spatial extent is limited to the region (Figure 1.4), and no comparable structures have been reported from either South Carolina or the North Carolina Piedmont. The most northerly mound is near Vanceboro on the north side of the Neuse River. It is a hemispherical structure which reportedly had been robbed of its content of secondary burials (as described by informants) some years before. An unpublished excavation of a sand dune on Bogue Banks by the University of North Carolina reclaimed a platform pipe, polished stone gorgets, triangular blades, and conch-shell cups typical of the Middle Woodland period, a situation which suggests substitution of a natural "high place" for burial instead of constructing a mound. Further research in both mounds and associated villages is needed to determine relationships of the mounds to the cultural phase that produced them and to correlate them with similar manifestations such as those on the Georgia coast.

No major excavations in sites of the Cape Fear phase have been reported, and most of the existing survey reports do not provide phase-specific site distributions in the South Coastal region. Given this situation, no meaningful statements can be made concerning settlement and subsistence patterns for the phase.

From A.D. 800 onward archaeological assemblages of the Late Woodland period in the North Coastal region can be related to ethnohistoric information and studies, thus providing the relative comfort of social and linguistic identities and the use of the direct historical approach. The South Coastal region is less well known both archaeologically and ethnohistorically, and correlation of historic with prehistoric data is more difficult.

The North Coastal region was the homeland of two distinct local cultures at the time of European contact, the Carolina Algonkians, who inhabited the Tidewater zone, and the Tuscarora, on the Inner Coastal Plain (Figure 1.8). The available ethnographic and historic data have been summarized by Mook (1944) and more recently by Feest (1978) for the Algonkians and by Paschal (1953) and Boyce (1978) for the Tuscarora and their two Iroquoian-speaking neighbors to the north, the Meherrin and Nottaway. While the political-territorial boundaries were originally set on the basis of ethnohistoric information, they can now be partially confirmed archaeologically, as shown in Figure 1.8. Two local phases have been established for these Late Woodland cultures of the North Coastal region: Colington is the phase name given the Algonkian culture of the Tidewater zone, and Cashie is applied to the territory of the Tuscarora, Meherrin, and Nottaway in the interior Coastal Plain.

The Carolina Algonkians were the southernmost representatives of a linguistic family distributed from North Carolina to Canada (Goddard 1978). They were exclusively adapted to the Tidewater environment in the middle and southern ranges of that distribution (Snow 1978).

The archaeological assemblage of the Colington phase (A.D. 800-1650), as it is presently and incompletely known, includes the Colington ceramic series, a shell-tempered ware divided into types on the basis of surface finishing techniques. In order of popularity these are fabric-impressed (Figure 1.9a-b), simple-stamped (Figure 1.9c-d), plain, and incised (Figure 1.9e-g). Rims are frequently decorated with incised linear and geometric patterns and less often with punctuations. Mockley cord-marking and net-impressing of the previous period did not survive the transition to the Colington phase. The range of vessel shapes is not yet well known but includes conoidal pots, hemispherical and simple bowls, and a small beaker form with everted rim. The shell used for tempering is either marine (oyster) or freshwater (mussel), depending on site location. Colington ware is the equivalent of the Townsend series and Roanoke

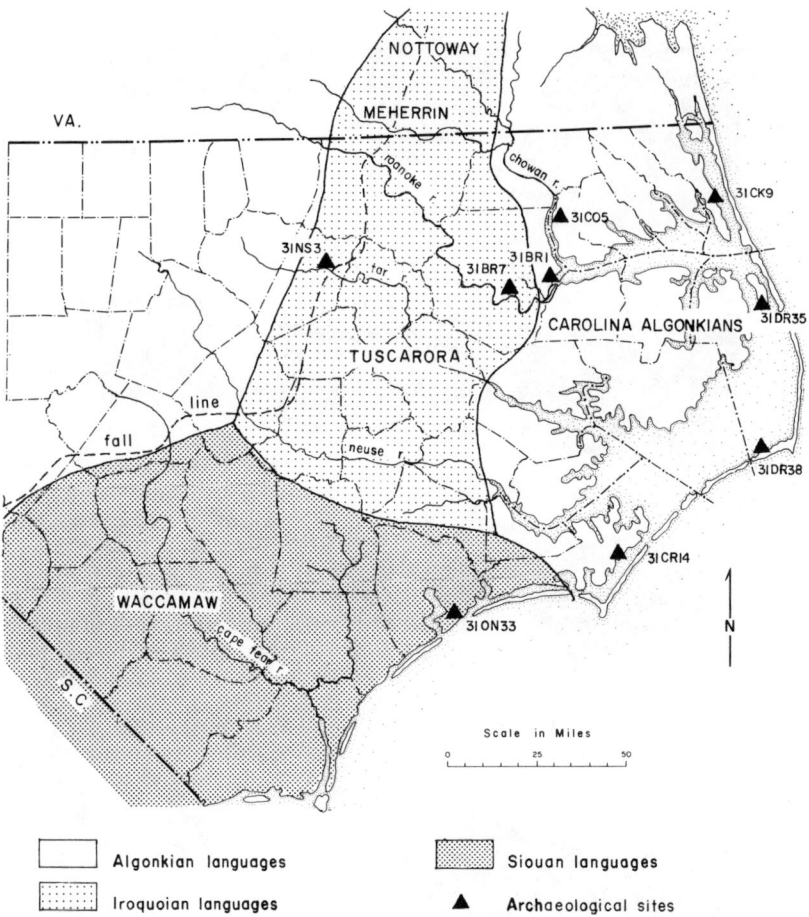

FIGURE 1.8. Distribution of protohistoric ethnic and linguistic groups in the Coastal Plain.

simple-stamped in southeastern Virginia. A second ceramic series is found as a trade ware in the Colington phase sites. This is a ware usually tempered with small pebble-size clastic material but often containing liberal amounts of sand and finished with the same surface treatments noted above for the Colington ware. Harrington (1962:45-46) reported the contemporaneity of these wares at Fort Raleigh, and Haag (1958:71) included some similar specimens in his "grit-tempered" types. The "grit" or pebble-tempered ware is more at home on the Inner Coastal Plain where it is known as the Cashie series (see Figure 1.12), and its presence in the Colington phase sites apparently resulted from extensive trade between the two cultures. The Cashie ceramics are found in higher frequencies in

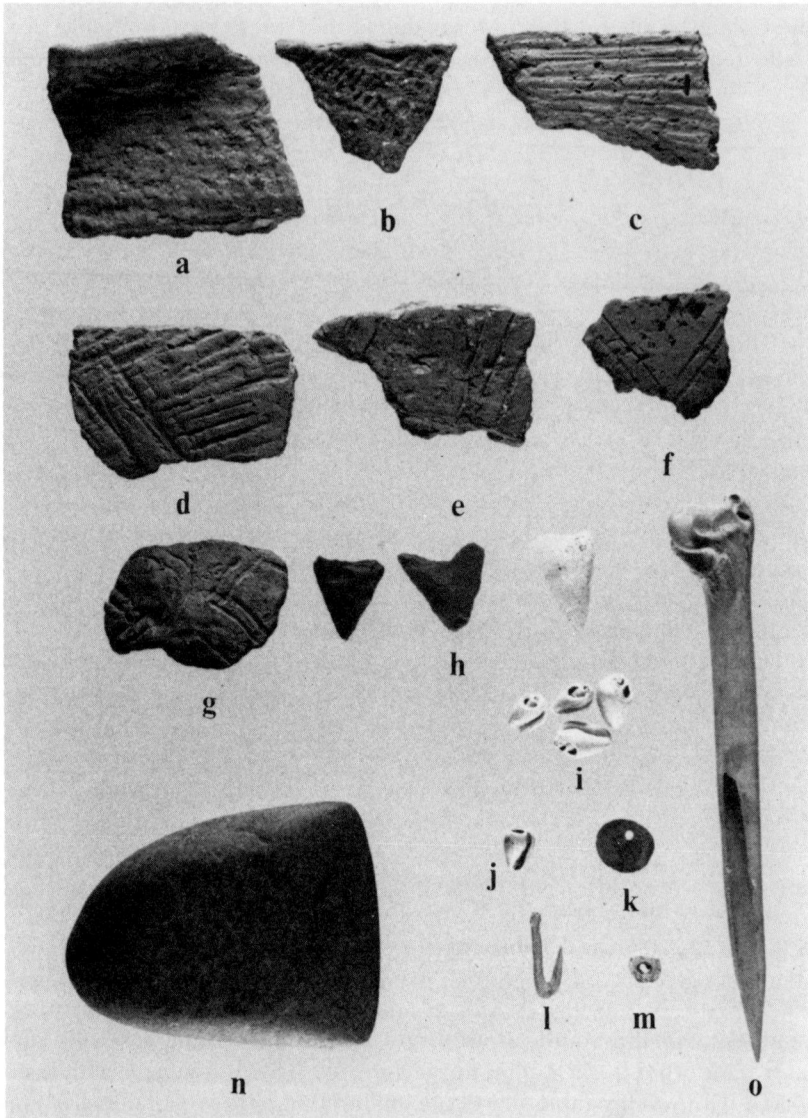

FIGURE 1.9. Artifacts of the Colington phase assemblage. Colington shell-tempered fabric-impressed (a-b), simple-stamped (c-d), and incised (e-g) sherds; the small variety of Roanoke triangular points (h); *Marginella* beads showing different methods of preparation for stringing by abrading away the shoulder of the shell (i) or removing the spire (j); a copper disc bead (k); bone fish hook (l); shell disc bead (m); small polished stone celt (n); and an awl made from a bird bone (o). Length of the celt (n) is 6 centimeters.

the Colington sites at the western edge of the Tidewater. Also found as a trade item are occasional sherds of a burnished plain, fine sand-tempered ware similar to Coe's (1964:33-34) Caraway Plain.

Projectile points are the small variety of the Roanoke triangular type (Figure 1.9h), with some occurrence of the smaller, equilateral triangular Clarksville (Coe 1964:112) points, Bifacial blades of various shapes, polished stone celts (Figure 1.9n), gorgets, sandstone abraders, and milling stones are part of the lithic assemblage. Busycon shell hoes or picks, ladles, columella beads of tubular shape, and *Marginella* shell beads (Figure 1.9i-j) are known, as are freshwater pearls from one site and a copper disc bead (Figure 1.9k) from another. Bone artifacts include antler flakers, fish hooks (Figure 1.9l), awls (Figure 1.9o) and punches of various shapes, bone pins (sometimes incised), and a panther mask. Ceramic pipes with bowls attached to stems either horizontally or at an angle are well known and have been previously illustrated (Haag 1958: Figure 10).

Current radiocarbon dates for the Colington phase assemblage are A.D. 860 ± 85 for the early Colington component at the Tillet site; A.D. 1045 + 65 and A.D. 1320 ± 80, which span the occupation at the Kitty Hawk Bay site; A.D. 1230 ± 65 at the White Court site; and A.D. 1315 ± 70 for the Baum site (Phelps 1977a; 1981b: Table 5).

The territorial range of the Colington phase (Figure 1.8) correlates with the distribution of Carolina Algonkian societies as they are known from ethnohistoric sources. The area included is the Tidewater zone of southeastern Virginia from Hampton Roads and the James River southward and the northern Tidewater zone of North Carolina. Recent discussions at the Symposium on the Middle Atlantic Culture Province held in Norfolk (January 1981) and comparisons of data with Virginia researchers indicate that the southeastern corner of that state is archaeologically more similar to the North Carolina Coastal Plain than it is to the area north of Hampton Roads. The southern boundary is presently conceived as a line drawn from New Bern to Cape Lookout, including the Neuse River estuary and northern Carteret County, but further research is necessary to define precisely this actual division.

Mook's (1944:181) definition of the area from ethnohistoric sources draws the line due south from New Bern to emerge at Bogue Inlet, but Snow's (1978:59) boundary coincides with that proposed above. Within this territory, exactly coinciding with geological definitions of the Tidewater region (Figure 1.1), were a number of social units organized as chiefdoms, although it is tempting to speculate that they were embryonic state systems because of the presence of a formal religion and priesthood. The settlement pattern was relatively dispersed; but probably not to the extent former researchers have suggested, with site locations concentrated along the sounds, estuaries, major rivers, and their tributaries. Site types should include capital villages, villages, seasonal villages, and camps for specialized activities. Also suggested is the farmstead, probably occupied by members of an extended family. Except for a seasonal site at Wanchese, a village site at Shipyard Landing (31Br1) in Bertie County, and shellfish collecting and fishing camps on Colington Island (Phelps 1981b), no sites have been extensively excavated. Villages on Hatteras Island (31Dr38), in Currituck County (31Ck9), and at Gloucester (31Cr14) have been tested, and others are scheduled for this operation in the near future. Villages of both regular internal organization with palisades and less formally structured open types were observed by the English explorers (Lorant 1965; Feest 1978: Figures 2, 8), but insufficient work has been done to elucidate this intrasite variability.

Except for the camps, which appear to be directly related to seasonal gathering of shellfish, fishing, and perhaps collecting, all seasonal and larger villages are located where agriculture, hunting, gathering, and fishing could all be accomplished within the site catchment area. The summer seasonal village at Roanoke Island visited by English explorer Arthur Barlowe in 1584 (Corbitt 1953:20) is an example. Gardens were planted here, and fishing was a major activity while the corn crop was maturing at the mainland capital village across Croatan Sound. Only one of the chiefdoms was located on the Outer Banks on Hatteras Island; most of the sites of this group reported by Haag (1958) have disappeared through modern development, but some evidence remains in the Hatteras Village site. Hatteras is one of the few barrier islands with sufficient area at its present south end to support the subsistence needs of a large population. Most of the large and small villages on the mainland are situated adjacent to streams or other bodies of water on high banks and ridges of sandy loams, the latter preferred for swidden agriculture. Oak-hickory forests interspersed with second-growth pine in previously cleared areas on the uplands, American beech forests, swamp forests, marshes, streams, and sounds provided ample resources. Subsistence data reclaimed from Colington phase sites include evidence of maize, hickory nuts, faunal remains of bears, deer, and a wide variety of small animals; alligators, terrapins, and turtles; fish, and both marine and riverine shellfish. The exploration period records indicate other cultigens (squash, sunflower, beans) and wild plants that were collected for food and for which future archaeological projects should search.

Perhaps the most striking trait of the Colington phase is the Algonkian ossuary form of burial (Figures 1.10 and 1.11). These mass interments are typical of both the Algonkian cultures and their Iroquian neighbors and appear to be part of a strong northern tradition (Ubelaker 1974). Five of these ossuaries have been recovered from village sites on the Chowan River (31Co5), in Currituck County (31Ck9), on Hatteras Island

FIGURE 1.10. Burial 1 (a) and Burial 5 (b) at the Baum site (31Ck9) are typical of the Colington phase ossuaries of the immediate coastal area. Both burial pits measured approximately two meters in diameter and contained secondarily deposited articulated skeletons as well as bundles and randomly scattered bones, all closely packed into the relatively small pits. Inclusive artifacts are infrequent with this type of burial.

FIGURE 1.11. A Colington phase ossuary at the Hallowell site (31Co5) with nine separate groups of secondarily deposited skeletons placed in a rectangular pit (3 x 4 meters) represents a variation of the ossuary pattern in the inner estuarine zone.

(31Dr38), and at Gloucester in Carteret County (31Cr14), the smallest containing 38 and the largest 58 persons (Phelps 1980b). The individuals range from newborn to old age and include both males and females. John White's watercolors (Lorant 1965) include a picture of a burial house or mortuary temple for storage of deceased political and religious leaders but provide no information on storage of the common population until the time of deposition. The ossuaries include incomplete bundles of bones, which had been stored for some time, as well as skeletons still articulated when deposited. Few artifacts accompany these burials; in one case some conch columella beads, in another bone pins and a panther mask, possibly indicating shaman status of one of the deceased. The known ossuaries occur in large and small villages, and future research is needed to determine: frequency of communal burial, especially this form; the range of site types in which these burials occur; and whether or not there are special burials in the capital villages for the religious and political hierarchy. Evidence from the Baum site (31Ck9) suggests a cemetery area near the northern site periphery, and this may be a standard part of the intrasite pattern in the Colington villages (Phelps 1980b). An intensive

Coastal Plain

study of one locality might utilize burial patterns to determine intersite relationships.

The Colington phase ends at ca. A.D. 1650 with the expansion of the European colonial frontier southward from Virginia into North Carolina. Twenty-five years later the Chowanoke, most powerful of the Algonkian tribes, were placed on a reservation in Gates County, and all mention of these people, except for a few thoroughly acculturated remnants, ceased in the colonial records by the middle of the eighteenth century.

West of the Algonkian distribution lay the territory of the Iroquoian-speaking Tuscarora, Meherrin, and Nottoway, closely related in culture to the Algonkians and probably originating from the same northern protoculture. The Tuscarora occupied the Inner Coastal Plain from the Roanoke to the Neuse rivers and from the western estuarine border to the fall line; the Meherrin and Nottoway occupied the river drainages of the same names, both tributaries of the Chowan River, in the northern North Carolina and southern Virginia Coastal Plain (Figure 1.8). The Late Woodland manifestation of these tribes is here designated the Cashie phase, contemporary with Colington from A.D. 800 but extending intact until A.D. 1715 when reservations were established for the Tuscarora and Meherrin after the Tuscarora War. Sociopolitical organization appears to have been at the village level, with each unit essentially autonomous (Boyce 1978:283) within the larger tribal society. A dispersed settlement pattern of small villages, farmsteads, and camps for specialized activities is the most plausible in light of the historic records and present archaeological evidence. Also there are the seasonal villages erected in the fall, winter "hunting quarters" (Boyce 1978:284), and the palisaded fortifications of European design from the war years. Excavations at one small village and a probable seasonal camp provided most of the current data, although minor excavations and tests have been accomplished at other sites.

The Cashie phase is defined by a ceramic series of the same name, taken from the Cashie River in Bertie County, the easternmost tributary of the Roanoke occupied by the Tuscarora. The series was first identified at the Jordan's Landing site (31Br7), the small village used for archaeological training of East Carolina University students, and includes Cashie fabric-impressed, simple-stamped, incised, and plain as the major types (Figure 1.12a-e). Vessel rims are frequently decorated with punctations and less often with incisions and finger pinching; some vessels have incised and punctated designs applied over the normal surface finish. While the Cashie ware is primarily tempered with small pebble-sized particles that often protrude through both side walls, sand tempering is often used in thin wall vessels and occurs as a free variation in many specimens. Cashie vessel shapes include conoidal pots, hemispherical and simple bowls, bowls with an ovate-triangular orifice shape and a flattened, extended lip at the apex, beakers, ladles, and dippers with long handles. The Gaston Simple Stamped type (Coe 1964:105-106) is equivalent to Cashie Simple Stamped, but the latter's late temporal position and existence as the sole type in the Gaston series raises many questions. Binford's (1964a) Branchville series in the Meherrin and Nottoway localities and the Sturgeon Head ceramics defined by Smith (1971) in his study of the Hand site correlate with Cashie ware but differ in the presence of cord-marked surface finish. The protohistoric position of these series suggest trade and other influences not present in prehistoric times, and future comparative work is needed to clarify their relationship to Cashie. The Cashie series duplicates the surface finishes of the Colington pottery, reinforcing the close relationship of these local phases. Colington ceramics, along with conch shells, *Marginella* shell beads, diamondback terrapin shells, and other items native to the coast (Figure 1.12f-h) have been found in Cashie phase sites on the lower Roanoke and indicate an extensive trading relationship between the two cultures. Other ceramic specimens include smoking pipes (Phelps 1980a: Figure 7.8) similar to those in the Colington assemblage, although some Cashie specimens may be painted red, and one example of a human figurine fragment with flat body and pinched, stylized arms has been found (Figure 1.12i).

Bone artifacts include awls and perforators, pins and a shaman's tool kit from one of the burials that contained two sets of deer antlers, whole and cut bear femurs, elk or deer scapulae cut into pointed, triangular objects, and carapaces of diamondback and Carolina terrapins. Beads made from *Marginella* shells (Figure 1.12h) are numerous and always accompany burials in which their quantity may be a status indicator; disc and barrel-shaped beads cut from conch shells are also part of the assemblage. The lithic complex includes small Roanoke and Clarksville triangular points, celts, bifacial blades, unifacial scraping tools, milling stones, and drills.

Two radiocarbon dates have been obtained for the Cashie phase so far; these are A.D. 1150 ± 65 (UGa-3143) from a feature at the Thorpe site (Phelps 1980a:71) (31Ns3b) and A.D. 1425 ± 70 (UGa-1086) from a well-defined cooking pit at Jordan's Landing (Phelps 1977a).

The Jordan's Landing site is probably a typical small village occupying approximately three acres of the northern margin of the Roanoke River. It is located at the confluence of a small stream with the river at a point where the channel is immediately adjacent to the bank. Oak-hickory forest occupies the bank ridge, and behind the site are long ridges of fertile sandy loam. The site has not been completely excavated, but some intrasite variability has begun to emerge. The village area appears to be roughly oval and is bounded on the north and west by a ditch, possibly

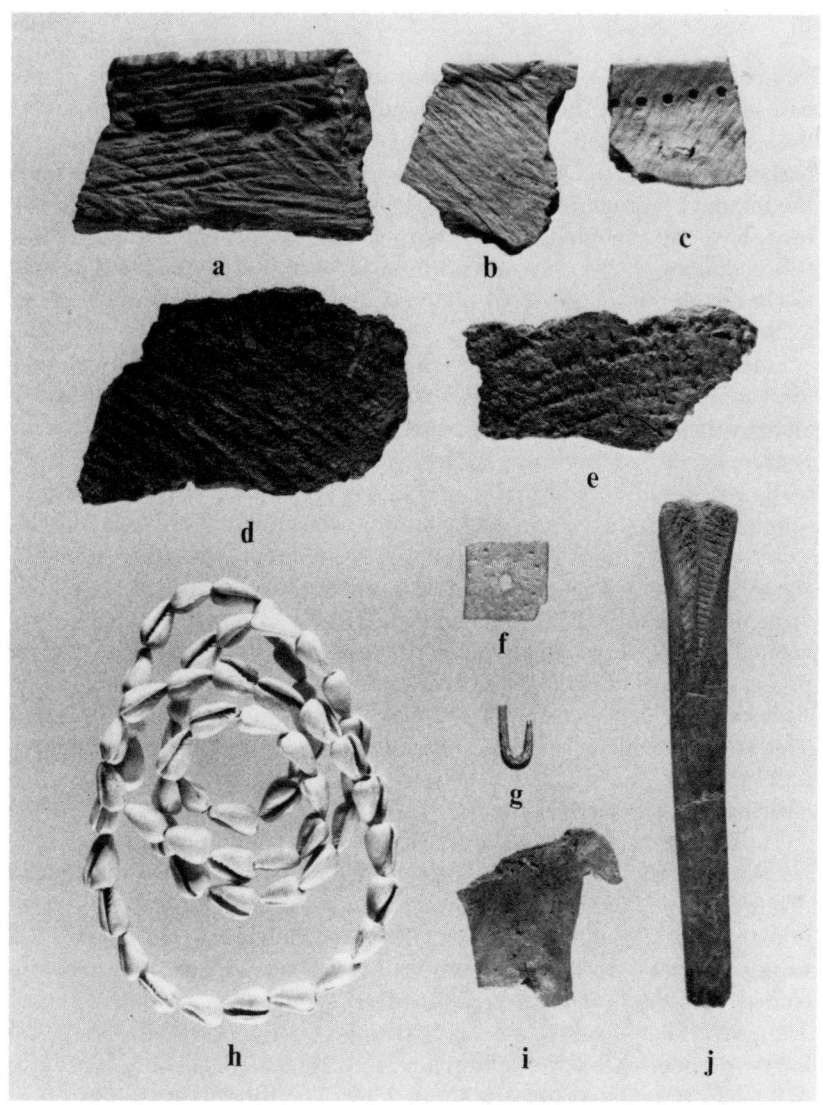

FIGURE 1.12. Artifacts of the Cashie phase assemblage. Pebble-tempered sherds of the Cashie simple-stamped (a-c) with typical rim punctations, and Cashie fabric-impressed (d-e). A cut shell bead with punctated decoration (f), bone fish hook (g), *Marginella* beads (h), ceramic figurine fragment (i), and a bone pin with incised decoration (j) from various sites. Length of the bone pin (j) is 10 centimeters.

originating from natural erosion or as the source of soil used to bank the base of a palisade. The ditch eventually became filled with refuse from the site; quite literally it was the village dump, identifiable from the first basket loads to the final overflow at the top. Within the village some fragmentary postmold patterns have been exposed, but no complete structures have yet emerged. Intact cooking hearths and pits are widely distributed along the western and northern sides of the site, and burials tend to cluster on the southeastern side, but much of the eastern area remains to be excavated.

Subsistence data from the site are typical of a multiple adaptive pattern; maize and beans have been reclaimed from the ditch and hearths, along with charred hickory nutshells, a wide range of fauna including bear, deer, raccoon, possum, rabbit, and other mammals; numerous fish; turtle and terrapin; and turkey and mussel. The wide variety of food resources clarifies the choice of site location where all of these natural foods were available, and arable land for agriculture was also adjacent. Agriculture in the Coastal Plain was not tied to floodplains, although this type may occasionally have been practiced; most of the villages are located on or near the loamy uplands along streams, regardless of size or proximity of floodplains. In this regard also the same uplands along streams were the mainstay of colonial agriculture and remain so today. The Tuscarora villages were particularly blessed, since they occupied that part of the Inner Coastal Plain containing the most productive agricultural soils in the state.

Typical Cashie burials are ossuaries by definition, in that they usually contain two to five individuals deposited as secondary bundle burials (Figure 1.13). This variation is similar in concept and origin but different in practice from the Algonkian pattern of the Colington phase in that the Cashie ossuaries represent family rather than community burials. Included with the burials are a few artifacts such as bone awls and always *Marginella* shell beads, some still in stringing order, others scattered. The lowest number of beads in a burial is approximately 200 and the highest, with the presumed shaman's burial, 2000. The different quantities may indicate social status or rank, but this pattern is not yet clear. One burial at Jordan's Landing differed from the normal type in containing a single extended inhumation in a large, specially prepared oval pit. Associated with the skeleton was a string of disc- and barrel-shaped beads. This special type of burial may also be indicative of status and rank.

Although a number of Cashie phase sites are now on record, no comprehensive study of settlement type and distribution has been initiated. One example of either a hunting-quarter village or a seasonal camp has recently been salvaged (Phelps 1980a) and adds a further dimension to the phase. Located at the falls of the Tar River, the Thorpe site final compo-

FIGURE 1.13. A typical Cashie phase ossuary, Burial 9 at the Jordan's Landing site (31Br7) contained the remains of four individuals. This bundled, secondary deposition also contained a large number of *Marginella* shell beads which may have indicated family or individual rank.

nent belonged to the Cashie phase. The features of that phase salvaged during the project suggested a pattern of autumn gathering and hunting, with the majority of the features containing large quantities of hickory nutshells and deer bones. A few features produced fish bones and minor amounts of mussel shell, but no structural or burial evidence was uncovered. While the work was limited to right-of-way salvage rather than the entire site, the interpretation favors a fall camp located to take advantage of available forest products and fauna and possibly a spring camp to exploit fish runs at the falls of the Tar River and shellfish below the falls.

The Colington and Cashie phases of the North Carolina region are local variants of the same basic cultural tradition, but the South Coastal Plain has been presumed to be Siouian territory since the beginning of the Woodland period (Snow 1978:60-61). The Late Archaic and Early and Middle Woodland data previously discussed certainly set the region apart, and the ethnohistoric accounts, although meager, argue for a Siouian-speaking culture distributed as shown in Figure 1.8. South (1976:5-8) has summarized the documentation for the Waccamaw, Cape Fear, and other groups in the region, presumably correlating these with his Oak Island complex, here adopted as the phase name for the Late Woodland in the South Coastal region.

The Oak Island phase is presently known best for the coast proper, where shell-tempered ceramics with cord-marked, fabric-impressed, and net-impressed surface finishes are diagnostic of the complex. Little else is reported except marine-oriented subsistence and a house pattern from the Uniflite site, 31On33 (Loftfield 1979), and surface surveys (Loftfield 1976; South 1976; Wilde-Ramsing 1978). Part of the problem is lack of data for the interior of the region and insufficient excavated data. While the existence of net-impressed ceramics may indicate a close relationship with Late Woodland Siouan phases in the Piedmont, most interpretations have used the Algonkian Colington phase for direct comparison (Loftfield 1976). In this respect, however, Loftfield's work has been primarily in the locality between the White Oak River and Cape Lookout, immediately adjacent to the presumed regional border. Coastal subsistence adaptations are generally the same from Chesapeake Bay to Florida, but the cultures exploiting these resources were considerably different. Similarly, some quite different cultures shared ceramic traits but varied significantly in other respects. Considerable work will be required in the South Coastal region before the Late Woodland period is clearly defined and can be submitted to regional comparison. Adding to the confusion are recently published radiocarbon dates (Loftfield 1979b:58) that have been interpreted as authenticating the beginnings of shell-tempered pottery in the Middle Woodland. However, two dates from one feature are 400 years apart, and the total range expressed by six dates is 1000 years. Two dates from Virginia were offered for comparison, and shell tempering certainly began in the Middle Atlantic subarea in Middle Woodland times and spread southward, but its impact on the south coast probably did not occur until the Oak Island phase.

The Oak Island phase may have differing local expressions in the Tidewater and Inner Coastal Plain, but the present level of knowledge for the latter precludes any meaningful statement at this time. The local phase in the narrow Tidewater zone appears to have been similar to the Colington phase but probably represents acculturation of south coast groups to north coast patterns. South's (1976:20) shell-tempered Oak Island ceramic series with cord-marked, net-impressed, plain, and fabric-impressed surfaces, in order of popularity, is the definitive complex for this phase, and the similar White Oak series (Loftfield 1976:157-163) has been subsumed under the Oak Island definition. The higher frequency of the fabric-impressed type and the presence of simple-stamped (Loftfield's "thong marked") sherds similar to Colington simple-stamped in northern Onslow and Carteret counties, the area of Loftfield's study, is a logical expectation near the regional boundary.

A recent study of an ossuary burial in New Hanover (Coe, et al.1982) concludes that the population represented in the ossuary is Siouan, and Oak Island ceramics in the burial fill confirm the phase identification. Other ossuaries in Carteret and Craven counties, nearer the northern boundary of the region, have been excavated and when finally studied may shed some light on the geographic range of coastal Oak Island and its exchange with the Colington phase and Algonkian populations.

CONCLUSIONS

In reviewing the content of this paper, two conclusions thrust themselves immediately to the fore: (1) archaeologists should know better than to repeat the mistakes of their own profession's past history, and (2) contemporary archaeologists of the "second" and "third" generations must adjust themselves to a structured, cooperative mutual effort in order to understand past culture and manage its diminishing resources. The first conclusion is obvious in that designed research addressing specific problems is the only means of achieving a fully accurate understanding of Coastal Plain prehistory; no longer can we afford the time to excavate a site here or do a survey there without first assessing the value of such research to current problems. There is nothing inherently wrong with data accumulation as long as there is a matrix in which to place it. The concept of designed research should apply to field schools and basic research projects initiated by university archaeologists and other agencies working in the region, and research continuity should be maintained.

The second conclusion relates directly to the perceived differences in orientation of basic as opposed to cultural resource research. Environmental projects are limited in scope and cultural space and seldom produce culturally meaningful results unless they are directly correlated with current archaeological information for the project area. Often new data, artifact types, major research concerns, realignments of previous models, and types of sites with National Register significance are not available in the published record, yet it appears that the published record is all that some environmental impact investigators depend upon to evaluate their results. Most archaeological facilities maintain collections, continuously accumulate and reinterpret data, and are willing to share this with any colleague since it is an integral part of professional ethics. Environmental project personnel have a responsibility to fit their data into the most accurate and current model and should avail themselves of the resident facilities and expertise in all stages of their projects from planning to publication. Another ethical practice of the not-too-distant past was the courtesy visit to archaeologists in the area of a research project to acquaint them with the project; this should be revived.

A concomitant of this problem is the significance of sites with respect to National Register criteria. An environmental project may have discovered a site presumed to belong to a particular phase and found it to have some minor remaining contextual deposits beneath an otherwise badly disturbed upper zone. Without particular knowledge of the area, the investigator may well evaluate the context as significant when, in reality, a number of sites of the same type and phase with better context may be known in the region, and some may even have been excavated although not yet published. All archaeological sites are significant, but their significance in terms of the National Register occurs in a priority ranking directly related to current knowledge of their value within a specific culture; if the cultural information is not known, the significance cannot be accurately evaluated.

More germane to the purposes of this paper, however, are the problems of culture history in the North Carolina Coastal Plain. Most of the problems have been addressed, either implicitly or explicitly in the preceding passages, but a summary of the more important issues is not amiss here. The key problems include:

(1) knowledge of Paleo-Indian period site distribution correlated with Pleistocene environment, which would result in settlement and subsistence models to be tested against those currently proposed;

(2) discovery and excavation of either single-component or stratified Paleo-Indian and Archaic period sites to provide more accurate descriptions of assemblages for each phase and to assay diachronic changes in the assemblages as well as changes in subsistence strategies and other cultural subsystems;

(3) location and excavation of sites that have preserved the transition from the Late Archaic to the Early Woodland to evaluate the impact of new technology introduced in the latter period;

(4) a study of changes in settlement and subsistence patterns during the Early and Middle Woodland periods in order to understand changes resulting from the introduction of cultigens; and

(5) excavation of sites that represent the range of types for each phase of the regional sequences to provide a complete culture history as a platform from which processual studies can be launched.

Beyond these problems designed to authenticate chronology and amplify culture history, the existing record permits identification of more specific areas of inquiry. A few examples of these problems are: (1) trade networks that existed across the Coastal Plain in the Late Woodland period and what commodities were passed along the networks. One example was the route along the Roanoke River-Albemarle Sound connecting the Colington (Algonkian) and Cashie (Tuscarora) territories with the Piedmont and Mountains, along which unmodified marine shells, shell beads, copper, pottery vessels, turtle shells, and probably many other items were traded. Can some sites be identified as "gateway" towns, and was the distribution of trade items even across each political territory or concentrated in the capital villages among the higher ranks of the society? (2) The relationship of the South Coastal region burial mounds to the culture that produced them and whether or not these are simply communal burial structures or reflect a degree of stratification in the society. How do these structures relate to surrounding regions, and what was the origin of this type of burial structure in the South Coastal region?

A listing of problems and hypotheses could consume many more pages, but the above sample should sufficiently illuminate the possibility of posing research problems from the available data. The most pressing needs for the moment are cooperative research, an efficient means of disseminating environmental archaeological reports, and an expanded mechanism to provide a synthesis of information from environmental archaeology and incorporate it into continuing regional studies.

The current culture history of the North Carolina Coastal Plain is, as previously stated, a working model to be modified as data accumulate, but even in its present form it should accommodate research designs for all objectives of modern archaeology. It will suffice for now if it generates research, both basic and environmental, to understand better the Coastal Plain and the cultures whose homeland it was in the past.

2

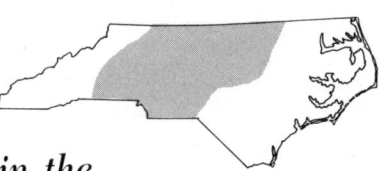

A Review of Archaeology in the North Carolina Piedmont: A Study of Change

H. Trawick Ward

INTRODUCTION

This paper will discuss ideas, feelings, and observations concerning what has been done, what is being done, and what are the major concerns that need to be recognized in charting the directions of future archaeological research in the North Carolina Piedmont. In order to accomplish this broad, rather august task, each of the major prehistoric periods will be summarized emphasizing the current level of understanding on such basic rungs of the archaeological ladder as typology, chronology, subsistence, and settlement analysis. Obviously these are hierarchically ordered and interrelated research concerns that only partially cover the total spectrum of contemporary archaeological thinking. These areas are, nonetheless, fundamental to most research and can provide a comprehensive framework for assessing what is known and what is not known, as well as outlining a set of realistic research objectives for Piedmont archaeology.

THE PIEDMONT ENVIRONMENT

In North Carolina the Piedmont is defined by some 39 counties separating the topographically monotonous Coastal Plain from the roller coaster terrain of the Blue Ridge escarpment. No attempt will be made to detail the various geological processes and formations that are responsible for the Piedmont topography; however, a review of some of the environmental features most important in shaping and influencing the cultural systems that have adapted to the area over the past 15,000 years is in order.

It is also appropriate to look at how the Piedmont landscape has been altered and changed in modern times. Too often archaeological sites are viewed as if their contemporary environs mirror a static condition that generally reflects the prehistoric scene both in the character of the surrounding geography as well as in the immediate site conditions. To understand the Piedmont site, however, it must be viewed as a component of an active, changing environmental regime, not simply as a constellation of artifacts frozen through time in their matrix.

The Piedmont defines an area that separates almost half the state of North Carolina not only physiographically but also politically, economically, and socially. This distinctiveness is reflected by past cultures as well as today's inhabitants. Physiographically the Piedmont is a highly dissected plateau that contains some 20,000 square miles. Elevation above sea level ranges from around 400 feet along the eastern border to roughly 2,000 feet at the edge of the Blue Ridge escarpment. The dominant topographic features are well-rounded hills and long rolling ridges trending northeast to southwest. This fairly uniform topography is interrupted occasionally by more prominent peaks such as the Uwharrie Mountains in Montgomery and Randolph counties, the Kings Mountain range in Cleveland and Gaston counties, and the Sauratown Mountains in the northern sections of Stokes and Surry counties (Figure 2.1).

The drainage systems of the Piedmont form a distinctive dendritic pattern with three main branches. To the north are the Dan River and its tributaries, while the Neuse, Tar, and Cape Fear rivers drain the central Piedmont area south of the Dan and east of the Yadkin basins. Important tributaries include the Haw and Deep rivers, which join to form the Cape Fear River in Chatham County. The final drainage system consists of the Yadkin, Broad, and Catawba, which flow through the southwestern section of the Piedmont. During prehistoric times this drainage pattern would have encouraged the north-south movements of people while inhibiting east-west travel.

Igneous, sedimentary, and metamorphic rocks comprise the Piedmont basement structures and are irregularly distributed at the surface throughout the area. Intense volcanic activity took place during the early Paleozoic period in the eastern Piedmont and forged what is commonly known as the Carolina Slate Belt. This formation runs the entire length of the state, covering part if not all of the counties between Granville to the north and Anson to the south. The slate belt with its lava flows, beds of breccia, ash, tuff, and slate provided the prehistoric inhabitants of the Piedmont with an abundant supply of raw materials from which to make their tools and implements (Stuckey 1965).

Not only was the Piedmont attractive to prehistoric peoples because of its abundant lithic supplies, it also offered a veritable smorgasbord of natural plant and animal resources. Of course, this bounty has not always been uniform as climatic changes have taken place during the past 15,000 years. By the end of the Pleistocene period, when man was beginning to adapt to the Piedmont, climatic conditions were moderating, and the area

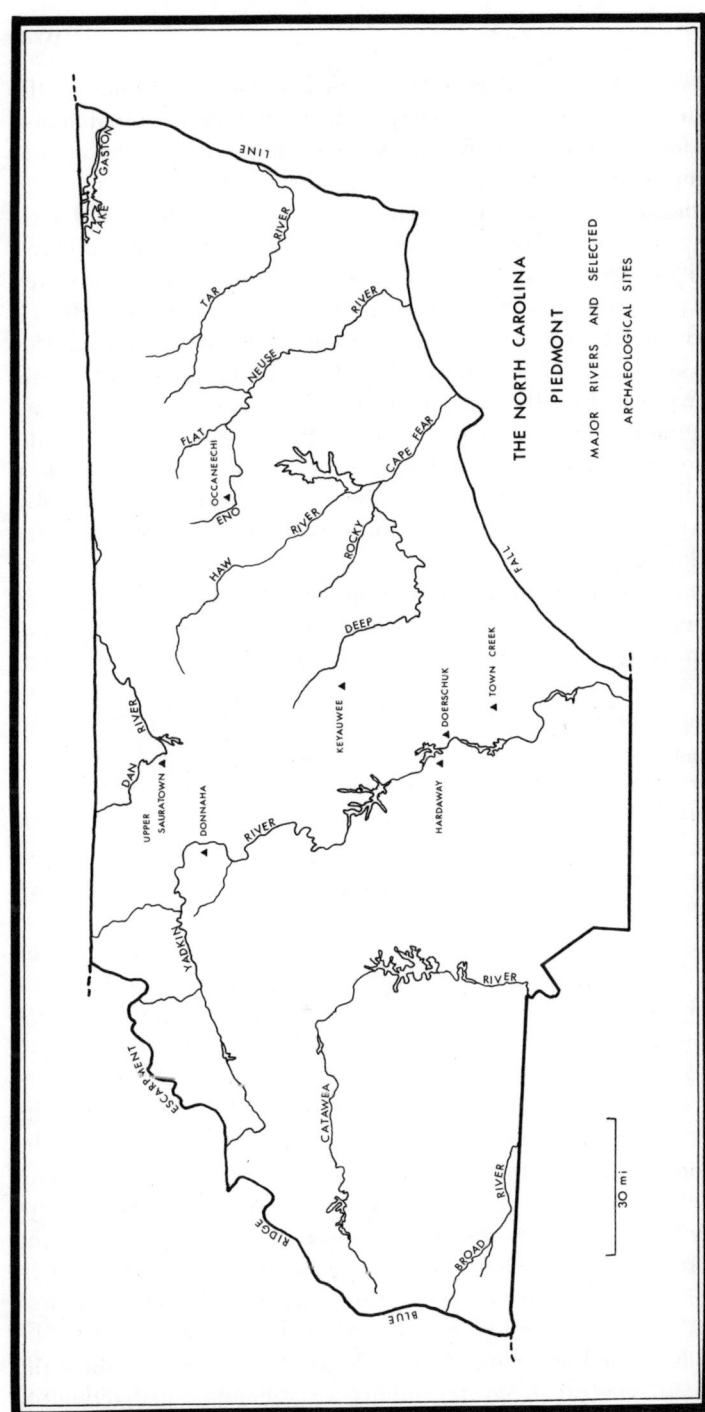

FIGURE 2.1. The North Carolina Piedmont, with major rivers and selected archaeological sites.

was probably dominated by stands of oak and hickory similar to the northern hardwood forests found today in the northeastern United States. As conditions continued to warm, this oak-hickory association was gradually replaced by a mixed forest dominated by oak and pine. These stands of pine and pine-hardwood mixtures are dominant today, although the relative abundance of pine has increased considerably in recent years.

Although changes took place, the aboriginal forest cover probably provided a more abundant supply of edible nuts and fruits as well as a more varied and richer habitat for game animals than is seen today. This assessment is certainly true for the late prehistoric and early historic periods as witnessed by the narratives of early explorers. John Lawson, traveling in the Piedmont in 1701, listed 27 different species of mammals, including several no longer found in the area today. Buffalo, panther, wolf, and elk were all inventoried by Lawson, and bear, which was ubiquitous during the early eighteenth century, is found only rarely today (Lawson 1967:120).

Lawson's much-quoted description of his journey from the Haw River to Occaneechi Town, located just north of present-day Hillsborough in Orange County, provides a vivid picture of the Indians as well as the land.

> Their Cabins were hung with a good sort of Tapestry, as fat Bear, and barbakued or dried Venison; no Indians having greater plenty of Provisions than these. The Savages do, indeed, still possess the Flower of Carolina, the English enjoying only the Fag-end of that fine Country (Lawson 1967:61).

Certainly a variety of resources was available for exploitation throughout the Piedmont. The major watercourses provided corridors for movement, trade, and communication and their floodplains, fertile, friable soils. The low rolling hills and ridges interspersed between the rivers and streams were laden with wild food resources as well as raw materials needed by the aboriginal economies. The Piedmont must indeed have been the "Flower" of the state, and for many it remains so today.

After extensive colonization, however, the flower wilted under the brutal onslaught of destructive cultivation practices. First the soils in the fertile bottoms were depleted and abandoned. Then the hills and ridges were cleared, farmed, and also abandoned at an astonishing rate as erosion became more and more severe. The soil from the uplands filled the river and stream channels with sediment and created wet, swampy conditions in areas that had once contained prime agricultural land. Because of these misguided agricultural practices, the Piedmont became one of the most severely eroded agricultural areas in the United States. Since the early eighteenth century in North Carolina, it has been estimated that the average depth of soil loss through erosion in the Piedmont was 5.5 inches (Trimble 1974:1).

Much of the soil destruction caused by early farming practices has been stopped through the use of commercial fertilizers and large-scale conservation measures. Regrettably, the impact of past cultivation practices on the archaeological record has been irreversible, and to some extent cultivation continues to disturb and destroy archaeological sites throughout the Piedmont. The impact today, however, can not possibly compare with the damage and destruction caused before the twentieth century. Consequently, most of the upland sites have become homogenized collections of tools and flakes with little or no associational context and spatial integrity, while many other sites in the bottoms have been buried deeply and are rarely discovered.

The destructive impact of agriculture and erosion on Piedmont archaeology is extremely important for an understanding of the complex web of factors ("site formation processes" to use Schiffer's [1976] terminology) that have stirred and shaped the record as it is preserved today. Cultivation and erosion are only two of these factors, but in the Piedmont they are pervasive and too often have been ignored by archaeologists, or considered of little consequence. Certainly any settlement pattern model or intrasite spatial activity analysis that does not include a detailed assessment of these disturbances runs the danger of being highly misleading.

EARLY WORK IN THE PIEDMONT

Southeastern archaeology was newly born when archaeological research began in the North Carolina Piedmont. The first statewide survey was initiated in 1934 by members of the North Carolina Archaeological Society, founded in 1933. In the Piedmont, Douglas Rights was responsible for the upper Yadkin Valley; Guy B. Johnson explored the New Hope Creek drainage in Orange and Durham counties; and Joffre Coe began work in Guilford County.

In the Piedmont this earliest work was primarily concerned with locating historic towns identified with the various Siouan groups. In 1935 the North Carolina Archaeological Society began excavations at the site of Keyauwee, located in Randolph County and visited by John Lawson in 1701 (Figure 2.2). This research continued in 1936 and eventually led to the identification of the Caraway and Uwharrie complexes. The following year marked the first season at the Frutchey Mound, later to become Town Creek Indian Mound State Park (Figure 2.3). During 1938 Siouan studies continued with excavations at Occaneechi and Saponi sites on the Roanoke River and Lower Saura Town on the Dan River. Additional excavations were also carried out at the village of Occaneechi on the Eno River near Hillsborough and at a Saponi site on the Yadkin River (Coe 1964:6).

FIGURE 2.2. North Carolina Archaeological Society camp at Keyauwee, 1935.

After World War II emphasis shifted to identifying some of the earlier complexes that had been isolated by surface survey. At this time it was assumed that "if a significant number of traits were found to occur together on a series of sites, then they were probably the physical remains of the activities of a particular group of people at a particular period of time" (Coe 1964:6). Coe (1964) later determined that these complexes represented everything but the activities of a particular group, and realizing the futility of seriations based solely on surface samples in developing

FIGURE 2.3. Preliminary trench excavated through the Frutchey Mound (Town Creek), 1936.

cultural sequences, he shifted research to the excavation of buried, stratified deposits. From this work during the 1950s and early 1960s at the Doerschuk, Hardaway, and Gaston sites, the cultural sequence of the Carolina Piedmont was firmly established (Figure 2.4). During this period excavations continued at Town Creek, and the reconstruction on the site was completed in 1960. The middle and late 1960s saw a shift in emphasis from the Piedmont to the Appalachians and the Cherokee. It was not until the early 1970s that research returned to the Piedmont with excavations at Upper Saura Town on the Dan River (Figure 2.5).

However, it is no overstatement to say that archaeology in general, and archaeology in North Carolina in particular, underwent dramatic changes during the early 1970s with the passage of national conservation legislation emphasizing cultural resource management (CRM). As a consequence, archaeologists have had to refocus many of their past perspectives

FIGURE 2.4. Preliminary excavations at the the Doerschuk site, 1948.

FIGURE 2.5. Excavations at Upper Saura Town, 1972.

concerning what they do—or are supposed to do. Even those in academia are no longer allowed the luxury of serene isolation behind ivy-covered walls where the only irritations come from an occasional pesty student or meddling dean. To be sure, the students and deans are still around, but they are welcome nostalgia compared with the hordes of planners, engineers, and bureaucrats with their realms of proposals, directives, guidelines, and forms that are now directly or indirectly involved in the archaeology business.

Over the last eight years most of the archaeological work in the Piedmont has resulted from CRM requirements. The emphasis has been on survey and settlement studies, with excavations being primarily limited to testing operations. Site intensive research has been extremely limited compared with the number of surveys and small-scale tests.

Although the main goals of CRM archaeology are to conserve and manage archaeological sites, methodological and theoretical concepts have also been developed that have had reverberations in the academic and research spheres as well. Today, more than ever, there is a need for cooperation and exchange between archaeologists primarily concerned with managing archaeological sites and those with more academically oriented research backgrounds. In the following pages the foundations for this mutual relationship will be addressed as well as some specific areas where divergence should be expected and is perhaps necessary for the growth of archaeology in general.

THE CURRENT STATE OF THE ART

Many recent reports dealing with Piedmont archaeology have in them somewhere a statement bemoaning the fact that very little is known. This assessment is totally erroneous. Since 1934 a great deal has been learned. Archaeologists working in other southeastern states appreciate how much is known since much of the typological and chronological backbone for the Southeast in general is directly tied to early work in the North Carolina Piedmont. This is not to imply that the total archaeological universe is understood nor that there are not problem areas, but there is a framework of knowledge that allows the formulation of questions that might appropriately be asked and points to directions that can profitably be investigated.

In order to be more specific, the major cultural periods will be reviewed from the standpoint of what is currently known and what are reasonable research objectives in light of the Piedmont data base. These remarks will of necessity be general but keyed to such specific and interrelated areas as typology, chronology, subsistence, and settlement patterning. Before beginning, a few brief comments are necessary to outline the temporal framework that will be used. This framework is meant to define only general chronological periods, not evolutionary or developmental stages (see Figure 2.6).

The Paleo-Indian period encompasses the temporal span between 12,000 and 8000 B.C. The beginning date is arbitrary, and evidence may eventually be found that places man in North Carolina before that time. The Hardaway complex occupies the earlier end of this period, and although there are no reliable dates for the Palmer complex, the 8000 to 10,000 B.C. range seems likely, thus placing Palmer at the later end of the Paleo-Indian period.

Following Coe (1964) and Phelps (1964) as well as others, the Archaic period is broken down into early, middle, and late subperiods. The Early Archaic period is seen as lasting from around 8000 B.C. until 6000 B.C. and is typified by the Kirk complex first identified at the Hardaway site. Recent radiocarbon dates place Kirk as early as 7200 B.C. (Chapman 1977:161). The Middle Archaic lasts from 6000 B.C. until roughly 2000 B.C. and is indexed by the Stanly, Morrow Mountain, and Guilford complexes. The Late Archaic is defined by the widespread Savannah River occupation, which persisted from around 2000 B.C. to perhaps as late as 500 B.C.

The Woodland period begins with the introduction of ceramics around the fifth century B.C. The Early Woodland, marked by the Badin and Vincent ceramic traditions, lasted until ca. A.D. 500. In the Uwharrie area Badin ceramics were replaced by Yadkin, while in the northeastern Piedmont the Vincent tradition persisted with little change until around A.D.

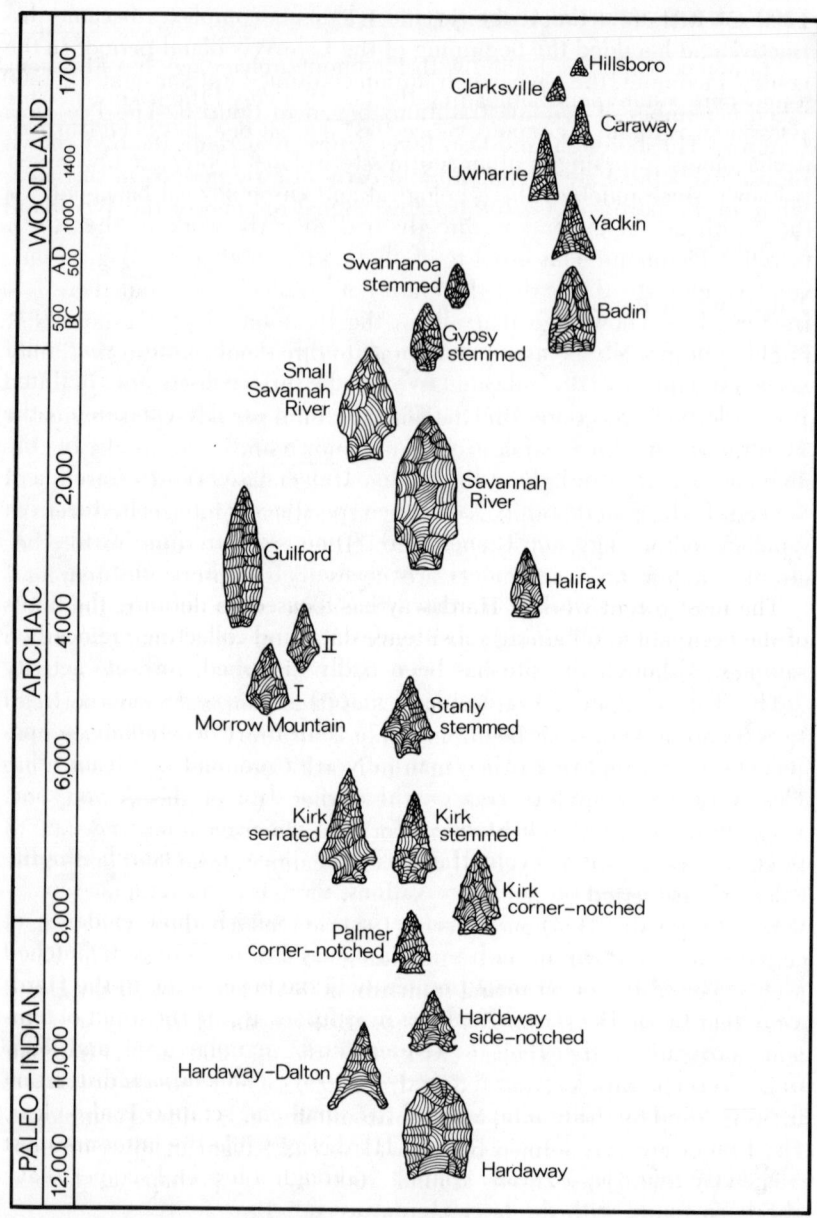

FIGURE 2.6. Generalized chronological sequence of projectile points in the North Carolina Piedmont (adapted from Oliver 1981b).

1200. At that time the Uwharrie and Clements complexes became distinctive and heralded the beginning of the Late Woodland period. In the central Piedmont, the Uwharrie tradition continued until around A.D. 1500 when a number of ceramic traditions began to flourish. The Pee Dee, Caraway, Hillsborough, and Dan River series are perhaps the best known indicators of the Late Woodland and early historic periods in this area, while to the northeast Gaston ceramics signal the end of the Woodland (Coe 1964).

Paleo-Indian Period

Paleo-Indian sites remain illusive ghosts in the Piedmont, but their presence is occasionally indicated by sporadic surface discoveries of fluted projectile points (Perkins 1971; 1973). The most notable exception is the Hardaway site, discovered in 1937 and excavated since 1948 by the Research Laboratories of Anthropology, University of North Carolina at Chapel Hill. Unfortunately, almost every serious relic collector from North Carolina, Virginia, Georgia, and Tennessee has also "excavated" the site, and today a great deal of its potential has been destroyed.

The most recent work at Hardaway has focused on defining the limits of the occupation, obtaining subsistence data, and collecting radiocarbon samples. Although the site has been badly disturbed, intrasite activity analyses are planned using statistical mapping techniques such as trend surface fitting (Ward 1980a; Davis 1973). For the Paleo-Indian occupation the first objective has been partially achieved, and one feature has yielded carbonized wood fragments that may date the Hardaway zone. Unfortunately, direct subsistence data have not been recovered.

At present the most recent Hardaway data have not been thoroughly analyzed; but based on field observations, there is a stratigraphic separation between the Hardaway blades (some of which show evidence of channel flake removal) and the Hardaway-Dalton and side-notched points. The blades occur most frequently in the lower levels of the Hardaway zone (Zone IV). The differences in morphology are the result of temporal variability rather than the sequencing of manufacturing and reuse stages as some have suggested (Goodyear 1974). The temporal distinction between the large side scrapers and the small end scrapers is also clear. The former are only associated with Hardaway while the latter are most frequently found in a Palmer context, although a few end scrapers have also been found with the later Hardaway varieties.

In terms of typology and chronology the Paleo-Indian period is fairly well understood. The diagnostic artifacts and the stratigraphic sequence outlined in 1964 have not changed; however, it is now felt that the Hardaway complex in its earliest form is at least as old as the Clovis fluted point tradition in the East (Coe, personal communication). This chronological position is based on recent radiocarbon dates from Early Archaic horizons in Tennessee and West Virginia (Chapman 1975, 1977; Broyles 1971), as well as morphologic and stratigraphic detail recently gleaned from the Hardaway site.

In 1979 a Hardaway side-notched point and a fluted Clovis-like specimen were reportedly found in the same stratigraphic context at 31Ch8, a site on the Haw River that has been inundated by the Jordan Reservoir. These specimens were, however, excavated by amateurs, and although the identification of the points has been verified, records were not sufficient to verify their stratigraphic context.

Also of potential importance for Paleo-Indian studies are recent excavations sponsored by the U.S. Army Corps of Engineers at 31Ch29, a multicomponent site also located in the Jordan Reservoir. Reportedly, a Hardaway occupation, which contains some degree of horizontal spatial integrity, has been isolated. Subsequent analysis should shed significant light on intrasite activity studies. At the very least an artifact inventory with good stratigraphic context will contribute to expanding the typology by investigating possible regional and functional variability within the Piedmont. When these data are studied in conjunction with other Paleo-Indian sites in the Jordan Reservoir, a regional settlement model incorporating intersite functional variability can perhaps be developed. Eventually such studies should provide some insight into Paleo-Indian ecology.

At present the development of settlement and subsistence models with a high degree of resolution for the Paleo-Indian period is a long way off in the Piedmont. The extant data are badly biased and lack floral and faunal remains that are requisite for direct dietary and subsistence analysis. It has been assumed the Paleo-Indians of the eastern United States lived in migratory bands that hunted and gathered wild resources available seasonally. Given the morphological and functional similarities between the projectile points from the East and the West, many have assumed that the megafauna associated with the western Paleo-Indian sites also have a primary importance in the East (Griffin 1967; Wormington 1957; Willey 1966).

Apparently the overall population at this time was small, as reflected by the relatively small number of sites. The fact that Paleo-Indian sites are spatially restricted and usually contain less dense concentrations of materials than later occupations also seems to support the assumption that a low level of sociopolitical integration is represented. Those statements, however, are about all that can be said without stretching the logical foundations of current assumptions to the point of creating a weak web of mere speculation. The seasonal round of resource utilization within a tightly scheduled procurement system cannot be substantiated and neither can the exploitation of late Pleistocene megafauna. Although it is difficult to tell what was hunted by the shape of the projectile point, the general typological continuity between the Hardaway, Palmer, and Kirk horizons appears to suggest a less specialized activity than the exploitation of megafauna.

Before more is known about Paleo-Indian ecology in the Piedmont, work needs to be done in defining and refining lithic tool variables in an effort to isolate temporal markers with the same or greater degree of sensitivity than the projectile points and scrapers that currently comprise the backbone of Paleo-Indian chronology. Detailed microscopic analyses of tool use and function may also help in understanding subsistence practices and may in fact offer the only avenue of subsistence reconstruction because of the extremely low preservation potential for ethnobotanical and faunal remains. Even if subsistence remains are found, such detailed lithic studies should be carried out to complement the more direct analyses.

If our understanding of cultural processes during the Paleo-Indian period is to increase, it is imperative that more stratigraphic work be initiated. This is not to imply that surface survey should be discontinued; certainly it should not. However, if research is to continue beyond rather simplistic, distributional studies that may or may not reflect some past reality, intact deposits with spatial integrity must be isolated and studied. Only at sites with stratigraphy can the complex stylistic, functional, and adaptive variability of Paleo-Indian cultures be brought to light. Once these kinds of sites have been studied in sufficient numbers, then perhaps some interpretive life can be breathed into the thin, shallow, eroded surface remnants usually encountered in the course of survey work.

Archaic Period

In contrast to the Paleo-Indian inhabitants, the bearers of Archaic culture covered the Piedmont landscape, leaving a network of tracks that is hard to miss. In almost every plowed Piedmont field some trace of the Archaic period can be found. The broad alluvial valleys, the rolling upland hills, and the banks of small streams were all occupied, visited, or utilized at some point during the 6,000 to 7,000-year span of the Archaic period. This is not to imply that an unchanging, homogeneous cultural system with simple adaptive machinery is represented. If anything, the opposite is true. The term Archaic probably covers more diversity and complexity than any other taxonomic construct applied to the Piedmont. Although there is a striking similarity throughout the area in the morphology of certain tools and implements, there is tremendous variety in site size, content, and function. This diversity is usually viewed as evidencing an ever-increasing adaptive radiation and specialization in a varied post-Pleistocene environment.

Typologically, the Kirk, Stanly, Morrow Mountain, Guilford, and Savannah River complexes still provide the index "fossils" for separating the Archaic period into early, middle, and late subperiods (Figure 2.6). These complexes are defined primarily on the basis of projectile point forms (or hafted bifaces), although other diagnostic tools such as scrapers, atlatl weights, chipped and ground stone axes, steatite vessels, and distinctive preforms or quarry blades can also be chronologically distinguished with a high degree of accuracy. The projectile points, however, are more ubiquitous and have had, by far, the greater chronological utility. Coe's (1964) Piedmont sequence has remained unaltered, and stratigraphic work in neighboring areas (Chapman 1975, 1977; Broyles 1971) continues to reinforce the chronological continuum identified two decades ago.

Lacking projectile points, many sites have been assigned to the Archaic period because they produced lithic debris and no pottery. Although specific tool kits might require unique lithic reduction and maintenance behaviors, there is much overlap in stone tool manufacture and use throughout the Archaic as well as Woodland periods. Consequently without a large sample of waste flakes, as well as a collection of associated diagnostic specimens, even the most general chronological or functional interpretations should be accepted with great caution. The position here is there is little difference between an Archaic and Woodland game processing site, and many of the sites identified as Archaic "extractive loci" could just as easily reflect Woodland or even Paleo-Indian activities (cf. Mathis 1979:26).

As with the Paleo-Indian period, direct subsistence data are extremely rare in the Piedmont. Recent work in Tennessee has resulted in the recovery of ethnobotanical remains that suggest a narrow range of botanical resource exploitation (acorn and hickory) as early as the Kirk period and lasting at least into the Middle Archaic (Chapman 1975:271). Yarnell postulates the cultivation of sunflower, sumpweed, and possibly chenopodium as early as 2000 B.C. (Yarnell, 1976a:268), and there is some evidence from Kentucky and Missouri that squash may have been cultivated at a similarly early date (Chomko and Crawford 1978). Nevertheless, wild plant foods (particularly hickory nuts and acorns) and white-tail deer continued as dietary mainstays during most of the Archaic period.

Most authorities see the Archaic period as representing a continuation of basic hunting and gathering patterns established during the Paleo-Indian period (Coe 1964; Griffin 1967). An increase in population occurred from the Early to Late Archaic period, and more and more diverse and specialized ecological niches were exploited as adaptive efficiency increased through time. This "forest efficiency" is generally believed to have been enhanced by scheduling resource procurement in a tightly structured seasonal round (Caldwell 1958).

In the North Carolina Piedmont this subsistence model is usually enmeshed with a settlement pattern comprised of two major site types, the base camp or "maintenance" site and the "extractive locus" where specialized activities associated with direct resource procurement took place. The former are larger in size, contain a wide variety of tool forms, and represent a more intense occupation. Maintenance sites are generally believed to occur primarily on the floodplains of the major Piedmont streams. The more specialized extractive sites, on the other hand, are generally small and contain fewer artifacts. Associated tool forms evidence functionally limited behaviors connected with specific resource procurement systems. The extractive sites are typical of the interriverine uplands (House and Ballenger 1976; Mathis 1979).

The larger base camps are believed to have been occupied during the spring, summer, and winter, while the smaller upland sites represent migratory fall camps resulting from deer hunting and nut harvesting activities (House and Ballenger 1976). Mathis has recently added an intermediate-sized Archaic encampment, which was putatively occupied during the warmer months when plant and animal resources would have reached maximum dispersion. These sites are situated along the smaller streams and tributaries (Mathis 1979:32).

During the Late Archaic period a trend toward a more sedentary life is normally suggested because of evidence of large sites replete with burials, steatite bowls, hearths, and floors. It should be added that most of these larger sites have been found in Georgia, Tennessee, Kentucky, and Alabama where the major streams are characterized by broad shoals. These shoals provided an ideal environment for the exploitation of freshwater mussels and other riverine resources, a practice that began as early as the Middle Archaic and continued through the Late Archaic period (Lewis and Lewis 1961; Webb and DeJarnette 1942). Although the mollusk remains are spectacular in many cases, late Archaic populations also relied heavily on deer and other mammalian species as well as fish and amphibians. No such sites have been discovered in the North Carolina Piedmont, although the Gaston and Doerschuk sites, situated by the falls on the Roanoke and Yadkin rivers respectively, would seem to have offered similar resource niches (Coe 1964).

The data, nonetheless, seem clear and point to the fact that an expanding population was characteristic during the Archaic period in the Piedmont. The general applicability of the seasonal transhumance settlement model evokes at least some healthy skepticism. From a theoretical standpoint, such a model is largely dependent on analogy with contemporary hunters and gatherers or on prehistoric data derived outside the eastern woodlands (e.g., Flannery 1968). In addition, there is no evidence to indicate a degree of resource marginality anywhere in the Piedmont comparable to that characteristic of modern hunter-gatherer territories.

Perhaps much of the ecological diversity seen in the Piedmont is more imagined than real and reflects a perspective pulled out of focus by the contemporary scene with its recently created back swamps, overgrown fields, pine thickets, and scrub oak stands (see Trimble 1974). This is not to imply that the area was uniformly blessed with natural foods and raw materials, but rather that the degree of seasonal diversity between the major floodplains and dissected uplands does not appear to have been sufficiently complementary to require dispersal and movements of migratory bandlike groups for maximum exploitation.

The presumed ecological diversity is usually expressed in terms of the alluvial bottoms being exploited primarily for fish, fowl, fruits, and berries during the warmer months in addition to providing a convenient trade and communications network. In contrast, the upland deciduous forest zone is seen as offering a plentiful supply of acorns and hickory nuts during the fall. In addition to attracting man, the fall mast production also attracted deer and other mammals, which further served to induce migrations out of the bottoms during this time.

There is no question that an oak-hickory or oak-hickory-pine forest dominated the interriverine uplands prior to European contact, and today oak and hickory still dominate all but the more recent successions. In reality, though, how much contrast is there between this ecological zone and the alluvial bottoms? There are expansive stands of huge oak and hickory along the banks of the Pee Dee River as well as the Dan, the Haw, and most other major Piedmont streams. A timber survey conducted in 1858 along the Deep River floodplain listed stands of white oak, chestnut oak, and overcup oak intermixed with hickory, ash, elm, and pine (Houck 1956). Another Piedmont survey in 1897 listed the dominant species along the larger floodplains as bitternut hickory, sweet and black gum, overcup oak, chestnut oak, sycamore, and hackberry. The broad flat river bottoms were described as being covered with stands of water oak, overcup oak, and willow oak while along their fringes were growths of white and black oak (Ashe 1897). A more recent botanical survey conducted in 1955 along the Deep River floodplain listed black oak, chestnut oak, swamp chestnut oak, red oak, and shagbark hickory as the dominant species (Houck 1956).

Based on this brief floral sketch, there is little difference, in terms of mast producing species, between the floodplain and upland zones. The differences that exist lie in the greater diversity of non-mast-producing species within the floodplain zone (Richard Yarnell, personal communication). As a consequence, the seasonal differences in floral mast production between the uplands and floodplains are minimal and do not support the assumptions of the seasonal transhumance model.

In the Piedmont there is also no evidence that the seasonal habits of deer vary much within a given region from year to year; neither do they appear to prefer the uplands over the lowlands. They do, however, enjoy edge-disturbed areas (Runquist 1979:170-171). Such areas would have been prevalent around the more sedentary habitation sites in the floodplains. In short, the alluvial bottoms probably offered an abundant supply of plant and animal food on a year-round basis.

From the standpoint of the archaeological record itself, there is a noticeable lack of evidence for seasonal procurement during the Archaic period. Seasonality is usually assumed because of such circuitous evidence as site size, artifact density, and inferred functional content, although most of the sites investigated, at least in the uplands, have been shallow, deflated, multicomponent occupations where diachronic variability can rarely be controlled. Granted the interriverine Piedmont is characterized by small, seemingly temporary sites, but numerous small sites are also located in the floodplains.

In light of these factors, Piedmont settlement patterns need to be broadened to include a model of relatively stable, sedentary hunters and gatherers primarily adapted to the varied and rich resource base offered by the major alluvial valleys. There is no doubt the interriverine zones were also extensively exploited, but instead of explaining such sites as fall procurement stations, alternate explanations should be expanded to include a wide range of adaptive responses. Such factors as territoriality, intersystemic conflict, population stresses, and environmental deterioration could provide the foundation for more regionally specific hypotheses that also need to be tested. The seasonal transhumance model and the sedentary model are opposite ends of a continuum, and in all likelihood variations on these two themes probably existed in different regions at different times throughout the Archaic period—and for that matter, on into the Woodland.

New ideas to stimulate new hypotheses are needed, but data that produce concrete information concerning subsistence, seasonality, scheduling, and sedentism are needed even more. Although a great deal of creativity and imagination have gone into formulating functional descriptions of surface or plow zone lithic scatters, these descriptions are becoming redundant. There are only so many ways the same phenomenon can be described or "explained." If the cultural processes operative during the Archaic period are going to be understood, more information is desperately needed than can be distilled from a temporally mixed handful of chips. As Chapman has stated:

> Although it is apparently passe in the 1970's to be concerned with cultural history and assemblages, these are the hard data for model building and processual studies. Too much has been written based on deflated sites and surface manifestations in which there were no con-

trols of the time span represented by the artifacts (Chapman 1977:125-126).

Woodland Period

Like the Archaic, most of the recent Woodland period research has involved surveys and limited excavations. These data have been applied to such problems as ceramic variability and settlement pattern change. The following remarks will review this research and attempt to provide some insight into which directions and approaches can most profitably be pursued in the course of future Piedmont Woodland studies.

Wake Forest University recently carried out limited excavations at the Donnaha and Parker sites located on the upper Yadkin River. Several interesting questions have been posed as a result of this work and other investigations in the Yadkin valley. The Research Laboratories of Anthropology at the University of North Carolina has concentrated on the Dan River drainage and continues to excavate extensively a historic village of the Saura Indians in Stokes County. In the southern Piedmont, Catawba College crews have tested a multicomponent Woodland site in Anson County.

The co-occurrence of Savannah River points and Woodland ceramics in surface collections has led some to hypothesize that the cultural discontinuity mentioned by Coe (1964) did not take place, but rather a basic Archaic tradition with large stemmed points persisted in some areas after the introduction of pottery (Woodall 1976). There appears to be some confusion concerning what Coe meant by a "discontinuity." His use of the term referred to the fact that there was no evidence of a transitional Archaic-Woodland zone at sites investigated up to that time, not that there was no transition. In fact, Coe stated,

> It is unlikely that there could have been such a widespread replacement of a population in such a short time and the explanation must be sought elsewhere. Perhaps this period of transition simply did not exist at the sites that have been studied. . . . (1964:124).

I, too, have observed the coincidence of Archaic remains and Woodland ceramics on many Piedmont sites. In fact, most large sites seem to produce both. It is also true that many aspects of the Archaic tradition persisted after the introduction of pottery. It should be pointed out, however, that the ceramic horizons were separated from the Savannah River occupations at the Doerschuk and Gaston sites by as much as 12 inches of sterile soil. Excavations at stratified Archaic-Woodland sites in the Jordan and Neuse reservoirs have also failed to reveal any overlapping between Savannah River and ceramic assemblages (Coe and Ward 1976; Wilson and Coe 1976). Today there is evidence of an Archaic-Woodland transition. Based on a reanalysis of the Doerschuk and Warren Wilson materials, a small stemmed projectile point bridges the typological gap. Research in this area is continuing, and a formal type description has been suggested (Oliver 1980).

One reason for the correlation between the occurrence of Late Archaic Savannah River materials, as opposed to Early or Middle Archaic specimens, and Woodland materials is the fact that Late Archaic occupational evidence is considerably more extensive throughout the Piedmont. Perhaps typological refinements such as those currently being carried out by Oliver will clarify the nature of the Late Archaic-Woodland transition. But certainly more stratigraphic evidence is needed as well.

Recent attempts have also been made to refine the Woodland ceramic typology developed by Coe (1952; 1964) and Coe and Lewis (1952). These studies have used sophisticated computer techniques and cluster analysis to explore a wide range of ceramic variables from sites in the northern Yadkin valley to see if the basic tenets of the "intuitive" typology were also scientifically correct (Barnette 1978; Newkirk 1978). The conclusion was that "key factors in this largely computerized ceramic analysis were generally the same as those observed by Coe in his primarily descriptive analysis of ceramics. . . ." (Barnette 1978:92).

This is not to say that the sequence Coe defined for the southern Piedmont should have universal applicability. In fact, there are marked distinctions between ceramics from the Buggs Island and Gaston reservoirs and the south-central Piedmont materials (Coe 1964:27). During Late Woodland times these regional differences increased markedly, reflecting varying degrees of northern and southern influences; protohistoric and historic population movements also clouded the ceramic picture with considerable diversity. However, there is some doubt as to the utility of cluster analysis and other schemes of numerical taxonomy in identifying and understanding this variability. As Thomas has recently observed, traditional, intuitive topologies work, and so far "number crunching" has failed to produce anything new or useful from a typological standpoint (Thomas 1978:236). Obviously, this viewpoint is not held universally. Newkirk argues:

> Despite the extensive variable list with no *a priori* knowledge inflicted on the data, the same attributes proved diagnostic in the clusters as those used in Coe's typologies. Does this mean that the cluster analysis is meaningless and simply a duplication of something that we already "intuitively" knew? The answer to that is yes and no; yes it did duplicate something that was already known (the Uwharrie prototype variables) but no it was not useless because although "intuitive" pottery types have been accepted for years as valid classification, they have not statistically been proven so (Newkirk 1978:60).

Several points concerning this statement should be mentioned. First, no statistic can be used to *prove* a relationship between a set of variables. The clusters derived from cluster analysis may be statistically sound yet lack typological or taxonomic validity. Also, Coe's classification does not need to be proven statistically or otherwise since it is based on irrefutable stratigraphic evidence. Even so, sites in the northern Yadkin valley would appear to be a poor choice to test statistically the southern Piedmont ceramic sequence. In fact, it is somewhat surprising that a high degree of coincidence was achieved. Also it is unclear how *a priori* knowledge was avoided. If the ceramic sequence had not already been developed, perhaps such a claim would be valid, but some familarity was necessary even to set up the study.

Perhaps these comments are overly critical, but too often the attitude today seems to be that if everything possible is measured and plugged into a canned computer program, there is no need to bother studying collections and sequences that have been developed and refined by years of research experience. I have been as guilty of this as anyone and can certainly understand the seductive lure of the computer. There are, however, no shortcuts, no magical formulae, and no substitutes for experience. This does not mean that computers and innovative techniques have no place in current Piedmont research. If anything the opposite is true, but new ideas and methodologies should use and build upon the foundation of current knowledge, not simply seek to make it "scientific."

Another concern that has been the subject of recent study is the role of maize agriculture in Woodland period subsistence and settlement. Although some indirect evidence of maize has been reported from the Donnaha site, evidencing primarily a Late Woodland occupation, no cobs or kernels have been recovered (J. Ned Woodall, personal communication). A small amount of cob and corn kernels was reported from the Parker site, occupied during Uwharrie times, but it may have been insignificant in the overall economic system because of the absence of hoes and other implements normally associated with agricultural production (Barnette 1978:93).

After testing several hypotheses interdigitating environmental variables considered important in the location of sites where agriculture was of primary importance, Barnette concluded that maize agriculture was not important to the subsistence of any of the Woodland inhabitants of the Great Bend area of the Yadkin River valley. This conclusion was based on the fact that the settlement systems do not show any particular shifts toward areas with increased agricultural potential during the Woodland period. As a result, a basic Archaic hunting and gathering pattern apparently continued until fairly late in the upper Yadkin valley (Barnette 1978:93).

Test excavations have been conducted in Anson County at the Trestle site (31An19), which contains Yadkin and Uwharrie components. So far, no evidence of maize has come to light. On the other hand, a large quantity of animal bone, particularly deer, has been recovered (Peter Cooper, personal communication).

These data suggest that maize agriculture was not particularly important even during the latter part of the Woodland period. Nonetheless, corn from the Parker site is a clear indication that maize was cultivated by Uwharrie times. At 31Ch29 located in the Jordan Reservoir, the Uwharrie component produced numerous chipped stone hoes but no direct evidence of corn (McCormick 1970; Wilson and Coe 1976). Of course, too much should not be made of the presence of "hoes" or other so-called agricultural implements because they could have easily functioned in any number of nonagricultural digging activities.

To summarize, maize agriculture was not important during the Early and Middle Woodland periods in the North Carolina Piedmont. In fact corn does not appear to have had much importance before A.D. 1000 (Coe 1964:51). Although people were growing corn by Late Woodland times, they were still relying heavily on hunting and gathering. A mixed economy probably prevailed where wild food production and agricultural resources complemented one another.

So far the emphasis of this discussion of Woodland subsistence has been on the importance of maize agriculture. The significance of other cultigens during the Woodland period is also important to subsistence and settlement analyses as well as to the more general questions of cultural evolution and adaptation. At present, however, there are too few excavated data for the Early and Middle Woodland subperiods to allow subsistence reconstruction. A complex pattern of mixed agricultural production is beginning to emerge for the later Woodland and historic periods where corn was significantly supplemented by beans, squash, and fruit production (Wilson 1977).

Although there has been relatively little excavation on Woodland Piedmont sites, a component of the historic Siouan village of Upper Saura Town (31Sk1) has been extensively excavated by the Research Laboratories of Anthropology since 1972. A detailed analysis of these data is currently in progress, and only a short summary of the more salient characteristics will be presented here.

To date over 13,000 square feet have been excavated uncovering 10 houses and 188 features. The houses are all circular and range in size from 20 to 30 feet in diameter with the average being around 25 feet (Figure 2.7). The wall posts are tightly spaced and seldom more than .5 foot apart. A wattle and daub facade was used to form the walls, while the dome-shaped roofs were probably thatched. Although center support posts have been tentatively identified within one structure, they have not been found inside the others. A bower-type construction was probably employed,

FIGURE 2.7. Overlapping circular structures at Upper Saura Town. Unexcavated stains represent large storage pits and burials.

whereby the upper sections of the wall saplings were simply pulled together and tied to form the roof (Joffre Coe, personal communication).

Five classes of features have been identified at the site. These include storage pits, earthen ovens, borrow pits, clay hearths, and refuse pits. Large storage pits occur with the greatest frequency (Figure 2.8). These are circular and range in size from a little over 2 feet up to 4.5 feet in diameter. The sides are usually straight, but some flare outward near the bottom producing the well-documented bell-shaped profile. Total depth below the base of the plow zone varies from 1 foot to over 4 feet. The average storage facility, however, is around 3 feet in diameter and 3 feet deep. Most have been refilled with stratified deposits of refuse.

Borrow pits occur almost as frequently as storage pits. These units probably reflect clay mining activities, and although they exhibit much variety in size and shape, the borrow pits are usually shallow and contain a relatively sterile, homogeneous fill.

Perhaps the most interesting features have been identified as earthen ovens (Figure 2.9). These units are large, usually shallow, and ovoid or circular in outline. They measure at least 4 feet in one dimension and are rarely over .7 foot deep. The fill from the ovens is the richest among the features and invariably contains wood charcoal and often large quantities of carbonized plant remains including corn, beans, squash, peach pits, and nutshells. Fire-cracked rock, burned cane fragments, and large

FIGURE 2.8. Profile of a large storage pit with stratified refuse fill; Upper Saura Town.

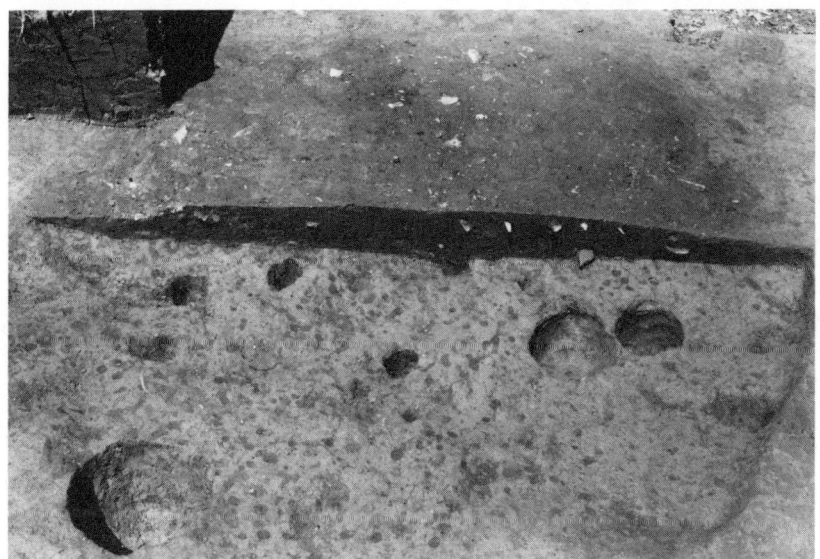

FIGURE 2.9. Profile of large earthen oven feature; Upper Saura Town.

amounts of animal bone are also characteristically found in the fill. Because the sides and bottoms of the ovens rarely show evidence of intense burning, the pits were probably covered and fires kindled on top of the covers.

Only a few pits were dug for the primary purpose of garbage disposal. These circular refuse pits are not as large as the storage facilities, usually measuring less than 3 feet in diameter and less than a foot in depth. The fill is normally homogeneous and uniformly rich in ethobotanical and faunal remains.

Unfortunately, the clay hearths have been plowed out of the structures, but in four instances circular burned areas mark former hearth locations. In one case a small section of a collared basin was preserved.

The ceramics from Upper Saura Town are typical of the Dan River phase, and although a detailed ceramic analysis has not been completed, considerable variation in paste and surface treatment has been observed. Net impressing predominates, but there are also large numbers of plain and burnished sherds. The minority surface treatments, in descending order, are curvilinear complicated stamped, corn cob impressed, simple stamped, and check stamped (Wilson, personal communication). A compact, fine sand-tempered paste is most frequently found, but temper ranges from almost none to an abundance of coarse sand with fairly large quartz particles. A few steatite-tempered specimens have also been recovered.

As mentioned previously, Woodland period subsistence activities involved a mixed economy, with hunting and gathering and agriculture sharing equal roles. Apparently, agriculture increased in importance as more European cultigens were incorporated into the plant food inventory. Peaches were an especially important late addition to the diet (Wilson 1977:115).

PROBLEM AREAS: AN OVERVIEW

From this brief review of the major cultural periods in the Piedmont, it is obvious that more is known about some periods than others and that more generally is known about typology and chronology than subsistence and settlement. The sequence of lithic forms defining the Archaic period is well established, and although some refinements are needed at the later end of the temporal scale, a good, working typology has been developed. Much of the Woodland ceramic sequence has been defined, and there are those who can type and chronologically order almost any pottery sample from the Piedmont. Although much of this ceramic information is not yet published, there are comparative collections available to those who seek an "intuitive" understanding of Piedmont pottery.

The recent flurry of cultural resource management studies have provided a tremendous amount of new distributional data from surveys in areas that have traditionally been uninvestigated. However, the overwhelming majority of these new sites are badly eroded and lack minimal horizontal or vertical stratigraphy. If they ever existed, features such as trash pits, storage facilities, burials, and architectural remains have long since been obliterated by plowing and erosion. Many of these sites consist of nothing more than a few chips and maybe a tool or two scattered over a vaguely defined area.

Although these sites usually lack minimal structural or contextual relationships, they may yet provide information upon which settlement patterns and models to infer ecological and subsistence parameters may be constructed. Problems arise only when the data potential contained in such sites is stretched beyond its logical limits by unfounded assumptions. When these eroded remains are assumed to represent discrete episodes of behavior functionally patterned as synchronous components of complex systems, adaptive models subsequently developed simply cannot be accepted (cf. Deetz 1968:282).

This two-dimensional jigsaw puzzle approach to intrasite structural analysis and settlement studies marks a resurgence of spatial-contextual assumptions that were discovered to be inadequate nearly 30 years ago (cf. Coe 1964:6). Apparently many of the lessons learned in the late 1940s and early 1950s have been ignored or forgotten by some today. As a consequence, archaeological "Frankensteins" such as the Badin and Guilford foci are being resurrected in such ecological disguises as synchronous components of adaptive systems or spatially contiguous collections of discrete, functionally diverse, but interrelated behavioral episodes.

In addition to erosion and plowing, there are many other biases resulting from site formation processes that must be dealt with when using surface survey data in reconstructing settlement and subsistence patterns. The most obvious is the fact that no matter how sophisticated the survey methodology or how complex the sampling scheme, differences in surface visibility are always going to favor the discovery of larger sites. In addition, many sites are deeply buried and will never be observed on the surface, while many others have been erased by meandering river channels and erosion. Amateur collectors are also a source of bias that is often ignored. Most Piedmont sites have been picked over for years, even those tucked away in the darker recesses of the most inaccessible terrain. The eagerness and savvy of the professional archaeologist is often paled by the resourcefulness and energy of the Piedmont collector. There is no doubt that if an archaeologist is brave enough to attack an inhospitable field, more than one collector has already searched it.

Problems in site interpretation from surface remains are also encountered in evaluating site significance relative to criteria for the National Register of Historic Places. There are many sites that present an unimpressive surface collection yet contain a wealth of buried, intact deposits. At 31Rk12, on the Dan River, the original surface survey produced less than 20 sherds and only a couple of flakes, although surface visibility was excellent. In 1972 the site was cut through by flood waters and several burials and trash pits were exposed. Today, after landfill operations, it is again virtually invisible from the surface. At 31Or11, Occaneechi Town, there is hardly any occupational debris on the surface, yet excavations uncovered an extensive village midden. In 1977 a large Woodland village in Chatham County was looted by relic collectors. Personnel from the Research Laboratories of Anthropology investigated and found evidence of numerous pits, features, and burials in the pits that had been dug. The destruction subsequently stopped, and the site was revisited in 1980. Although it had been continuously cultivated and collecting conditions were excellent at the time, the total surface sample consisted of 3 sherds and 2 chips, hardly an endorsement for the National Register.

The problems of site evaluation and significance determination based on surface appraisal and limited testing can frequently be avoided through experience and archaeological common sense. There are, nonetheless, situations where no easy solutions are evident. If midden is absent, and the only intact deposits are contained in pits and features below the plow zone, a surface inspection or small test pit usually will not provide an accurate appraisal. This obvious conclusion is amply supported by the simple fact that of all the CRM reports reviewed in preparing this paper (all the major ones were covered), in only two instances did tests indicate the need for site avoidance or further mitigation. Except for these two sites, not a single undisputed, intact cultural deposit—midden, feature, or posthole—was recorded. No additional work was recommended at any of the sites, and no new information, other than the fact that nothing was there, could be added to the data gathered in the course of the initial survey.

So far only the shortcomings have been pointed out when using data from survey and limited tests to answer questions of settlement and subsistence and to evaluate significance. What then are the positive contributions of such studies? As long as the limitations previously discussed are realized, low level explanations concerning settlement and population shifts are possible. Broad trends in adaptive responses through time and over space may be identified as well as increases and decreases in populations. But the main potential of these data lies in formulating questions and hypotheses, not in answering and testing them. Many interesting hypotheses have been derived from survey data gleaned over the past eight years as a direct consequence of CRM. However, as long as data retrieval stops there, and intensive excavations are not carried out at selected sites, there will continue to be many more questions than answers.

Some researchers have a different view and suggest that the questions are not being answered because they have not been asked the right way. Specifically, this viewpoint holds that processual explanations for the Piedmont are weak and general because they are wholly inductive, and these inductive statements or assumptions tend to be accepted uncritically. I do not agree that induction is the problem, nor do I feel that inductive statements can be equated with assumptions. The former are logically derived from empirical data while the latter, in many instances, are born from nothing more than a fertile imagination. Nevertheless, the hypothetico-deductive (H-D) method has been suggested as an alternative where the validity of formal hypotheses can be measured against a series of implication statements or tests deduced from the hypotheses (Woodall 1979:3-5).

What is not discussed, however, is the fact that test implications are nothing more than assumptions themselves, and just because they are used to test hypotheses does not necessarily increase their epistemological veracity. It should also be pointed out that the H-D approach is, strictly speaking, inductive since it involves accepting a conclusion containing more information than the premises. In fact, most archaeological test implications are not deduced from hypotheses but rather derived inductively through inference (Salmon 1976:377-378).

I would further argue that much of the recent emphasis on deductive hypothesis testing ultimately results not so much from a desire to be scientific—at least according to the rules of Hempelian logic—but from a lack of hard data. If sites are not excavated or only superficially tested, the amount of direct (inductive) evidence concerning subsistence, architecture, stylistic variability, and a host of systemic parameters is severely limited. As a consequence, these kinds of information are being sought inferentially by using various versions of the H-D approach where logical assumptions and test implications replace charred corn and posthole patterns.

Certainly the hypothetico-deductive approach has linked CRM studies to the processual goals of current archaeological theory, but because of the limited data contained in the majority of sites encountered doing CRM work, implications and assumptions are too often substituted for context and association. However, these two conditions are basic for any sound archaeological research and cannot be replaced by hypothetical constructs.

These comments are made not so much as substantive criticisms, but rather to point out the fact that problems in understanding the cultural-systemic processes operative in the Piedmont do not revolve around whether questions are asked before or after the data are gathered or whether assumptions are called inductive statements or test implications. The problems are with the data base: the extent of what is preserved in a site and the integrity of its spatial context. Southeastern archaeological sites in general and Piedmont sites in particular, under the best conditions, contain only traces of a small fraction of material technology. If the chances for answering the more complex questions are to be maximized, efforts must be concentrated at sites that have maximum data for such questions (cf. Clarke 1977:15). Simply rephrasing the questions will only continue to befuddle the issues.

CONCLUSIONS

I have tried to review where we stand today in the Piedmont, but this short paper on such a broad subject can only be superficial at best. I am sure research is going on that I have overlooked, and some I have not covered in the detail it deserves. As stated in the introduction, we all have our biases, and mine have no doubt shown through. I have attempted, however, to be objective and offer constructive, alternative suggestions in areas where I feel we have serious shortcomings.

One theme that has been stressed is the need for intensive research projects at sites with maximum data potential. I am fully aware of the funding shortages for such projects, but I firmly believe they are necessary not only to fill voids in our understanding of Piedmont prehistory but also to train and prepare students to interpret and assess sites under field conditions. Too often I have seen the research potential of sites based on naive assessments of basic archaeological principles, and too often I have read excavation reports where obvious formation processes have been overlooked or misinterpreted. The finer points of site interpretation—isolating structures, determining spatial-temporal associations, and the mechanics of stratigraphy—rarely come to light in a one-meter pit excavated in arbitrary levels.

This emphasis on intensive research projects is not meant to diminish the importance of cultural resource management studies and certainly not a call for a de-emphasis in the conservation effort. Data will accumulate from CRM investigations, and they may stimulate provocative ideas about Piedmont prehistory. On the other hand, such studies usually mark the beginning of a complex research process, where the data requirements dictate explorations at sites in areas not endangered by the construction of highways or the development of housing projects.

Finally, there is no one theoretical approach that can solve all the problems. From a planning standpoint, it can certainly be argued that a research design with specific problem domains and hypotheses can be helpful. A research design, however, is again only a starting point and cannot guarantee valid and significant research results. The questions and hypotheses may be framed deductively or inductively, but if progress is to be made, they must be built on a firm foundation of data and derived from a sound set of assumptions.

3

Ancient Mountaineers: An Overview of Prehistoric Archaeology of North Carolina's Western Mountain Region

Burton L. Purrington

INTRODUCTION

For more than a century the Southern Appalachian Mountains have been romanticized in fiction, song, the public mind, and even scholarly studies. Indeed, this diverse region with its steep, narrow ridges; dense forests; deep, fog-shrouded valleys; and distinctive plant, animal, and human populations and communities is a natural magnet to both romantic and scientific curiosity. Archaeologists too have been lured by the siren call of "the hills" albeit somewhat sporadically and, with a few notable exceptions, recently—perhaps because of the superficially unspectacular nature of the region's record of the past.

One of the earliest of the Appalachian subregions to feel the archaeologist's spade was the Appalachian Summit, the southern section of the Blue Ridge Mountain chain which includes western North Carolina and small adjacent portions of southwestern Virginia, eastern Tennessee, northern Georgia, and northwestern South Carolina (Figure 3.1). Although the Appalachian Summit was long-recognized as the homeland of the Middle, Valley, and Out towns of the Cherokee Indians, it generally was considered to have been something of a cultural backwater in prehistoric times or, as the anthropological historian John Swanton (1946:37) characterized it, a "marginal area . . . occupied rather through necessity than by choice." Nevertheless, the earthen mounds and interesting artifacts of the region's native American inhabitants attracted both scholars and museum representatives as early as the 1880's, and, in 1935, Joffre Coe of the University of North Carolina at Chapel Hill began what has become nearly a half-century of research which has soundly dispelled any notions that the Appalachian Summit might be deficient in distinctive and important archaeological, anthropological, and historical data.

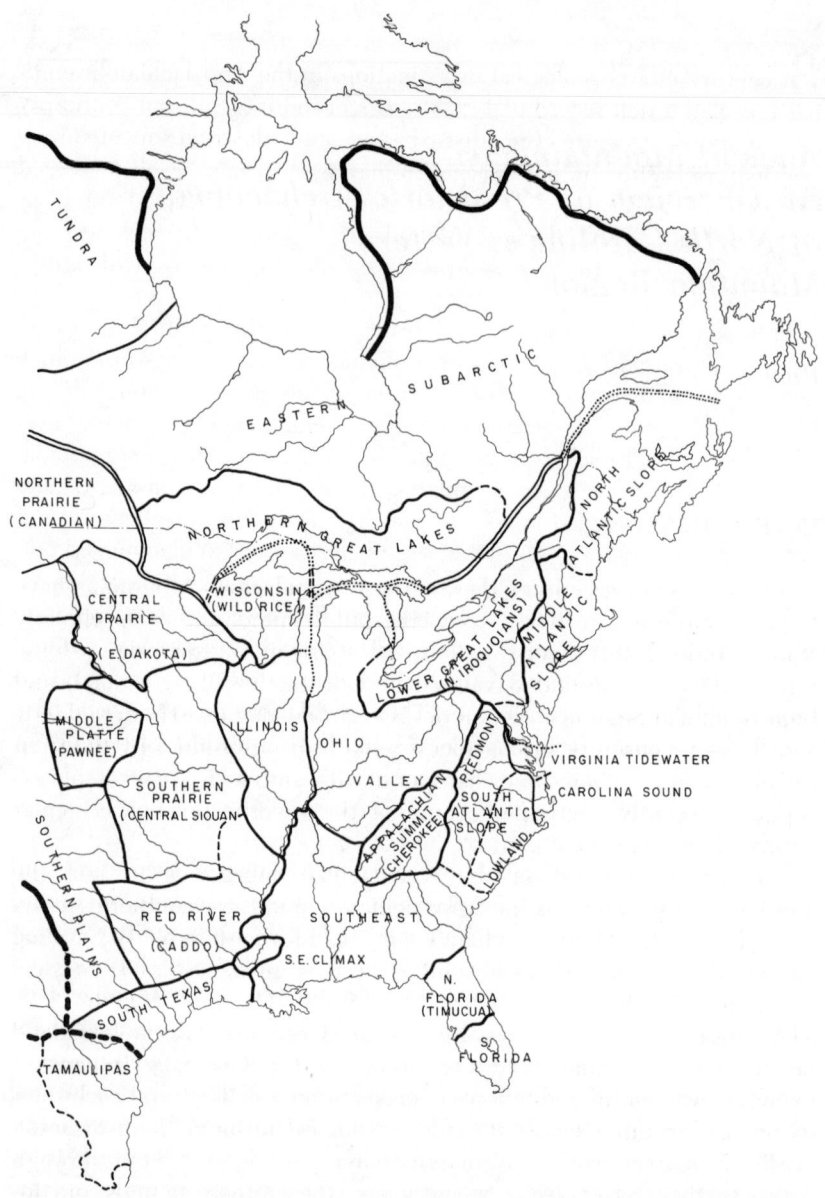

FIGURE 3.1. The Appalachian Summit and other culture areas of eastern North America (after Kroeber 1939:Map 6). Note that the Appalachian Summit as defined by Kroeber encompasses the entire Cherokee area, including the southern half of the Blue Ridge province and adjacent portions of the Appalachian Plateau, Ridge and Valley, and Piedmont provinces. Following Dickens (1976:4) and Keel (1976:1) the boundaries of the Appalachian Summit region in this study are essentially confined to the southern Blue Ridge province.

A century of archaeological investigations in the Appalachian Summit has revealed a rich record of 11,000 years or more of cultural continuity and change. Despite the disturbance and destruction of many archaeological sites by natural and human agents, many well-preserved sites in a wide variety of natural settings have survived, and, as archaeological techniques and methods of data recovery become more sophisticated, even the less well-preserved sites promise to yield significant information.

However, as in other regions of the world, the cultural resources (archaeological, historical, architectural, and cultural) of the Appalachian Summit are being rapidly lost to land modification and erosion resulting from urban expansion, second home and recreational development, farming, mining, lumbering, and other needs of expanding consumer populations. In addition, an alarming number of sites are being plundered and their scientific records forever lost because of the uncontrolled and unscientific recovery methods of many collectors as well as commercial pothunters. In the face of the relentless and accelerating depletion of this nation's prehistoric and historic archaeological record, federal legislation and mandates have been issued to manage and preserve our cultural resources by regulating projects which are supported by federal funds or require federal permits or licenses. These regulations provide a legal base for the preservation or recovery of a small but significant portion of our cultural heritage, but in order to accomplish these ends, careful planning, coordination, and cooperation between federal agencies, state offices of historic preservation, developers, and archaeologists are essential.

Of particular importance is the need to develop a theoretical and methodological framework for planning and decision making in cultural resource management for, as Dunnell (1979:448) notes, archaeology is presently "in danger of being structured not by the limits of its theory and methods, but by administrative regulation and book keeping conveniences." One of the most important concepts used in the management of cultural resources under current legislation is that of "significance." Broadly stated, a cultural resource is significant if it has been determined to be eligible for nomination to the National Register of Historic Places, and such a determination is ultimately necessary if the resource is to be protected or adverse effects upon it are to be mitigated under federal guidelines.

However, at the present time the criteria of significance are so broadly defined as to cause problems for archaeologists and those involved at various levels of cultural resource management. The *Code of Federal Regulations* (36 *CFR* 1202) states that a cultural resource is eligible for inclusion in the National Register and thus significant if it possesses "integrity" and, among other things, if it has "yielded, or may be likely to yield, information important in prehistory or history." A conflict over definitions thus may well result. To the developer, the city manager, the engineer, and some federal agencies many archaeological sites are nothing more than "a few chips" or "a couple of arrowheads." From the perspective of these individuals artifacts and other archaeological remains are simply discrete objects with little, if any, intrinsic value. On the other hand, to most archaeologists all archaeological resources, including single flake finds, are of at least potential importance for developing an understanding of the lives of people of the past, and the site definition currently used by the Archaeology Branch of the North Carolina Division of Archives and History reflects this assumption (Mathis 1979:7-8).

Nevertheless, it is obvious from both research and management standpoints that the research value of sites is relative, and this factor must be a major consideration in determining research and management priorities. Unfortunately, in many cases the assessment of relative site importance and research and management priorities has been an essentially subjective process or has been based on a relatively narrow range of research goals. Often a disproportionate number of large sites with impressive artifact yields are assessed as "significant" at the expense of smaller, less productive sites such as shallow upland lithic scatters. However, despite their unimpressive appearance, such small, low-density sites may contain unique archaeological data, and omitting such sites from major data recovery programs may leave unnecessary gaps in our picture of past social and cultural systems. On the other hand, it is a very real fear of many developers and planners (and some archaeologists) that an overemphasis on the significance of small sites will ultimately lead to a multi-million dollar project being held up while its adverse effects on the locus of a single redeposited chert flake are being mitigated (see Trinkley 1980b).

A major cause of this dilemma is the fact that the National Register criteria of significance per se are too general to ensure protection of a representative sample of the nation's cultural resources. In part this problem can be alleviated by assessing the significance of archaeological sites in a more explicitly defined context that will allow a clearer definition of what information is "important in prehistory or history." As King (1976) and others have noted, a site is not automatically eligible for inclusion in the National Register simply because it has yielded a large number of diagnostic artifacts and has undisturbed deposits nor are sites lacking such characteristics automatically ineligible. The key to assessing the significance of a site and determining whether or not it merits preservation or data recovery, perhaps at public and/or private expense, is the determination of its research potential (see Woodall 1981). King (1976:8-9) has recommended that the potential significance of a site should be evaluated within the context of local and regional research questions, and Raab and Klinger (1977) state that the management and research goals of archaeology can be most effectively accomplished when site significance is assessed within the context of explicit, problem-oriented research designs which are regional in scope (see also Schiffer and Gumerman 1977). Furthermore, as Sharrock and Grayson (1979) and Lynott (1980) have pointed out, significance is a dynamic concept which must continuously adapt to newly developing research questions.

As of 1979, archaeological research and cultural resource management in North Carolina were being conducted in the absence of explicit, problem-oriented regional research designs. To be sure, many institutions and individual archaeologists in the state followed clearly defined research interests and carefully developed research strategies when investigating questions related to their concerns, but in general such interests, including my own, were relatively narrow in scope (e.g. site, period, locality, or problem specific), and, therefore, generally less useful than regional research designs for assessing the significance of a site and, ultimately, determining its fate.

Since this problem also has existed to a greater or lesser degree on a nationwide scale, the federal government has mandated that the individual states will develop statewide master plans for the management of their cultural resources. The North Carolina Division of Archives and History has been in the forefront in developing a statewide archaeological survey (Mathis 1979). A key to the creation of such a planning tool is the development of sets of criteria against which the significance of the state's archaeological resources can be evaluated. As Mathis (1979:20) notes, however, the federal criteria of significance, which are the fundamental basis for site evaluation in the state, "are of minimal value when used outside of a known context (i.e., a synthesis of local, regional, and/or state history and prehistory)."

This paper has been prepared at the request of the Division of Archives and History to meet the need for regional syntheses. However, a synthesis would be a massive undertaking given the environmental and cultural diversity of the Appalachian Summit, and a presumptuous one on my part as well, given the fact that the term of my research in the region (9 years) is only one-fifth of that of Joffre Coe. Moreover Coe's work has been conducted on a far larger scale than mine, and a regional synthesis is ultimately his right—and responsibility.

Nevertheless, the backgrounds of Coe's and my research are quite different and they will undoubtedly affect our perspectives on the region. First, although Coe and his coworkers (no pun intended) have located and recorded thousands of sites in a wide range of environmental settings, their intensive excavations have been concentrated on large, often deeply stratified, sites such as Garden Creek, Coweeta Creek, Townson, Warren Wilson, and Tuckasegee. My work, on the other hand, has been at considerably smaller, less impressive sites including excavations at several upland sites. Therefore, Coe's data base is much more extensive than mine, his sites are more complex, and the record of the cultural sequence tends to be clearer. Second, the bulk of the archaeology conducted by the Research Laboratories in Anthropology at the University of North Carolina at Chapel Hill, under Coe's direction, has been in the south central and southwestern portion of the Appalachian Summit in a major area of Cherokee settlement, while most of my work has been in a much more remote and restricted area, the upper Watauga valley in the northwestern corner of the state. Finally, while the published reports of the projects directed by Coe have been essentially descriptive and culture-historical (e.g. Dickens 1976; Keel 1976) the major emphasis in my work has been on reconstructing settlement patterns and, ultimately, subsistence, settlement, and social systems. My work is clearly dependent on the typological and cultural sequences developed by Coe, Dickens, Egloff, Holden, and Keel.

This paper then is an overview rather than a synthesis, although opportunities to indulge in generalizations and intraregional comparisons will not be ignored. The basic goals of this essay are: 1) to briefly describe the Appalachian Summit environment, to identify some of its potential influences on prehistoric cultures, and to propose geographical-environmental study units based on stream drainages; 2) to summarize the past and current state of archaeological research in the region; 3) to summarize the region's known prehistory and, when possible, discuss intraregional similarities and variability; 4) to identify local and regional research questions and recommend courses of future research; and 5) to propose a preliminary set of criteria for the assessment of archaeological site significance in the region. This paper is intended to be a preliminary to the development of regional syntheses. Undoubtedly it will serve as a target for cannons at Chapel Hill and elsewhere. If it generates some published responses which introduce new data to southeastern historians, it will have been well worth the effort.

THE NATURAL ENVIRONMENT

The natural environment is one of the major influences on human societies, particularly preindustrial ones. In the North Carolina mountains the environment has been especially important in human activities and existence because it has presented human populations with both opportunities for and limitations on development. An in-depth description of the environment of North Carolina's Appalachian Summit region is beyond the scope of this paper. Detailed descriptions of local environments and the cultural implications of such settings should be a major component of any study of local prehistory including cultural resource management studies.

The Appalachian Summit region is one of the most rugged settings in the eastern United states. The term "Appalachian Summit" was used by Kroeber (1939:95) to designate a cultural and natural area comprising the highest portion of the Appalachian Mountain chain. The region is part of Fenneman's (1938) Blue Ridge physiographic province and it is bordered on the west by the Ridge and Valley and Interior Plateau provinces and on the east by the Piedmont Plateau province (Figure 3.2).

The bulk of the region's drainage follows a relatively gradual slope to the west to the Tennessee River, or in the case of the New River, to the Ohio. However, the eastern side of the region is a steep escarpment whose streams descend rapidly into Piedmont rivers which in turn flow more sluggishly into the Atlantic or the Gulf of Mexico. In comparison with surrounding regions, the Appalachian Summit has greater relief, a more temperate climate with extended periods of cold weather, narrower stream valleys, greater local variability of microhabitats, and a much less consistent pattern of drainage and topography (cf. Thornbury 1965:103-108).

The Appalachian Summit is a true highland relative to surrounding terrain with main valley floors ranging from about 1200 to 3000 feet above mean sea level (amsl) and many mountain peaks exceeding elevations of 6000 feet. The Great Smoky Mountains form a barrier that for 54 miles never drops below 5000 feet (Sharpe 1954:471). Although the Appalachian system is ancient and the profile of the mountains is generally not rugged, topographic relief in the Appalachian Summit is in general quite pronounced, and the dense dendritic drainage has created a labyrinth of deep, narrow, steep-sided valleys separated by narrow ridges (Figure 3.3). In the uplands level areas suitable for human habitation are found at gaps, saddles, upland flats and at some summits, ridge lines, spur ridges, and stream valleys. Streams descend rapidly from the uplands to the more gently flowing rivers, but even in the major river valleys floodplains seldom exceed a mile in width, and riffles, rapids, and gorges are common. Natural levees and both recent and older terraces appear along the major rivers. While the topography of this ancient uplift area is largely defined by drainage, important exceptions are found in the relatively broad intermontane "basins" such as those around the modern communities of Asheville, Canton, Hendersonville, and Murphy, North Carolina (Dickens 1978:17).

The geology of the area is predominantly igneous and metamorphic with granites, schists, gneisses, quartzites, and quartzes predominant. In addition to quartzites, which are sporadically distributed, and quartz, which is virtually ubiquitous, other local rocks and minerals that were

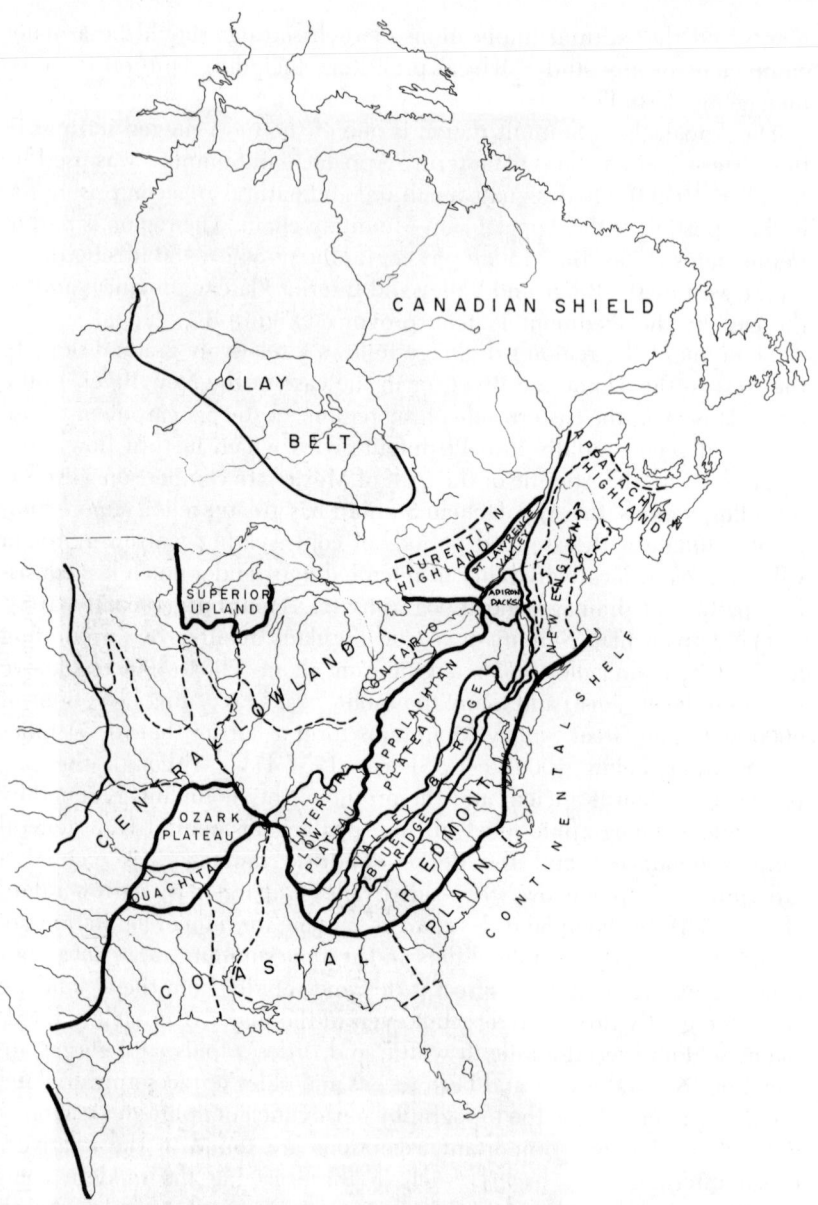

FIGURE 3.2. The Blue Ridge and other physiographic areas of eastern North America (after Kroeber 1939:Map 7).

FIGURE 3.3. The typically rugged topography of the Appalachian Summit. A view of the Cove Creek valley (Watauga River watershed), Watauga County, North Carolina, from the Wakeman 2 site (31Wt175).

utilized by the region's prehistoric inhabitants include soapstone, slate, chalcedony, felsite, mica, and chlorite schists. Chert, the prehistoric Indians' principal lithic raw material resource, is found in a few localized limestone deposits but it is much more abundant immediately west of the Appalachian Summit in the fossil-bearing limestones of the Ridge and Valley province of eastern Tennessee (King 1968:2-10). Rhyolite occurs just north of the study area at Mount Rogers, Virginia.

Reconstructions of the climates and environments of the Appalachian Summit suggest that the region was quite cold during the Pleistocene (Whitehead 1973), with periglacial geomorphic processes occurring at higher elevations (Clark 1979), and widespread boreal-like forests and possibly extensions of tundra and park-tundra at higher elevations during the full glacial (Delcourt and Delcourt 1979). Between 14,500 and 10,500 B.C., spruce, pine, and fir forests declined in importance in the midlatitudes of the Southeast (Delcourt and Delcourt 1979) and deciduous species began to migrate northward and into higher elevations such as the Appalachian Summit. Given the topographic and altitudinal diversity of the region it is likely that it was characterized by a mosaic of plant communities even at full glacial times (Purrington 1976). By the time of the earliest known intrusions of humans into the region, about 9000 to 10,000 B.C., the climates and biotic communities may have been only slightly to moderately more northern than today. The record of climatic-environmental stability and change in the region over the past 12,000 years is of major interest to archaeologists, but, unfortunately, it is not yet well understood.

The modern climate of the Appalachian Summit is humid, warm-temperate, and continental. Summers are generally mild with average July temperatures ranging from 68 to 74 degrees Fahrenheit. Winters are often quite cold, averaging 36 to 42 degrees Fahrenheit in January, with temperatures occasionally dropping below zero degree Fahrenheit and with snow remaining on the ground for several days or occasionally from December to early April. Temperatures vary substantially with elevation. The average annual frost-free season ranges from 150 to 190 days (Lee 1955:10-12), and late and early frosts are common.

Mean annual precipitation for much of the region falls within the range of 50-60 inches. However, the quantity, intensity, and seasonality of rainfall vary locally. The heaviest rainfall in the eastern United States occurs along the southern portion of the eastern escarpment of the Blue Ridge, while in the region's interior to the west many localities are much drier. For example, Rockhouse in Macon County, North Carolina has recorded a 25-year average of 82.96 inches per year, while Asheville, about 60 air miles to the northeast, averaged 38.47 inches per year during the same period (Keel 1976:6). Prolonged torrential rainstorms frequently occur, and they often cause local flooding. The productivity of modern crops is significantly reduced on occasion by long periods of cool, foggy weather or drought during the growing season.

The soils of the Appalachian Summit reflect local climate, topography, lithology, and vegetation. The area's soils include: 1) red-yellow podzolics (e.g. Hayesville, Hiwassee, and Talladega) at lower elevations and in intermountain valleys; 2) gray-brown podzolics on older terraces and colluvial aprons and fans in mountain covers and along valley margins (State, Tate, and Tusquitee), on some high mountain slopes (Ashe, Porters), and in broad plateaus and intermountain valleys at higher elevations (Watauga); 3) brown forest soils (Burton) on the higher mountain slopes and crests and alluvial soils near streams that have parent material rich in bases; 4) lithosols and shallow soils with incipient gray-brown podzolic characteristics (Ramsey) on hilly to very steep mountain slopes; 5) and alluvial soils (Congaree and undifferentiated alluvium) in the active floodplains (cf. Perkins and Gettys 1947:59-65; Lee 1955:77-97).

The better soils are moderately fertile, but they are much less productive than the soils of many outside areas such as the Illinois River Valley (cf. Zawacki and Hausfater 1969; Roper 1978). Soils of moderate fertility which have been rated as Class I or II soils by the U.S. Department of Agriculture Soil Conservation Service because they have few or no agricultural limitations (stoniness, impermeability, steep slopes, excessive or slow drainage, susceptibility to erosion) comprise less than 10% of the soils in most Appalachian Summit localities.

The Appalachian Summit is in Braun's (1950) oak-chestnut forest region. Because of the significant local variability in topography, elevation, drainage, microclimates, soils, and lithology, plant communities in the Appalachian Summit are highly diverse in their species composition, productivity, and season of availability as resources for human use. Although the productivity of the region's food plants is somewhat limited by low to moderate soil fertility and the steepness and shallowness of many soils (cf. Cowan 1978a), a situation very similar to the Ozark Highland (Roper 1978, 1979b), the diversity in kinds, species composition, and environmental settings of plant communities as well as variations in seasonality and productivity between species and within specific populations (depending on natural setting) probably supported a higher biomass of animals, including humans, than a more homogeneous environment.

The historic and modern Cherokees have made use of a wide range of native wild plants (Hamel and Chiltosky 1975; Perry 1974; Witthoft 1977). Undoubtedly a much greater variety was used in the prehistoric past not only for food but for medicinal and ceremonial purposes and as raw materials for tools, containers, clothing, and shelter. The region's most common trees, including oaks, hickories, chestnut, black and white walnut, and beech, produce large numbers of nuts which are nutritious and easily stored but also available on a seasonal basis only and annually variable in production. The nature of these important food sources undoubtedly had a significant influence on the movement and social organization of the region's human and animal populations.

The following information on the general distribution of plant communities in the Appalachian Summit has been taken from a number of sources including Bass (1977), Braun (1950), Leighty, et al. (1944:57), Perkins and Gettys (1947:9), Stupka (1964), Ware (1973), and Whittaker (1956). It must be recognized that a great deal of local and subregional diversity, particularly in community composition, existed and that some prehistoric plant communities may have been completely unlike modern communities. In addition, the kinds, composition, distribution, and extent of various flora communities have undoubtedly changed in response to climatic shifts as well as human and other influences over time. Plant communities of the Appalachian Summit include:

High mountain peaks: Frazer fir and red spruce occur between 5,000 and 6,000 feet with almost pure stands of the former above that elevation. Heath and grassy balds occur on some of the summits (Bass 1977:8) but may not have been present in precolonial times (Bass 1977:98-99).

Ridges and slopes with shallow soil: Pitch pine and table-mountain pine occur at higher elevations (generally above 3,500 feet) with post oak and scrub oaks dominant at lower elevations.

Mountain forests: 1) Upland hardwood forests are on south and west facing slopes and drier north and east facing slopes. Chestnut; chestnut, black, red, white, and northern red oak; and hickories (probably bitternut, mockernut, and pignut with shagbark occasionally occurring) are dominant with scarlet oak, tulip poplar, red maple, black locust, dogwood, and sourwood in association. 2) Cove hardwood forests are in moist environments in narrow coves on north and east facing slopes. Chestnut and yellow poplar are dominant with basswood, white, and northern red oaks, black birch, red and sugar maples, white ash, hemlock, and black locust also important. 3) Northern hardwood forests are in mesic environments at intermediate to moderately high elevations, ca. 3,500-5,000 feet. Beech, red and sugar maples, and northern red oak predominate.

Valley uplands and terraces: Oaks, hickories, small pines, sourwood, dogwood, and black locust are common. Prior to extensive timbering, this habitat was dominated by oaks and pines (Perkins and Gettys 1947:9).

Colluvial slopes near the bases of mountains: Chestnut, chestnut oak, black walnut, butternut, honey locust, red maple, yellow poplar, and buckeye predominate.

Bottomlands: River birch, sycamore, water oak, elm, ironwood, and a few hickories dominate this setting.

The Appalachian Summit is included in Shelford's (1963:38-42) oak-deer-chestnut faciation. Important mammals included white-tailed deer, black bear, mountain lion, gray wolf, bobcat, groundhog, cottontail rabbit, raccoon, squirrels, gray and red fox, beaver, striped and spotted skunks, muskrat, and the ubiquitous marsupial opossum. Bison and elk were present into early historic times, but apparently were not very numerous (Linzey and Linzey 1971:74, 77). Important game birds included turkey, grouse, and passenger pigeon, but migratory waterfowl were uncommon. A variety of fish, turtles, amphibians, and shellfish was found in the rivers and streams.

The rugged, deciduous forested Appalachian Summit environment presented both opportunities and limitations to native and early Euro-American inhabitants. Limitations would include: 1) restricted mobility because of the rugged topography and limited navigability of streams due to numerous riffles and rapids; 2) a relatively short growing season; 3) occasional threats to food resources and physical safety because of droughts, floods, lengthy periods of cool rainy weather, high winds, periods of extreme cold, blizzards, and forest fires; 4) limited amounts of good farm land; 5) the general absence of local sources of chert; 6) a relatively small amount of level, habitable space, and 7) locally diverse but relatively limited wild food resources compared to neighboring regions such as the Ridge and Valley province of the Piedmont.

Environmental potentials for human populations would include: 1) access to neighboring valleys by way of ridges and gaps; 2) a growing season of sufficient length in most years for productive horticulture; 3) moderately fertile and easily tillable bottomland soils; 4) an abundance and variety of widely distributed raw material resources including plant fibers, woods, animal products, clays, and workable quartz; 5) nearby sources of chert outside the region and localized regional sources of soap stone, quartzite, rhyolite, and other lithic raw materials which could be obtained through exchange networks following ridges and/or rivers; 6) easy access to drinking water in most locations; 7) small and sporadically-distributed but habitable rock-shelters; 8) a moderate abundance of wild food resources; 9) a variety of natural habitats within short distances of each other on different landforms, soils, elevations, and microclimatic settings; 10) seasonal and local variability in kinds and quantities of wild food resources; and 11) raw materials such as mica, quartz crystals, soapstone, and possibly copper that were in demand outside the region.

Of particular importance are the characteristics of limited mobility and ready availability of a variety of wild food resources since both would have tended to restrict human contact within and outside the region and reinforce local self-sufficiency. Local, perhaps cyclical, mobility of social units and diversity in diet would have also been reinforced by seasonal and geographical variability of wild food resources. According to Flannery (1968) the scheduling of mobile, seasonal subsistence activities tends to produce self-regulating sociocultural systems and reinforce social and cultural stability. It is clear that in order to understand past cultural systems of the Appalachian Summit, the full range of habitats and resources available to resident and transient populations as well as stability and change in climatic and environmental variables over space and time must be identified.

Given the ruggedness of the Appalachian Summit terrain it is likely that topographic features such as major valleys and ridges tended to channel human transportation and migration routes and, to an extent at least, isolate social groups within major watersheds. In order to analyze the degree and kind of internal diversity within a region it is useful to divide the larger geographical area into smaller units. Such geographical units have analytical utility since they can help verify or invalidate models relating to the influences of rugged topography and other environmental variables on human populations.

River systems have had strong influences on the movement, adaptive strategies, and social interaction of past groups (Peterson 1976:61; Watanabe 1972:463-466) and they provide a relatively objective set of criteria for subdividing the landscape (Schmits 1978; Weichman n.d.). The following hydrological units (Figure 3.4) will be referred to in the text, but they should be considered preliminary until their utility is tested:

1. Hiwassee-Valley rivers
2. Southeast Escarpment (Chatooga-Whitewater-Toxaway rivers)
3. South Central Escarpment (Broad River)
4. North Central Escarpment (Catawba River)
5. Little Tennessee-Tuckasegee rivers
6. Pigeon River
7. French Broad River
8. Nolichucky-Toe-Caney rivers
9. Watauga River
10. New River
11. Northeast Escarpment (Yadkin River)

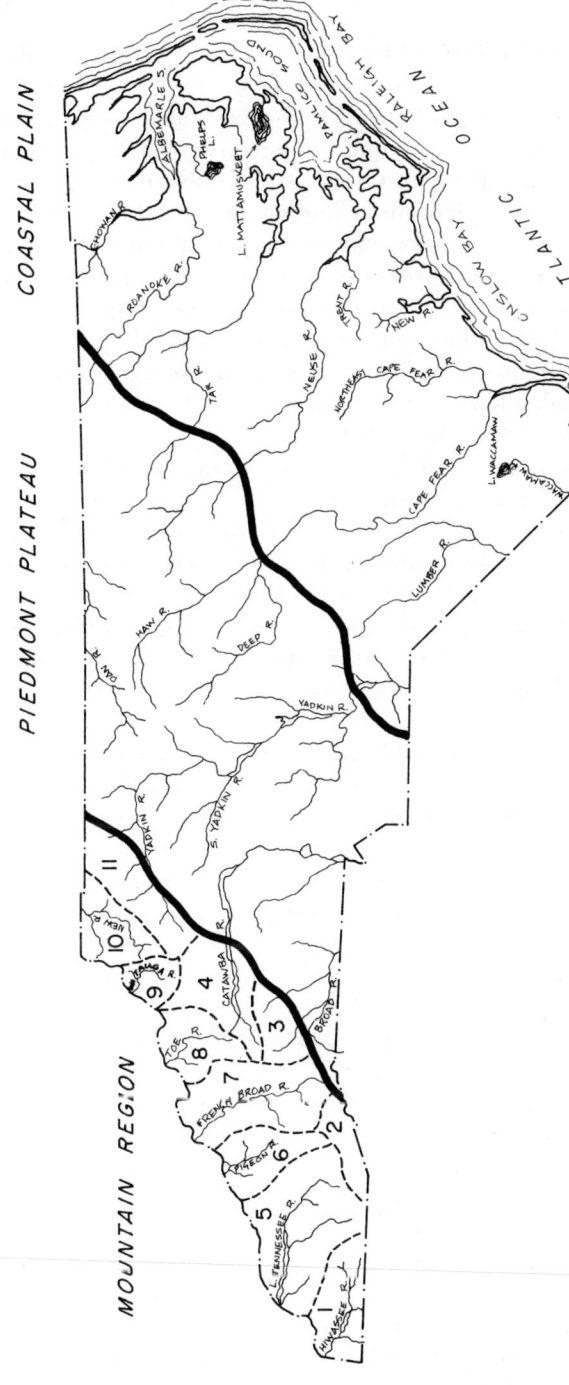

FIGURE 3.4. Proposed hydrological units of the Appalachian Summit in North Carolina.

HISTORY OF INVESTIGATIONS

In a sense the year 1980 marked the centennial of archaeological research in the Appalachian Summit. In January, 1880, Mr. and Mrs. A. J. Osborne began excavations at Garden Creek Mound No. 2 (31Hw2), a late Middle Woodland platform mound on the Pigeon River in Haywood County, for the Valentine Museum in Richmond, Virginia (Keel 1976:71). Over the years the museum removed artifacts from several other mounds in western North Carolina. Although no adequate publications resulted from their work, the Osbornes kept relatively detailed field records, and most of their field notes, journals, and letter books have been studied at the Research Laboratories of Anthropology at the University of North Carolina in Chapel Hill (Keel 1976:12-13).

The 1880s also saw some of the more systematic archaeology of the period being conducted in western North Carolina. Several mounds were excavated under the general direction of Cyrus Thomas of the Bureau of American Ethnology of the Smithsonian Institution. Data from these and other sites in the eastern United States enabled Thomas to invalidate the prevailing theory that the thousands of mounds and earthworks in the East had been constructed by an advanced race of non-Indians, the so-called "Mound Builders," and he demonstrated that they were the handiwork of Indians (Thomas 1887, 1891, 1894).

Organized, well-financed collection of museum specimens returned to the Appalachian Summit and the Garden Creek site in 1915 and for several years thereafter as George G. Heye and his workers sought fine specimens for Heye's Museum of the American Indian. Apparently relatively little useful information can be gleaned from the field records and reports of these projects (e.g. Heye, Hodge, and Pepper 1918), although, as Keel (1976:13) notes, Mark R. Harrington (1922) produced an interesting and important interpretive report on the archaeological remains of the upper Tennessee River valley.

The only scientific archaeology conducted in the Appalachian Summit during the first half of the twentieth century included the 1933-1934 excavations at the Peachtree site on the Hiwassee River in Cherokee County by the Smithsonian Institution (Setzler and Jennings 1941) and excavations at the Connestee, or Puette, site (31Tr1) in Transylvania County in 1935 by Joffre Coe (Keel 1976:14). WPA-supported archaeology recovered massive quantities of data in much of the East, but in North Carolina it was largely confined to the Piedmont and Coastal areas except for surveys conducted by Harold T. Johnson in Buncombe County and elsewhere as part of a statewide survey. Plans to excavate several sites in western North Carolina with WPA crews were terminated with the outbreak of World War II.

One of the major concerns of southeastern archaeologists has been the identification of the tribal groups responsible for various assemblages of archaeological remains. Many archaeologists believed that the late prehistoric archaeological remains from the Appalachian Summit and neighboring areas were those of the Cherokees, but there was a great deal of disagreement over the extent and age of such remains (cf. Dickens 1979:3-11). In 1961 Coe recommended that the only way to understand the origins and character of prehistoric and early historic Cherokee culture was to look at the Cherokee heartland, the area of the historic Middle, Valley, and Out towns in the Appalachian Summit. The Cherokee Archaeological Project followed in 1964 and lasted until 1971, with extensive archaeological surveys and intensive excavations of historic Cherokee and earlier sites.

The history of fieldwork conducted as part of the Cherokee Archaeological Project has been summarized by Dickens (1976:8-9) and Keel (1976:15-16). Large quantities of data were carefully collected as a result of this project, but to date relatively little information has been published. Several masters' theses (Holden 1966; B. Egloff 1967; K. Egloff 1971) and doctoral dissertations (Dickens 1970; Ferguson 1971; Keel 1972) have been written as a result of the project, and two of the dissertations have been revised and published (Dickens 1976; Keel 1976). The emphasis in these studies is on detailed description of cultural remains, the identification and definition of archaeological phases and culturally-temporally diagnostic artifact types, and the development of cultural chronologies. This emphasis is certainly appropriate given the dearth of such basic descriptive information up to the 1960s, and these studies provide an indispensable data base and cultural-temporal framework for more theoretical studies of the future. Limited attempts at reconstruction of social organization were made by Dickens and Ferguson. Subsequently Dickens has published several interpretive papers on the area including a comparison of the archaeological cultures of the Cherokees of the Middle and Valley, Overhill, and Lower towns and their prehistoric antecedents (1979), an analysis of the settlement patterns of the historic and prehistoric Cherokees (Qualla and Pisgah phases respectively) (1978), and a study of ceramic diversity and culture change during the Woodland period in the Southeast (1980). Although environmental data were gathered and analyzed as part of the Cherokee Archaeological Project (Wing 1976; Yarnell 1976b), they have not yet been extensively used as part of an analysis of Cherokee cultural ecology, nor have explanatory studies of cultural processes in the area been published. Specialized studies of raw material resources in the Southern Appalachians include papers on sources of mica (Ferguson 1974), copper (Goad 1976), and soapstone (Holland, Pennell, and Allen 1981).

Since 1972, archaeological research in the Appalachian Summit has primarily been conducted as part of environmental assessments, mitigation of the adverse effects of federally funded or licensed projects, state and federally funded surveys, and summer field schools. Most of this work has been conducted by the University of North Carolina at Chapel Hill under the direction of Joffre Coe; Western Carolina University by Susan Collins, John Dorwin, Peter Miller, Charles Michael Baker, and Ann Rogers; and Appalachian State University by Harvard Ayers, L. Jill Loucks, and Burton Purrington. However, few reports have been published, a notable exception being Collins' (1977) report of mitigation at the Macon County Industrial Park site. The Archaeology Branch of the North Carolina Division of Archives and History has become actively involved in the region in the past few years. Major reports of their studies include a survey in the Wild and Scenic Rivers portion of the New River in Ashe and Alleghany counties (Robertson and Robertson 1978) and highway right-of-way surveys in Ashe and Wilkes counties (Mathis 1979). Many unpublished reports of these projects are on file at the Archaeology Branch (see Hargrove 1980, 1981; Bollinger 1982).

Collins (1977) report is unusual for archaeology in the Appalachian Summit because it describes a project in which the Phase III (mitigation) research design included the testing of explicitly stated hypotheses. The report attempts to test deductively hypothetical reconstructions of prehistoric social organization in the region and, Trinkley's (1977) criticisms notwithstanding, it is a major contribution to research in the region.

The North Carolina portion of the Appalachian Summit obviously did not exist in a vacuum, and studies of portions of the area outside the state and in neighboring physiographic regions are pertinent to this review. In the Virginia portion of the Blue Ridge, Holland's descriptive study (1970) of archaeology in the southwestern portion of the state is relevant as are the surveys and test excavations conducted in the proposed Mount Rogers National Recreation Area by Douglas Boyce (1976) and Harry and Jackie Piper (1977; H. Piper 1977; J. Piper 1977), the New River valley (Custer 1979), and Shenandoah National Park (Hoffman, et al. 1979; Hoffman and Foss 1980; Foss 1977, 1980). Like Harry Piper (1977), Quentin Bass (1977) in his survey of the Tennessee and North Carolina portions of the Great Smoky Mountains National Park attempts to identify site functions and activities on the basis of artifact types present, develops a preliminary typology of sites, and utilizes lithic raw materials and technology of non-diagnostic artifacts to assist in the identification of cultures present at various site types to show changing patterns of site utilization over time. Changing patterns of site utilization have also been studied in the upper Watauga River valley in northwestern North Carolina in unpublished papers by Purrington (1979) and Purrington and Douthit (1976, 1977). In 1981, a "Symposium on Upland Archaeology in the East" was organized by George Tolley, Michael Barber, and Clarence Geier. Fourteen papers on the Blue Ridge and Ridge and Valley provinces were presented.

Numerous river basin salvage projects have been conducted in the Ridge and Valley province of Tennessee since the 1930s. A large number of pertinent recent studies have been conducted in the Tellico Reservoir on the lower Little Tennessee River (e.g. Chapman 1973, 1975, 1977) and in the Normandy Reservoir on the Duck River (e.g. Faulkner and McCollough 1977). In West Virginia, Broyles' (1971) excavations at the St. Albans site and Wilkins' (1978) investigation of upland "bear wallow" sites are of special interest. Particularly relevant reports from the Carolina Piedmont include Coe's (1964) classic report of excavations at the Hardaway and Doerschuk sites in North Carolina in which the typological sequence which is now basic to the culture history of the Appalachian Summit was developed, House and Ballenger's (1976) Interstate 77 (South Carolina) survey report, and House and Wogaman's (1979) report of excavations at the Middle Archaic Windy Ridge site in the South Carolina Piedmont.

Archaeologists working in western North Carolina's mountains have generally followed a culture history approach which emphasizes data recovery, description, and developing and refining typological and cultural chronologies. Occasional reports include environmental and/or cultural reconstruction, but attempts to identify and explain cultural processes are still largely in the talking stage. A major contribution by the area's archaeologists has been the amassing of large quantities of well-controlled archaeological data, which have thereby been spared from the bulldozer's blade and the pothunter's shovel. These data will provide grist for scholarly research for decades.

A second major contribution by the region's scholars is the relatively well-defined and apparently sound typological sequence for the region developed by Coe (1964) and his students and colleagues, particularly Dickens (1976) and Keel (1976) with contributions by Egloff (1967), Holden (1966), and others. The regional sequences of projectile points/knives (hereafter "points") and ceramics are particularly well-defined and far more precise than those from many other regions in the East such as the Ozarks. The temporal spans of some types and the stylistic and technological ranges of others remain uncertain, but, even with their rough edges, these "index types" or horizon markers are critical for dating sites and identifying archaeological cultures (phases). Without this baseline information, settlement pattern and community pattern studies would not be particularly informative and we would have a very limited perspective on the nature and rates of culture change. As a result, access to dynamic areas of past cultural systems such as settlement, subsistence, demography, resource procurement, and social organization would be extremely limited.

Third, we have learned a great deal about the material culture and, to a lesser extent, the organizational characteristics of the Cherokees and their predecessors in southwestern North Carolina. And finally, these studies have revealed the potential of the Appalachian Summit to contribute to the investigation of major archaeological, anthropological, and historical research questions. As a result it will be much more difficult in the future to write off the prehistory of this and other "backwater" areas as insignificant.

A major strength of Appalachian Summit archaeology has also been its major weakness. While the emphasis on excavation of impressive sites, preferably with deep strata and/or discrete components, has made it possible to develop one of the more tightly controlled chronologies in the East, small sites and sites in the uplands have largely been ignored until recent times. To be sure, thousands of these less impressive sites have been located and recorded, but in general they were not intensively or systematically studied. For example, in his summary of the culture history of the Appalachian Summit, Keel (1976:216-244) makes some general observations on the nature of settlement patterns in the region, but presents no statistics on site distribution over time to support his generalizations (cf. Haynes 1976), and Holden's survey of Transylvania County is essentially a catalogue of sites with only a minimal attempt to discuss settlement patterns or their cultural implications (Holden 1966:89-91).

However, in the past decade a systemic approach has been followed by many of the region's archaeologists. This approach emphasizes the study of "whole" cultural systems which are evident in the archaeological record as the complete range of environmental zones which yield observable archaeological remains of a given period. In order to better understand many aspects of past cultures such as subsistence, demography, social organization, and resource procurement, it is critical that their full range of observable site types be investigated. Recent studies in the Appalachian Summit (e.g. Ayers 1976; Baker 1979; Bass 1977; Dickens 1978; Loucks 1981, 1982; Mathis 1979, 1981; Purrington and Douthit 1976, 1977; Robertson and Robertson 1978; White 1972, 1976) have emphasized this approach.

CULTURAL SEQUENCE AND SUGGESTED RESEARCH QUESTIONS

As is evident in the preceding discussion, archaeology in the western North Carolina mountains is in a transitional stage. Past archaeological research has been characterized by an emphasis on careful, well-controlled data recovery, taxonomy, and culture history. These studies have provided an indispensable foundation for the development of "explicitly scientific" (Watson, Redman, and LeBlanc 1971) research designs to employ in reconstructing nonmaterial culture, past environments, and cultural processes. In the not-too-distant future it should be possible to develop and test hypothetical explanations for past cultural phenomena and processes in the region and apply them to the development of general laws of human behavior. In particular, recent studies, many of which have been conducted as cultural resource management projects, have begun to investigate patterns in community structure, local and regional settlement, and subsistence and other aspects of resource procurement within the context of environmental, social, and cultural systems (e.g. Collins 1977; Dickens 1978).

In the prehistoric past the Appalachian Summit exhibited a significant degree of internal variability. However, the region's cultures also shared a large number of stylistic, technical, and behavioral traits which are particularly evident in the apparently contemporaneous region-wide distribution of distinctive projectile point and ceramic techniques and styles. In addition, the region's cultures appear to have followed similar evolutionary trends. Therefore, given the geographical unevenness of our knowledge of Appalachian Summit prehistory, an overview is most appropriately focused on region-wide archaeological cultures or phases and they will be the basic cultural-temporal units in this discussion. However, when possible, similarities and differences between localities within the region will be described and their implications in terms of local and regional cultural processes will be discussed.

The state of archaeological knowledge of the Appalachian Summit will be discussed chronologically beginning with the earliest phases or stylistic-technological complexes. Each cultural unit will be described in terms of typical material traits, known local cultures, inferred nonmaterial cultural characteristics, and pertinent research questions. A general regional sequence of diagnostic projectile point/knife types is shown in Figure 3.5.

It will be evident that the basic cultural chronology and the descriptive information used in this paper come from the landmark studies conducted in the southwestern portion of the state by Joffre Coe and his students and colleagues, notably Dickens (1970, 1976), B. Egloff (1967), Holden (1966), and Keel (1972, 1976). Moreover, many gaps in our archaeological knowledge of the region have been filled in recent years. In particular, the discussion will rely on Quentin Bass's (1977) survey in the Great Smoky Mountains National Park and nearly a decade of research, carried out by Ayers and Purrington in the upper Watauga valley, largely through field schools and cultural resource management studies.

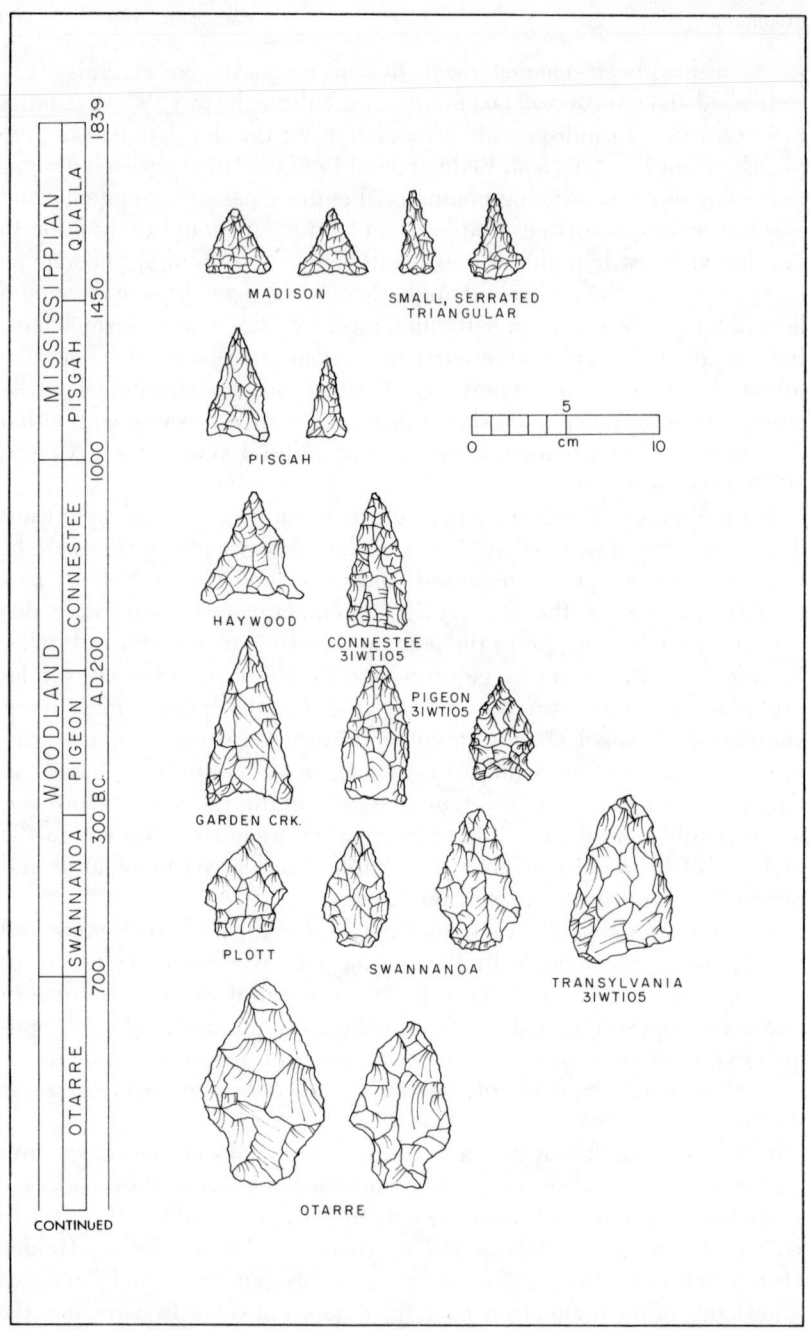

FIGURE 3.5. Generalized chronological sequence of projectile point/knife types in the Appalachian Summit. Unless otherwise noted, all points are from the John Hodges site (31Wt184), Watauga County, North Carolina.

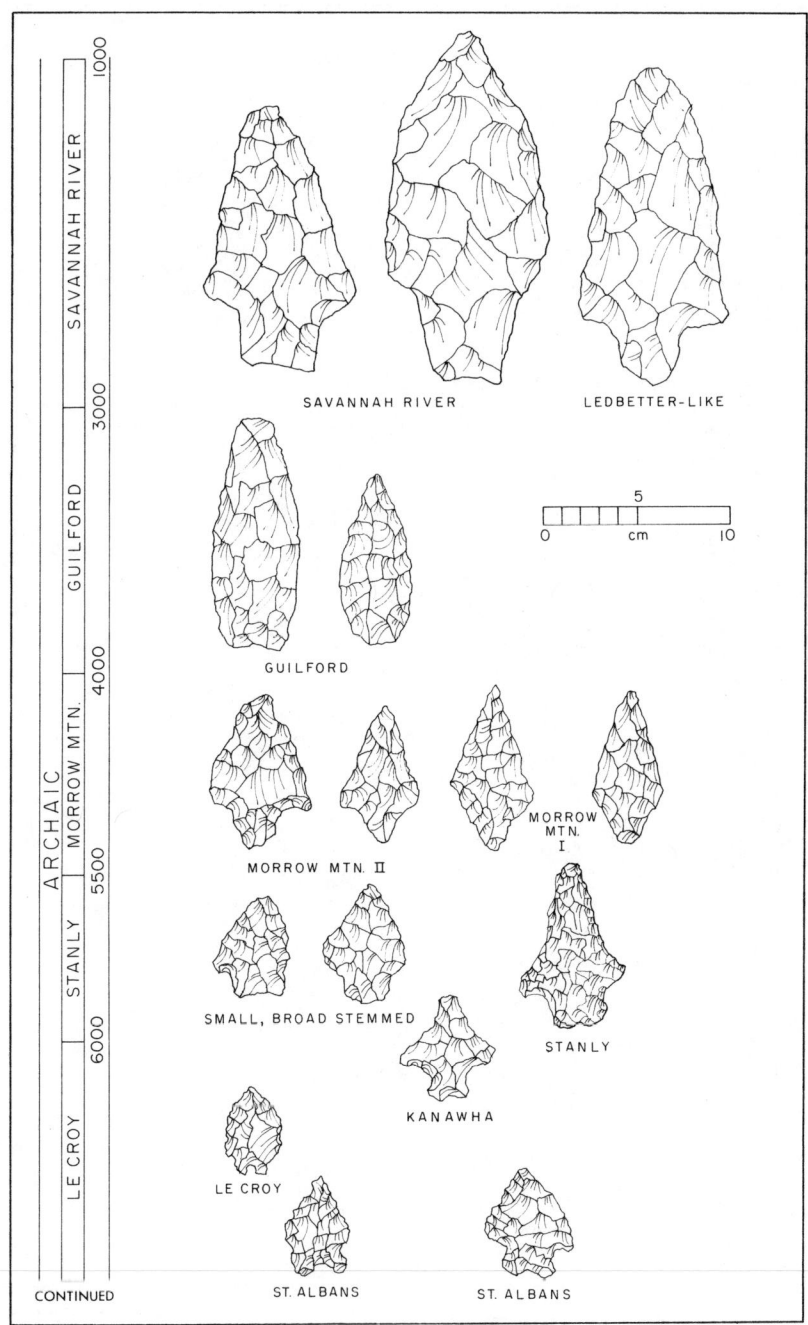

FIGURE 3.5. Continued

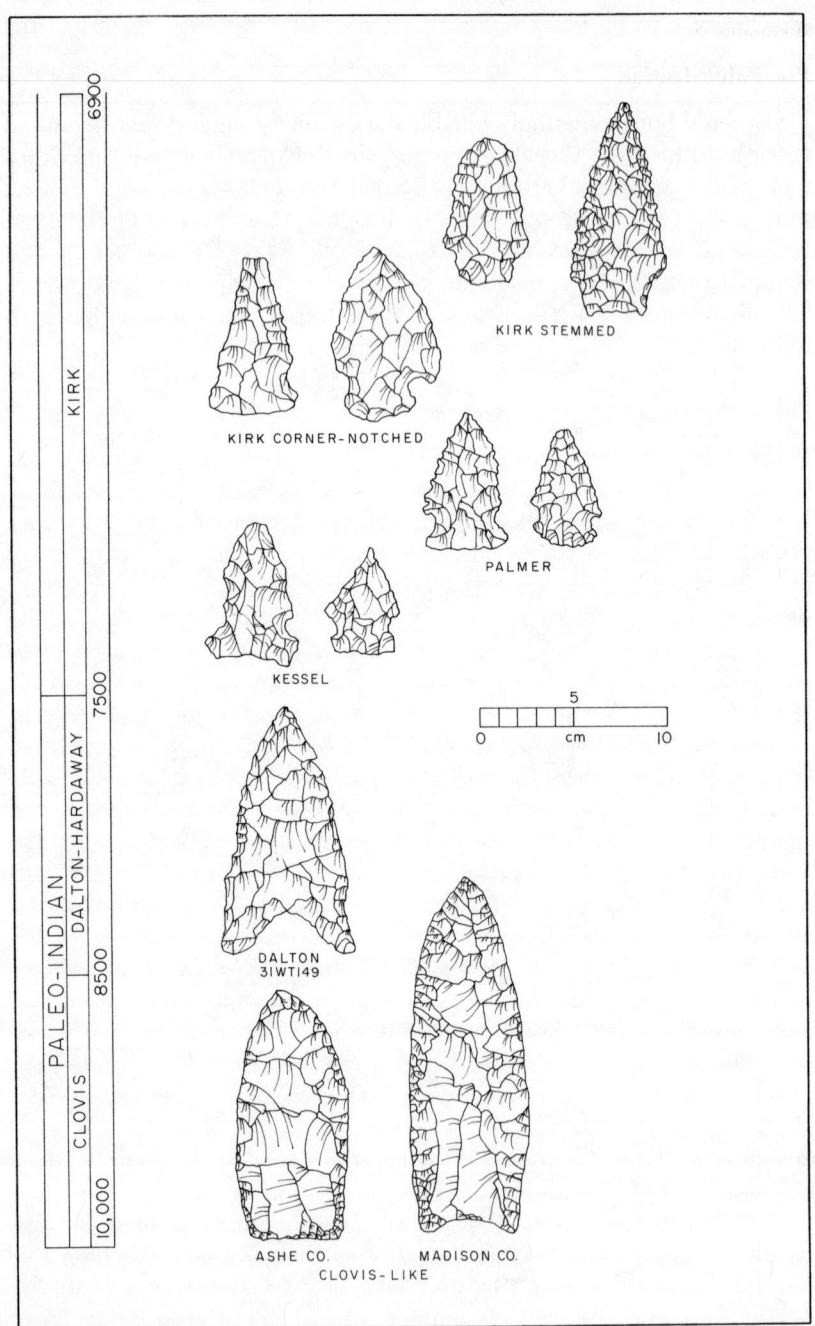

FIGURE 3.5. Continued

Pre-Paleo-Indian

Scattered but increasingly reliable data strongly suggest that the initial entry into the New World of the ancestors of today's native Americans took place sometime between ca. 18,000 and 26,000 years ago. Several sites in the eastern United States such as the Meadowcroft Rockshelter, Pennsylvania (Adovasio et al. 1978), and Wells Creek Crater, Tennessee (Dragoo 1973), are possible evidence of such an occupation. No evidence for the presence of such early groups in the Appalachian Summit has been recognized.

Paleo-Indian

Clovis. Clovis-like fluted and unfluted lanceolate projectile points and knives from the Paleo-Indian period (ca. 10,000-8500 B.C.) occur as rare and thus far virtually isolated finds in the Appalachian Summit. Such data provide little basis for a reconstruction of Paleo-Indian life. In general, their life-style has been characterized as that of band-level societies consisting of small, nomadic groups who emphasized hunting, possibly of big game, as a subsistence pursuit and had a highly sophisticated lithic technology. Evidence of mastodon hunting in eastern Missouri (Graham 1980), hunting of white-tailed deer, wapiti, small game, and birds in western Pennsylvania (Adovasio et al. 1978:647-648), and consumption of fish and hawthorne fruit in eastern Pennsylvania (McNett, Marshall, and McDowell 1975), suggest a varied diet and an early adaptation to the characteristic wild food resources of the Eastern Woodlands. In the northern Shenandoah Valley of Virginia, Gardner (1974:41-44) has identified a Paleo-Indian settlement system that is characterized by "territorially restricted mobility." In this system base camps are located near outcrops of high quality cryptocrystalline stone and hunting sites are located in the uplands. Gardner (1974:42) notes that "native lithic raw material was utilized almost exclusively when it was available." It is evident that in some, if not most, localities of the Eastern Woodlands these people did not conform to the popular model of free-wandering followers of Pleistocene megafauna but were already in incipient, if not well-developed, stages of efficient adaptation to the forested Eastern Woodlands area (cf. Caldwell 1958).

The extremely sparse distribution of Paleo-Indian remains in the Appalachian Summit renders interpretation of their lifeways extremely difficult. Assuming, however, that the rarity of Paleo-Indian remains in the Appalachian Summit reflects limited use of the region rather than destruction and/or burial of sites by post-Pleistocene erosion (which remains to be verified), a pattern of limited use, but use nevertheless, of the region is apparent. These sparsely scattered remains may represent short term forays (probably in pursuit of game since there are very few local chert sources for them to seek) by small groups (perhaps all male) who generally resided outside the region (probably in the Ridge and Valley province to the west). However, as we shall see, most fluted points from the region which have been described are produced from local stone which may indicate that local populations were present.

Paleo-Indian distribution in the Appalachian Summit remains unclear. Keel (1976:17) noted that all fluted points for which he had provenience data occurred in the southwestern mountains south of a hypothetical line drawn by Michalek (1969) from east to west through Asheville, North Carolina. Michalek suggested that this line roughly separated a periglacial climate to the north and a milder climatic regime to the south during the final Wisconsin glacial periods. However, this pattern may simply reflect the far greater intensity of archaeological research and avocational collecting in the southern part of the region since several recent investigations describe points which have been found north of this line. A Clovis-like point from a site on a terrace on the New River in Watauga County has been observed in a private collection (Purrington 1976); Perkinson has reported Clovis-like points from the middle French Broad valley in Madison County (Perkinson 1971:30-32) and the New River valley in Ashe County (Perkinson 1973:46-47); and the Archaeology Branch's New River survey reported four "Cumberland or variant Guilford types" which "were located on the second terrace above the New River" (Robertson and Robertson 1978:81). The points from the New River survey were made from a local "coarse-grained felsite" which Robertson and Robertson (1978:81) note is very common to the Middle Archaic Guilford complex. The Watauga County point noted above is made of quartzite and seven of the eight points described by Perkinson (1971, 1973) are apparently made of local material including jasper (Buncombe County), local chert (Madison County—two points), quartzite (Cherokee County), rhyolite (Ashe County), clear quartz (Cherokee County), and silicified dolomite (Cherokee County). The predominant use of local material in the production of these artifacts suggests that despite the infrequent recovery of Paleo-Indian remains in the Appalachian Summit, they may represent small, local populations with limited access to raw materials from outside the region.

Site locational information on many Paleo-Indian finds is ambiguous and the sample from known contexts is so small that reconstruction of settlement patterns would be sheer guesswork. The New River finds have been made on a hillside overlooking the river (Perkinson 1973:46) and on terraces in the main valley (Purrington 1976; Robertson and Robertson 1978). However, Max White (1976:2) notes that the majority of Paleo-Indian points found in the Balsam Range in the Little Tennessee-

Tuckasegee watershed come from higher elevations and he suggests that this may reflect hunting of upland grazers in a tundra habitat. The mosaic of tundra, parkland, closed coniferous, and northern and southern hardwood forests, which probably typified the Appalachian Summit at this time, would have provided a richly varied habitat for Paleo-Indian residents or visitors.

Our limited knowledge of the Paleo-Indian period in the Appalachian Summit suggests a number of fundamental research questions.

1. What artifacts including projectile points/knives and other categories are diagnostic of Paleo-Indian culture in the Appalachian Summit? Of course this question can be asked of all prehistoric cultures in the region.
2. Were the more temperate portions of the Appalachian Summit more intensively utilized by the Paleo-Indians than the colder localities in the higher elevations and to the north? Were two or more different biomes (e.g. park-tundra and deciduous forest) included in the Paleo-Indian subsistence-settlement system? Were edge habitats (ecotones) adaptively significant?
3. Do the sparse Paleo-Indian remains in the Appalachian Summit reflect the presence of outside groups, local groups, or both? What is the significance of the apparently intensive use of a wide range of local lithic raw materials? An analysis of Paleo-Indian lithic raw materials and their sources would be highly desirable.
4. Are Paleo-Indian sites in the Appalachian Summit predominantly hunting/butchering stations or were other activities carried out in the region, too?
5. Does the rarity of Paleo-Indian remains reflect low population density or site destruction and/or burial?
6. What was the extent of tundra, park-tundra, and boreal forest biomes in the Appalachian Summit during the Paleo-Indian period? Did climatic-environmental change influence the Paleo-Indians?

Dalton-Hardaway. The period of about 8500-7500 B.C. in the Appalachian Summit is represented by the Dalton and Hardaway point types. These semi-lanceolate forms are technically and stylistically transitional between earlier Paleo-Indian points and later Archaic corner-notched and side-notched forms. For this reason and the fact that these points were present during a period of environmental change over much of the eastern United States, it is often assumed that the Dalton phase or complex represents a transition between the Paleo-Indian and Archaic ways of life. However, as evidence accumulates that Paleo-Indian subsistence was more generalized than previously assumed, the perception of Dalton as transitional between a specialized hunting economy and a broad spectrum hunting and gathering way of life may be invalidated.

In some areas of the Eastern Woodlands, such as Northeast Arkansas and the lower Tennessee Valley, Dalton remains far outnumber those of Paleo-Indian times, but in the Appalachian Summit the increase, if any, is slight. Hardaway and Dalton artifacts occur infrequently and in both upland and bottomland habitats in the Appalachian Summit, but these remains are so sparse that they provide few insights into the way of life of their makers and users. The two known Hardaway points from the upper Watauga valley are made from nonlocal chert and local quartz respectively. Assuming that there has not been extensive destruction of Dalton-Hardaway sites in the region, it would appear that population density as well as frequency and duration of occupation of specific sites were quite low during this period or that the region was only temporarily occupied by specialized activity groups (e.g. hunting parties).

Many of the questions to be asked regarding the Paleo-Indian period are pertinent to the Dalton period as well. Other important research questions include:

1. Are the cultures represented by Dalton and Hardaway points transitional between two distinctive ways of life or do they represent progressively effective adaptations to an essentially modern Appalachian Summit environment?
2. Why are Dalton-Hardaway remains so sparse in the Appalachian Summit given their abundance in many other areas of the Southeast?
3. To what extent, if any, are the technological changes associated with the Dalton-Hardaway complex related to environmental change?

Archaic Period

Kirk. The Early Archaic Kirk phase (7500-6900 B.C.) is characterized by Palmer corner-notched points and Kirk corner-notched and stemmed points. Big Sandy I or Kessel side-notched points (cf. Tuck 1974; 75-76) occasionally appear. Serration, repeated sharpening and beveling of blades, and grinding of bases, stems, and/or notches are frequent attributes of the projectile points/knives of this period. At the Mitchell Branch site, possibly a single component Kirk site in the uplands of the Toe River Valley in Yancey County (Figure 3.6), the sparse artifact assemblage includes a Kirk small corner-notched point, a serrated flake (denticulate), a unifacial end scraper with the bit on the thick end of an elongated flake, a side scraper on a decortication flake, a flake perforator,

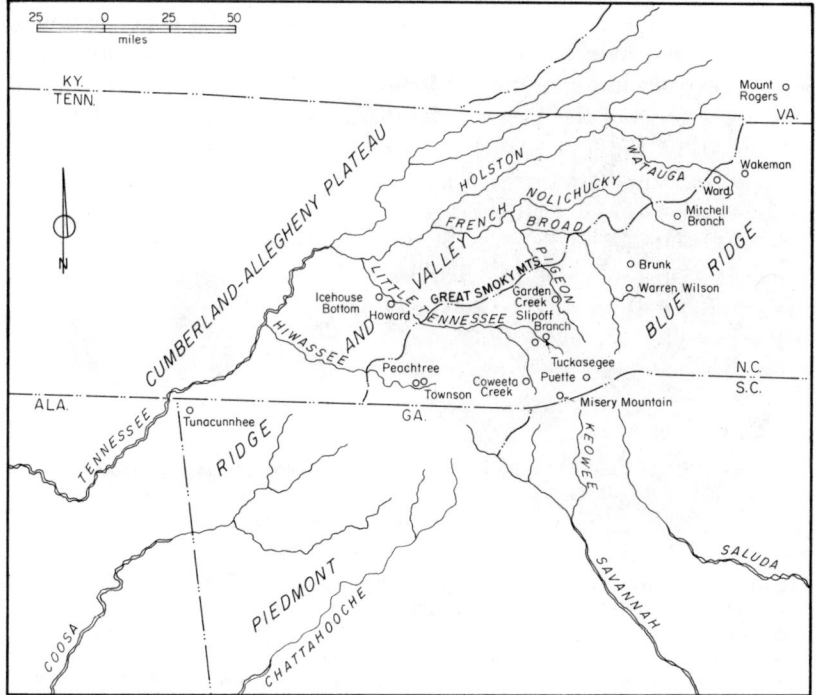

FIGURE 3.6. Some important archaeological sites and localities in and near the Appalachian Summit.

an angle graver on a blade-like flake, and a possible mano (Figure 3.7; Purrington 1980). These artifacts all fall into classes which occur in undisturbed Early Archaic strata in the lower Little Tennessee valley (Chapman 1975, 1977). Identification of Kirk phase artifacts and their stratigraphic/temporal position is based largely on Coe's (1964) excavations at the stratified Hardaway site in Piedmont North Carolina, Chapman's (1975, 1977) excavations of several stratified sites in the lower Little Tennessee River valley in the Ridge and Valley province, and Broyle's (1971) excavations at the deeply stratified St. Albans site in the West Virginia mountains. To date no undisturbed Kirk strata have been reported in the Appalachian Summit. In the Piedmont, Palmer points occur stratigraphically below Kirk horizons (Coe 1964:Figure 55), while the two types appear to be contemporaneous in the Ridge and Valley province in eastern Tennessee (Chapman 1977:48).

Archaeological evidence of the Kirk phase is relatively uncommon in the Appalachian Summit, but, nevertheless, it is far more abundant than the remains of preceding periods. Settlement pattern studies in the Great Smoky Mountains of southwestern North Carolina (Bass 1977) and in the

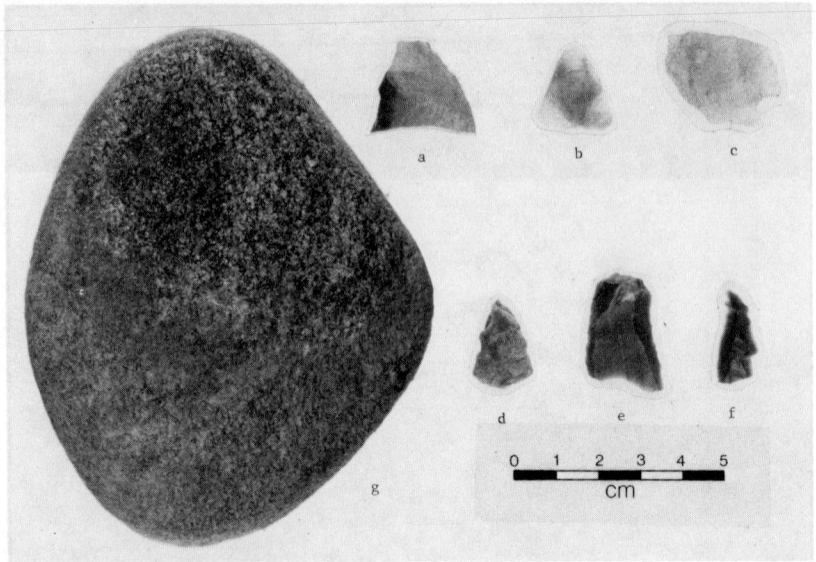

FIGURE 3.7. Artifacts from the Mitchell Branch site, a possible single component Kirk phase upland site in the Nolichucky-Toecane watershed, Yancey County, North Carolina: a, side scraper on a decortication flake; b, perforator on a worked flake (bit is broken off); c, Kirk corner-notched point; d, serrated flake; e, unifacial end scraper with bit on the thick end of an elongated flake; f, unprepared graver on a blade-like flake; g, cobble tool/mano.

upper Watauga valley in the northwestern part of the state (Purrington and Douthit 1977) lend insights into the nature of Kirk life and also suggest substantial intraregional variation in adaptive strategies. In the Great Smoky Mountains, Bass (1977:52, 60) found Kirk points to be made predominantly of chert from the Ridge and Valley province and to be few in number; he suggested that they came from local limited activity sites of Early Archaic visitors from the east Tennessee river basins. At the briefly occupied Mitchell Branch site in the Toe River uplands to the north the exclusive use of chert and fine-grained quartzite from east Tennessee also suggests short-term occupation by outside groups (Purrington 1980).

On the other hand, in the upper Watauga valley a substantially higher percentage of Palmer, Kirk, and Big Sandy I points are made of local quartz as well as rhyolite from Mount Rogers to the north. A similar practice of using local as well as nonlocal stone occurred on the Southeastern Escarpment (see Figure 3.4). Here the Palmer and Kirk points collected by the Misery Mountain survey in the uplands above the Thompson River valley in Transylvania County were of intermediate quality local vein quartz and they had been reworked to near exhaustion (Purrington 1981a). Palmer points of quartz, quartzite, and chert were collected by Holden (1966:50) during her survey of Transylvania County which included the Southeastern Escarpment and French Broad watersheds. These examples of intensive use of relatively poor quality local stone suggests resident Kirk populations in these localities. The Kirk phase appears to have represented a time of gradual establishment of permanent occupation of the Appalachian Summit with some localities being occupied by resident groups and others on a temporary basis.

Kirk sites in the Appalachian Summit occur in a wide range of upland and main valley habitats which suggests an extremely mobile population. The variety of habitats occupied in the upper Watauga valley suggests a broad-spectrum adaptive strategy which supports the previously proposed hypothesis of a resident Kirk population (Purrington and Douthit 1977). However, over 70% of the Kirk phase sites in the upper Watauga valley (sites with Big Sandy/Kessel, Palmer and/or Kirk points) occur in upland settings, which is 10 to 50% higher than any subsequent phase (Tables 3.1 and 3.2). Although it might be argued that the relatively higher frequency of Kirk phase sites in the uplands may simply be a statistical illusion created by more frequent burial of the earlier Kirk components in floodplain sites, one statistic from the upper Watauga valley clearly indicates relatively intensive use of upland habitats by Kirk people: six Kirk phase sites (14.6% of the total number of Kirk sites) are found at elevations of 4,000 feet or greater; the next closest are the Middle Archaic Morrow Mountain and Early Woodland Swannanoa phases with five sites each (8.8% and 6.7% of their respective totals) at or above 4,000 feet (Purrington and Douthit 1977). Further support of a model of relatively intensive use of the Appalachian Summit uplands by Kirk phase people comes from the fact that eighteen (72%) of the Early Archaic sites from the Great Smoky Mountains survey occur in the upland zones and most display a wider range of activities than bottomland and valley margin sites from the same period (Bass 1977:66). On the other hand, Robertson and Robertson (1978) found that in the upper New River valley, Kirk sites occurred more commonly in floodplains and secondarily on the higher ridges. Intensive use of the main valley floodplain of the lower Little Tennessee River by Kirk phase people has been demonstrated by work in the Tellico Reservoir (Chapman 1975, 1977).

Among the most important questions to ask of the Kirk phase data are those related to the cultural implications of the apparent intraregional variations in local settlement-subsistence systems and the significance of an apparent relatively intensive use of upland and high elevation sites during this period presumably by both local and visiting groups.

1. Did some Kirk groups inhabit the Appalachian Summit year-round while others were transient populations from neighboring regions such as the Ridge and Valley province of east Tennessee?

TABLE 3.1. Distribution of prehistoric and protohistoric phases by general landform categories, upper Watauga valley, North Carolina.

Component[a] Site Type	Main Valley Fertile Bottoms (#) (%)[c]		Main Valley[b] Limited Bottoms (#) (%)		Main Valley Margins (#) (%)		Main Valley Uplands (#) (%)		Upland Valley Bottoms and Margins (#) (%)		Upland Valley Uplands (#) (%)		Ridgetops (#) (%)		TOTAL (#)
Hardaway (O)	-	-	-	-	-	-	-	-	1	50.0	-	-	-	-	1 (2)
Hardaway (R)	-	-	-	-	1	50.0	-	-	-	-	-	-	-	-	1
Big Sandy/ Kessel (O)	2	28.6	-	-	1	14.3	1	14.3	2	28.6	-	-	1	14.3	7 (7)
Big Sandy/ Kessel (R)	-	-	-	-	-	-	-	-	-	-	-	-	-	-	-
Palmer (O)	1	10.0	-	-	1	10.0	-	-	3	30.0	-	-	4	40.0	9 (10)
Palmer (R)	-	-	-	-	-	-	-	-	1	10.0	-	-	-	-	1
Kirk (O)	1	4.2	-	-	4	16.7	4	16.7	5	20.8	1	4.2	4	16.7	19 (24)
Kirk (R)	-	-	-	-	2	8.3	-	-	1	4.2	2	8.3	-	-	5
Bifurcate Base (O)	5	25.0	-	-	4	20.0	2	10.0	5	25.0	1	5.0	1	5.0	18 (20)
Bifurcate Base (R)	-	-	-	-	1	5.0	-	-	1	5.0	-	-	-	-	2
Morrow Mountain (O)	14	24.6	-	-	8	14.0	5	8.8	16	28.1	3	5.3	7	12.3	53 (57)
Morrow Mountain (R)	-	-	-	-	2	3.5	-	-	1	1.8	1	1.8	-	-	4
Guilford (O)	5	12.5	-	-	9	22.5	2	5.0	13	32.5	3	7.5	3	7.5	35 (40)
Guilford (R)	-	-	-	-	2	5.0	-	-	2	5.0	1	2.5	-	-	5

(continued)

TABLE 3.1. Continued

Component Site Type	Main Valley Fertile Bottoms (#) (%)	Main Valley Limited Bottoms (#) (%)	Main Valley Margins (#) (%)	Main Valley Uplands (#) (%)	Upland Valley Bottoms and Margins (#) (%)	Upland Valley Uplands (#) (%)	Ridgetops (#) (%)	TOTAL (#)
Connestee (O) (ceramic)	5 71.4	- -	- -	1 14.3	- -	- -	- -	6 (7)
Connestee (R) (ceramic)	- -	- -	1 14.3	- -	- -	- -	- -	1
Connestee (O) (non-ceramic)	1 7.7	1 7.7	7 53.8	- -	1 7.7	1 7.7	- -	11 (13)
Connestee (R) (non-ceramic)	- -	- -	- -	- -	1 7.7	1 7.7	- -	2
Pisgah (ceramic) Village	12 100.0	- -	- -	- -	- -	- -	- -	(12)
Pisgah (ceramic) Farmstead	3 33.3	- -	5 55.5	- -	1 11.1	- -	- -	(9)
Pisgah (R) (ceramic)	- -	- -	2 66.7	- -	- -	1 33.3	- -	(3)
Pisgah (O) (non-ceramic)	6 20.7	1 3.4	4 13.8	2 6.9	7 24.1	1 3.4	3 10.3	24 (29)
Pisgah (R) (non-ceramic)	- -	- -	2 6.9	- -	- -	3 10.3	- -	5
Qualla (O) (non-ceramic)	12 54.5	- -	1 4.5	- -	3 13.6	- -	1 4.5	17 (22)
Qualla (R) (non-ceramic)	- -	- -	4 18.2	- -	- -	1 4.5	- -	5

(continued)

TABLE 3.1. Continued

Component Site Type	Main Valley Fertile Bottoms		Main Valley Limited Bottoms		Main Valley Margins		Main Valley Uplands		Upland Valley Bottoms and Margins		Upland Valley Uplands		Ridgetops		TOTAL
	(#)	(%)	(#)	(%)	(#)	(%)	(#)	(%)	(#)	(%)	(#)	(%)	(#)	(%)	(#)
Savannah River (O)	13	16.2	4	5.0	24	30.0	5	6.2	13	16.2	7	8.8	6	7.5	72 (80)
Savannah River (R)	–	–	–	–	4	5.0	1	1.3	2	2.5	1	1.3	–	–	8
Otarre (O)	5	20.8	–	–	7	29.2	2	8.3	4	16.7	–	–	4	16.7	21 (24)
Otarre (R)	–	–	–	–	1	4.2	–	–	1	4.2	1	4.2	–	–	3
Swannanoa (O) (ceramic)	8	17.0	2	4.3	11	23.4	3	6.4	4	8.5	1	2.1	2	4.3	31 (47)
Swannanoa (R) (ceramic)	–	–	–	–	6	12.8	1	2.1	2	4.3	7	14.9	–	–	16
Swannanoa (O) (non-ceramic)	7	25.0	1	3.6	6	21.4	2	7.1	5	17.9	5	17.9	2	7.1	28 (28)
Swannanoa (R) (non-ceramic)	–	–	–	–	–	–	–	–	–	–	–	–	–	–	–
Pigeon (O) (ceramic)	3	30.0	–	–	1	10.0	–	–	–	–	–	–	–	–	4 (10)
Pigeon (R) (ceramic)	–	–	–	–	4	40.0	–	–	1	10.0	1	10.0	–	–	6
Pigeon (O) (non-ceramic)	8	30.8	–	–	8	30.8	3	11.5	3	11.5	1	3.8	3	11.5	26 (26)
Pigeon (R) (non-ceramic)	–	–	–	–	–	–	–	–	–	–	–	–	–	–	–

TABLE 3.1. Continued

^a O = open air site
R = rockshelter
(ceramic) = ceramics representing designated component present at site
(non-ceramic) = ceramics representing designated component have not been recovered from site

^b General landform categories include:

a. *Main Valley, Fertile Bottoms*—Undifferentiated floodplains (T-O) and natural levees of 5th to 7th order streams. Soils are classified as 1-A with few or no agricultural limitations. Elevations range from about 2600 to 2800 feet amsl.

b. *Main Valley, Limited Bottoms*—Backswamps and other features of floodplains (T-O) with agricultural limitations on 5th to 7th order streams. Soil capabilities limited by stoniness, frequent flooding, poor drainage, clay pans, etc. Elevations range from about 2600 to 2800 feet amsl.

c. *Main Valley Margins*—Landforms on the edges of stream valleys 5th to 7th order including terraces (T-1, T-2, etc.), alluvial and colluvial fans and aprons, and rockshelters 80 feet or less above the main stream or major tributary. Elevations range from about 2640 to 2880 feet amsl.

d. *Main Valley Uplands*—Knolls, low ridge spurs, and hill slopes on the edge of a main valley (5th-7th order) and 80 feet or less above the main stream or major tributary, and rockshelters immediately above and more than 80 feet above a main valley. Elevations range from about 2680 to 2920 feet amsl.

e. *Upland Valley Bottoms and Margins*—Landforms in 1st to 4th order stream valleys including bottoms and terraces, alluvial and colluvial fans and aprons, rockshelters 80 feet or less above the main stream, and level areas at streamheads and the heads of hollows. Elevations range from about 3000 to 4120 feet amsl.

f. *Upland Valley Uplands*—Knolls, low ridge spurs, and hill slopes on the edges of upland valleys (1st to 4th order) and 80 feet or less above the main stream, and rockshelters immediately and more than 80 feet above an upland valley. Elevations range from 3040 to 4120 feet amsl.

g. *Ridgetops*—Peaks, ridgelines, gaps, saddles, and ridge spurs greater than 80 feet above permanent water, and rockshelters on or immediately below a ridgetop landform. Elevations range from about 3060 to 4560 feet amsl.

^c Percentages based on the total number of open air and rockshelter sites for each phase.

TABLE 3.2. Distribution of prehistoric components in the upper Watauga Valley, North Carolina, by main valley and upland settings.

Component[a] Site Type	Main Valley Fertile Bottoms (#)	(%)	Main Valley[b] Marginal Settings (#)	(%)	Upland[c] Valleys (#)	(%)	Upland[d] Ridges (#)	(%)	Total Main Valleys (#)	(%)	Total Uplands (#)	(%)	Total (#)
Hardaway	-	-	1	50.0	1	50.0	-	-	1	50.0	1	50.0	2
Big Sandy/ Kessel	2	28.6	1	14.3	2	28.6	2	28.6	3	42.9	4	57.1	7
Palmer	1	10.0	1	10.0	4	40.0	4	40.0	2	20.0	8	80.0	10
Kirk	1	4.2	6	25.0	6	25.0	11	45.8	7	29.2	17	70.8	24
Bifurcate Base	5	25.0	5	25.0	6	30.0	4	20.0	10	50.0	10	50.0	20
Morrow Mountain	14	24.6	10	17.5	17	29.8	16	28.1	24	42.1	33	57.9	57
Guilford	5	12.5	11	27.5	15	37.5	9	22.5	16	40.0	24	60.0	40
Savannah River	13	16.2	32	40.0	15	18.8	20	25.0	45	56.2	35	43.8	80
Otarre	5	20.8	8	33.3	5	20.8	6	25.0	13	54.2	11	45.8	24
Swannanoa (ceramic)	8	17.0	19	40.4	6	12.8	14	29.8	27	57.4	20	42.6	47
Swannanoa (non-ceramic)	7	25.0	7	25.0	5	17.9	9	32.1	14	50.0	14	50.0	28

(continued)

TABLE 3.2. Continued

Component[a] Site Type	Main Valley Fertile Bottoms (#)	(%)	Main Valley[b] Marginal Settings (#)	(%)	Upland[c] Valleys (#)	(%)	Upland[d] Ridges (#)	(%)	Total Main Valleys (#)	(%)	Total Uplands (#)	(%)	Total (#)
Pigeon (ceramic)	3	30.0	5	50.0	1	10.0	1	10.0	8	80.0	2	20.0	10
Pigeon (non-ceramic)	8	30.8	8	30.8	3	11.5	7	26.9	16	61.5	10	38.5	26
Connestee (ceramic)	5	71.4	1	14.3	–	–	1	14.3	6	85.7	1	14.3	7
Connestee (non-ceramic)	1	7.7	8	61.5	2	15.4	2	15.4	9	69.2	4	30.8	13
Pisgah Village (ceramic)	12	100.0	–	–	–	–	–	–	12	100.0	–	–	12
Pisgah (ceramic) Farmstead, Shelter	3	25.0	7	58.3	1	8.3	1	8.3	10	83.3	2	16.7	12
Pisgah (non-ceramic)	6	20.7	7	24.1	7	24.1	9	31.0	13	44.8	16	55.2	29
Qualla (non-ceramic)	12	54.5	5	22.7	3	13.6	2	9.1	17	77.3	5	22.7	22

[a] (ceramic)=ceramics representing designated component present at site.
(non-ceramic)=ceramics representing designated component have not been recovered from site.
[b] Includes limited bottoms, valley margins and rockshelters on valley margins.
[c] Includes bottoms, margins and rockshelters in upland valleys.
[d] Includes open sites and rockshelters in main valley and upland valley uplands and ridgetops.

2. If both outside and local groups were present, can functional, adaptive, and sociocultural similarities and differences be identified in their archaeological records?
3. What was the nature of social interaction between resident and outside groups as well as between various resident populations?
4. Are there temporal and/or functional differences between Palmer, Big Sandy I, and the various forms of Kirk points?
5. Did Kirk people use the upland and higher elevations more intensively than subsequent groups? If so, does this reflect a greater subsistence utilization of upland resources such as elk (which are upland grazers), deer, wild turkey and other mast-consuming fauna, and nuts? Was there relatively little utilization of bottomland resources (with the possible exception of game)?

LeCroy. The Early Archaic LeCroy phase (6900-6000 B.C.) is characterized by bifurcate-based projectile points/knives including (from earliest to most recent) MacCorkle, St. Albans, LeCroy, and Kanawha. The temporal relationships of these types to each other and to points from other periods have been identified by excavation of stratified sites on the lower Little Tennessee River (Chapman 1975, 1977) and on the Kanawha River in West Virginia (Broyles 1971). These points have not yet been recovered in stratigraphic context in the Appalachian Summit, and no single component sites have yet been identified.

Bifuracte-based points have been found in small numbers in most subregions of the Appalachian Summit. Generally they are outnumbered two times or more by Kirk phase points and even more substantially by points from subsequent phases. Bifurcate-based points recovered by the Great Smoky Mountains Survey were made only of Ridge and Valley chert (Bass 1977:52), but in the upper Watauga valley these types occasionally were made of local vein quartz. As with the Kirk phase these local variations in types of lithic raw materials used may reflect the difference between non-local and resident populations.

Although LeCroy phase sites in the Great Smoky Mountains follow the Kirk settlement pattern with an emphasis on upland habitats (Bass 1977), in the upper Watauga valley there is a decided shift toward bottomland and valley margin habitats (Tables 3.1 and 3.2). This settlement shift appears to have remained largely unchanged throughout the remainder of the Archaic period (Tables 3.1 and 3.2; Purrington and Douthit 1977). This situation may reflect substantially increased utilization of riverine and floodplain resources during the seventh millenium B.C. in the upper Watauga valley—a major adaptive achievement, which probably took place earlier (Kirk phase) in the lower Little Tennessee valley (cf. Chapman 1975, 1977) and later (Morrow Mountain phase) in the Great Smoky

Mountains (cf. Bass 1977). Among the key research questions that remain are:

1. What factors motivated and reinforced the apparent broadening of the LeCroy subsistence base which is suggested by the increased frequency of LeCroy sites in floodplain habitats?
2. Why was there an apparent time lag from one Appalachian subregion and locality to the next in the establishment of year-round human residence?
3. Why are fewer LeCroy phase points found in the Appalachian Summit than Kirk phase points since the phases are of roughly equal duration.
4. What was the nature of the procurement or exchange systems that brought nonlocal chert to resident LeCroy phase groups?

Stanly. The Stanly projectile points/knives, representative of the Middle Archaic, Stanly phase (6000-5500 B.C.) have been found in undisturbed early Middle Archaic strata in the North Carolina Piedmont (Coe 1964) and in the lower Little Tennessee Valley (Chapman 1975, 1977). As yet they have not been identified in single component contexts in the Appalachian Summit.

Stanly points apparently occur with even less frequency in the Appalachian Summit than the earlier LeCroy phase types although they are abundant in the neighboring Ridge and Valley and Piedmont provinces (cf. Chapman 1977; Coe 1964). A general depopulation of the region, a trend that could have begun during the LeCroy phase, may have taken place. In the upper Watauga valley where people may have been resident for perhaps 1,500 years and a set of adaptive strategies that was to persist for 5,000 years or more apparently had evolved, there is very little evidence of the Stanly phase. However, it is also possible that archaeological assemblages from this period simply have not been recognized, have been destroyed, or have been buried by natural forces. For example, some Stanly phase points may have been mistakenly classified as Terminal Archaic or Early Woodland types (see Bass 1977:66, 69; Cridlebaugh 1977:51; and discussion below) which would seriously skew our perception of population density during this period.

In the Great Smoky Mountains where Early Archaic occupation was ephemeral, Stanly points were made entirely of local vein quartz and quartzite which would suggest the initial appearance in this locality of a resident population, albeit one that was much smaller than the succeeding Morrow Mountain phase population (cf. Bass 1977:53). Stanly points were also produced from local stone in other Appalachian Summit localities which may indicate that even if a general reduction in the region's population took place, some local groups remained.

These patterns suggest the following kinds of questions:

1. Is the density of the Stanly assemblage significantly lower in the Appalachian Summit than in the neighboring Ridge and Valley and Piedmont provinces? Is it lower than preceding and succeeding phases? Does this pattern reflect a lower population density or simply a failure to correctly associate some artifact classes with this phase?
2. What factors led to the apparent initial occupation on a permanent basis of the Great Smoky Mountains during the period of the Stanly phase?
3. Were some localities such as the upper Watauga valley abandoned during the period of the Stanly phase?
4. Was there a population movement from the northeastern Appalachian Summit to the southwest, or were some localities abandoned and new localities colonized?

Morrow Mountain. The Middle Archaic, Morrow Mountain Phase (5500-4000 B.C.), as represented by Morrow Mountain projectile points/knives, is characterized by a heavy dependence on local lithic raw materials to the virtual exclusion of nonlocal stone. When only quartz is locally available, it was used almost exclusively. Chert, felsite, quartzite, and rhyolite were used when locally available. Tools from the Slipoff Branch site, a single component Morrow Mountain hunting/butchering camp in the uplands of the Tuckasegee valley (Purrington 1978a), are exclusively of local vein quartz and quartzite. They include contracting stemmed Morrow Mountain points and knives; crude bifacial ovate knives and choppers; amorphous end, side, and flake scrapers; serrated flakes (denticulates); and combination tools (Figure 3.8).

Whereas the LeCroy and Stanly phases appear to represent formative attempts at increased efficiency in the utilization of local food and lithic resources of the Appalachian Summit, the Morrow Mountain phase represents a resounding region-wide success. Virtually anywhere one looks in the region there is a manifold increase in Morrow Mountain artifacts over recognized remains of preceding phases (Table 3.1; Bass 1977:53; Holden 1966:50-51; Purrington and Douthit 1977).

However, the archaeological evidence for the settlement patterns of this phase is somewhat ambiguous. Bass (1977:109) notes that in the Great Smoky Mountains "total utilization of the environment is indicated by the distribution of sites of this period in every physiographic zone." He also tentatively suggests that "the lack of significant differences in activity sets between sites implies that all physiographic zones of the Great Smokies were exploited similarly." Should this second inference stand up under testing, the sociocultural implications would be extremely significant.

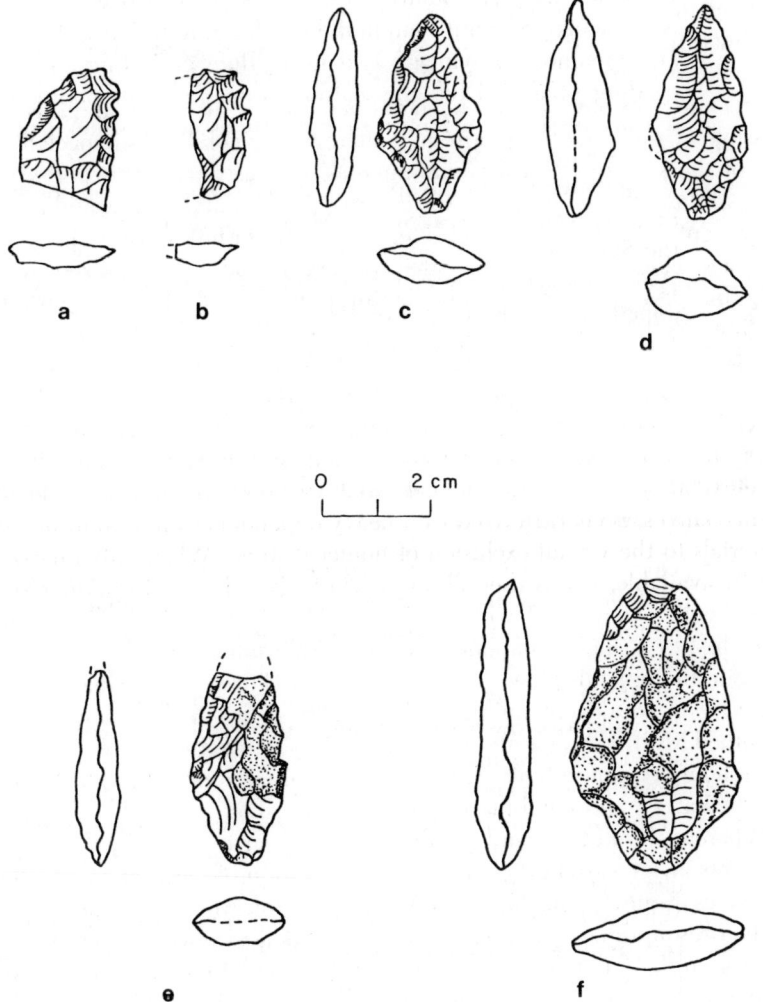

FIGURE 3.8. Artifacts from the Slipoff Branch site, a single component Morrow Mountain phase upland site in the Little Tennessee-Tuckasegee watershed, Swain County, North Carolina; a,b, serrated flakes; c-e, Morrow Mountain projectile points/knives; f, Morrow Mountain knife. All artifacts are white quartz

Such a settlement pattern suggests a very generalized subsistence system with whole, presumably small, social units (primarily extended families?) making unspecialized and perhaps nonseasonal use of a wide range of habitats. In the upper Watauga valley the complete range of recognized habitats was also utilized but, unfortunately, functional typologies of artifacts and sites have not yet been defined for this subregion and it is not possible at this time to determine if there was generalized or specialized use of the variety of local environmental settings during this period.

Possible evidence of a specialized Morrow Mountain occupation may be present at the Slipoff Branch site, about 30 river miles east of the Great Smokies (Figure 3.6). This site appears to be a specialized hunting/butchering camp where maintenance of tools and perhaps preliminary hide preparation also took place. The small number of artifacts at the site and the absence of evidence of either long-term habitation or a wide range of activities suggest that this was a short-term, special-use site. However, this finding does not necessarily invalidate Bass's hypothesis since earlier Archaic phases in the region exhibit an apparently substantial degree of local variation. Further research should address the following kinds of problems:

1. Does the dramatic increase in Morrow Mountain artifacts represent an increase in the region's population? Is this an increase in population density alone or an increase in size of social units as well?
2. What were the causes of this apparent population increase?
3. Why did Morrow Mountain stoneworkers rely entirely or nearly so on local raw materials?
4. Was the primary adaptive strategy of Morrow Mountain people in the Great Smokies one of generalized, nonseasonal utilization of a variety of habitats by microbands? Was this pattern present elsewhere?
5. What was the role of apparently special-use, short-term hunting/butchering sites such as Slipoff Branch in Morrow Mountain subsistence, settlement, and social systems?

Guilford. Thick, lanceolate Guilford projectile points/knives characterize the Middle Archaic, Guilford phase (4000-3000 B.C.). In this phase there was continued use of predominantly local stone particularly quartzite and quartz in the Great Smoky Mountains (Bass 1977:53) while the proportion of nonlocal quartzite increased in the upper Watauga valley. No single component strata or sites have been identified.

The Guilford assemblage was first recognized in the North Carolina Piedmont and described by Coe (1964:43-44). This technological complex may be primarily a Piedmont and Appalachian Summit phenomenon for, although the Guilford point is common in the Appalachian Summit, it is virtually nonexistent in the Ridge and Valley province immediately to the west (Bass 1977:60). In the upper Watauga valley Guilford settlement patterns appear to be essentially a continuation of Morrow Mountain settlement with a wide range of habitats being utilized (Table 3.1). There may be a slight decline in bottomland utilization with a corresponding increase in utilization of valley margins and upland stream bottoms (Table 3.2). Essential questions remain to be answered:

1. Why is the Guilford type point generally absent west of the Appalachian Summit?
2. What are the technological, functional, and sociocultural implications of the increased use of quartzite by the Guilford phase people in the upper Watauga valley?
3. Is Guilford basically a continuation of the Morrow Mountain way of life?

Savannah River. The major diagnostic artifacts of the Late Archaic, Savannah River phase (3000-1000 B.C.) are large, broad-bladed, straight-stemmed projectile points/knives (Figure 3.9) which are generally made of quartzite (Savannah River or Appalachian Stemmed points). In the upper New River and Watauga River valleys a similar type of point, which more closely resembles the Tennessee Ledbetter type, is made of rhyolite. Large triangular blades, possibly preforms for Savannah River points, are also made of quartzite. In the Great Smoky Mountains, where quartzite is locally available, and in the upper Watauga River valley, where it was probably imported from the Ridge and Valley province, quartzite comprises the sole raw material in most Savannah River assemblages. Soapstone bowls and jars, occasionally with lug handles, also characterize this phase and reflect the apparent introduction of semi-permanent (until broken) cooking/storage containers to the region. Keel also associates bar gorgets, groundstone grooved axes, large elbow pipes, notched stones ("net weights"), pitted and pebble hammerstones, large crude bifaces, and flake scrapers with this phase (Keel 1976:231).

Savannah River remains have been found in a stratigraphic context below Early Woodland Swannanoa remains and above Morrow Mountain remains at the Warren Wilson site (Keel 1976:Table 24), and they appear in early contexts at both Tuckasegee and Garden Creek (Keel 1976:231). The remains of this phase are among the most abundant in the Appalachian Summit which may suggest increased population density as well as increased visibility of archaeological remains. It is clear that there were significant local variations in settlement systems and adaptive strategies during this period. For example, in the Great Smoky Mountains Late Archaic settlement patterns are much more restricted than Middle Archaic settlement patterns (Bass 1977:69), while in the upper Watauga

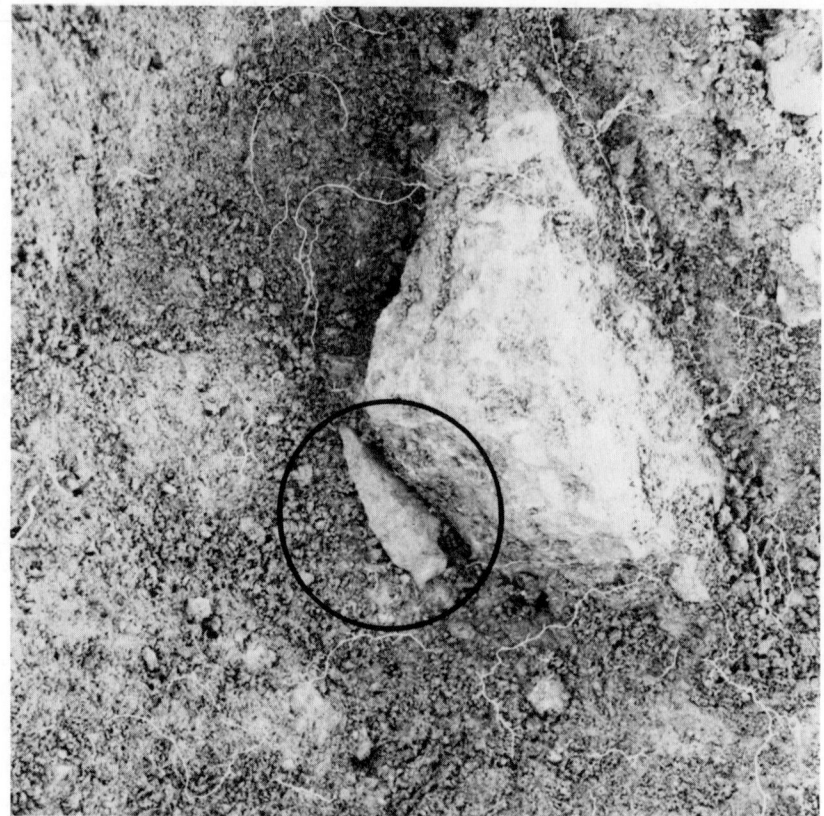

FIGURE 3.9. A Savannah River point in a large, subrectangular pit, possibly a burial, at the Bynum Taylor site, Watauga River watershed, Watauga County, North Carolina. Charcoal from this feature has been radiocarbon dated at 1851 ± 80 B.C. (UGA-1060).

valley both Middle and Late Archaic sites are found in a wide range of habitats (Tables 3.1 and 3.2; Purrington and Douthit 1977).

In the Great Smoky Mountains, Bass found that Late Archaic sites occur mainly within the larger river valleys, the only local areas where quartzite outcrops occur, and that local Savannah River artifacts are made exclusively of quartzite (Bass 1977:54, 69). A decided shift from the generalized Middle Archaic settlement patterns of the Great Smokies is evident in the increased percentage (69.5%) of Savannah River sites in the valley zone and in the fact that a much wider range of activities is represented in floodplain sites (food processing, hunting, butchering, wood, bone, and primary chipped stone working) than the coves and "benches" of the upland zone and the upper valley areas of the valley zone. Sites in the latter settings exhibit less evidence of food processing (soapstone vessel fragments and grinding slabs) and wood and bone working (axes, adzes) activities than the floodplain sites. The ridges, balds and gaps of the upland zone reflect only hunting and hunting-related activities. Bass (1977:77) has developed a three-component settlement model for the Late Archaic period of the Great Smoky Mountains suggesting that these patterns probably reflect:

> activity- or season-specific segmentation of the Late Archaic population within these areas—larger populations on the floodplain area seasonally dispersing to the upper valley and coves and "benches." The sites located in the gaps and ridges and balds of the Upland Zone were apparently hunting camps extended from a base camp in valley sites.

The "decided collapse of human habitation onto the floodplains of the valley floors" (Bass 1977:109), which characterizes the Late Archaic period of the Great Smoky Mountains, does not appear to have occurred in the upper Watauga valley. There both Middle and Late Archaic peoples seem to have made use of the same wide range of habitats, and, if anything, the Savannah River people made greater use of valley margin sites and less use of floodplain sites than Middle Archaic people (Table 3.2). Moreover, there is substantial evidence of plant food storage and/or processing in Late Archaic high gap and saddle sites such as the Wakeman 2 site and the Rich Mountain Gap site in Watauga county (Figure 3.10). Soapstone vessel fragments have been found in Savannah River contexts at both sites, and grinding stones and charred black walnut and hickory shells have been identified at Wakeman 2. However, there is a proportionate increase in main valley sites over upland sites (Table 3.2). Whether or not there are functional and/or seasonal differences between Savannah River sites in the various habitats of the upper Watauga valley cannot be determined until analyses and use-wear and technical attributes of artifacts are performed and functional artifact types and other activity indicators are identified.

Another important difference between the Savannah River remains of the Great Smoky Mountains and the upper Watauga valley is that although quartzite was exclusively used in the former locality and nearly so in the latter, the patterns of procurement were quite different. In the Great Smoky Mountains quartzite outcrops are locally restricted to "nick points" along streams in the larger river valleys, and Savannah River sites are located mainly within these areas (Bass 1977:48, 69). Bass (1977:69) suggests that the fact that Savannah River artifacts are made exclusively of quartzite "appears to be a function of the fact that sites for this period are located mainly within the larger river valleys." This shift to exclusive use of local raw materials is believed to exemplify "the more intensive exploitation of smaller areas" and "the valley-oriented, semisedentary nature of the settlement and subsistence patterns" of the Late Archaic

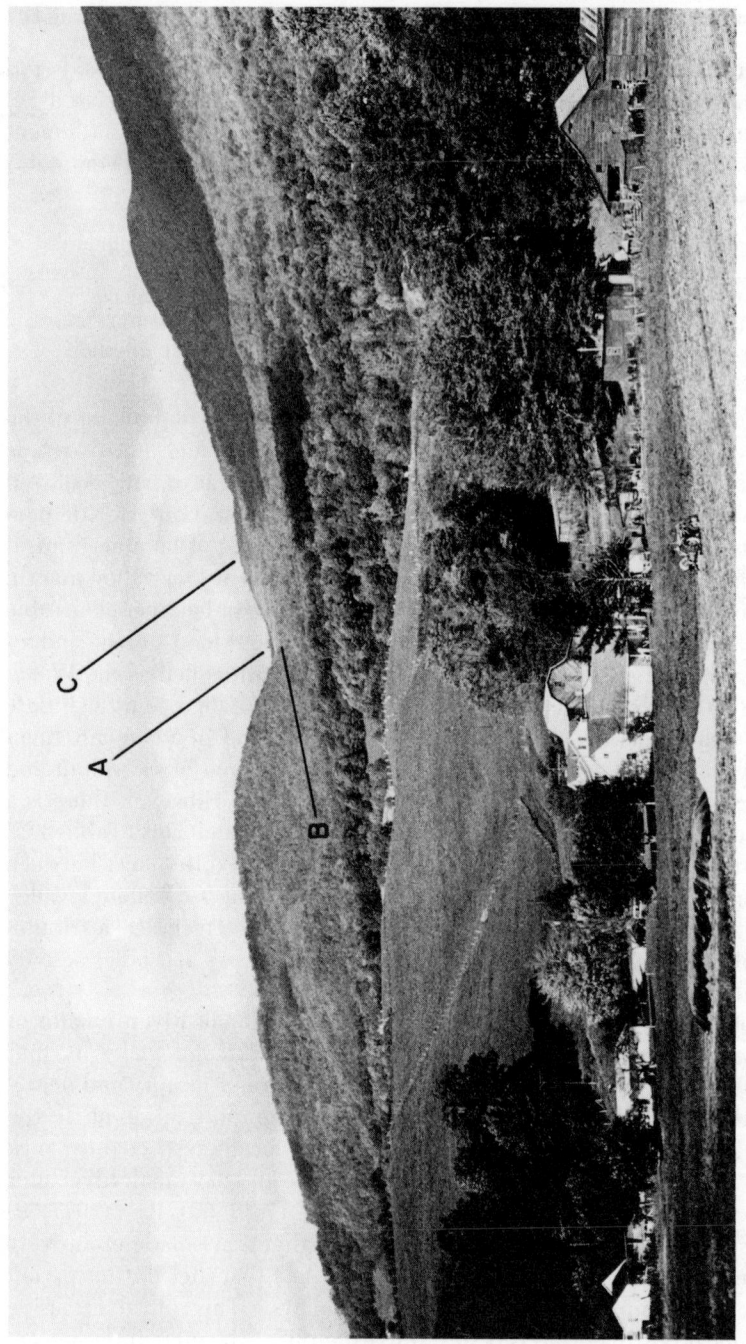

FIGURE 3.10. The Wakeman sites, Watauga River watershed, Watauga County, North Carolina. Wakeman 2 (A) is located in a saddle between Ellison and Rich mountains at an elevation of about 4200 feet (AMSL); Wakeman 3 (B) is in a small, south-facing hollow at a springhead at about 4000 feet; and Wakeman 4 (C) is on the point of a ridge spur at about 4560 feet.

period (Bass 1977:113). Bass's (1977:113) suggestion that the progressive increase in use of nonlocal chert following the Late Archaic period in the Great Smokies is "indicative of its direct procurement from eastern Tennessee or, more likely, expanding trade networks with that region" implies that the local Middle and Late Archaic populations were relatively isolated and self-sufficient. An interesting parallel in a topographically similar region occurred in the Fishtrap locality in eastern Kentucky's Cumberland Plateau where Late Archaic groups shifted to exclusive or nearly exclusive use of locally available siderite while succeeding Woodland period groups gradually resumed use of nonlocal chert (Dunnell 1972:32).

However, in the upper Watauga valley the near-exclusive use of quartzite does not appear to be a function of its availability in preferred habitats since it occurs locally only on high, resistant outcrops such as Grandfather Mountain (Leighty, Perkins, Croom, and Davis 1958:55) and further to the west in the Ridge and Valley province (Ayers 1976), whereas vein quartz is locally abundant. Instead it appears to be a preferred raw material which was probably procured from the scattered local outcrops and imported from the Ridge and Valley province. The Wakeman 2 site is a clear example of this preference. Unlike high gap sites in the Great Smokies where evidence of Savannah River presence is generally represented by a single quartzite point (Bass 1977:48), Wakeman 2, which is probably 40 miles and 3000 vertical feet from a quartzite source (Ayers 1976), is literally a quartzite pavement. Thousands of quartzite flakes, flake tools, and an occasional Savannah River point occur in the top few inches of soil over much of the site.

One reported Late Archaic site in the region, the Evans Gap site in the Tuckasegee watershed, deviates from the previously described patterns of lithic resource utilization. This site is located in a saddle at 4,000 feet elevation in Jackson County, North Carolina where outcrops of quartz and quartzite are immediately available. However, nearly all of the Savannah River points and other Late Archaic chipped stone tools at the site are made of quartz (White 1972).

Many research questions remain:

1. Are these increases in sedentism, size of social units (at least at times of seasonal aggregation), and/or population density in the Great Smokies and other localities in the region? If so, why?
2. Is the substantially increased occurrence of Savannah River artifacts in floodplain habitats in the Great Smokies the result of increased utilization of floodplain food resources (riverbank and wetland plants, floodplain commensal plants, fish, and/or shellfish), the emergence of horticulture, concentration near sources

of a preferred raw material (quartzite), higher visibility of archaeological remains, or what?
3. Is the Late Archaic settlement-subsistence system of the upper Watauga valley basically a continuation of the Middle Archaic pattern?
4. What was the nature of the procurement system that brought quartzite to Late Archaic groups such as those in the upper Watauga valley who lacked local sources of the stone?
5. Was quartzite used out of preference, easy access to local sources, the absence of exchange or procurement systems for obtaining nonlocal raw materials, geographical and social isolation, or what?
6. How extensive are the patterns of settlement and resource procurement described above?

Otarre. The Terminal Archaic, Otarre Phase (1000-700 B.C.) is characterized by the Otarre stemmed projectile point/knife which is a smaller, more formally variable version of the Savannah River stemmed point. Keel, who defined the Otarre Stemmed type (1976:194-196), considers it "to be the latest point type produced in the Southern Appalachians prior to the introduction of ceramics" and "the lineal descendant of the Savannah River Stemmed point." However, the temporal position of Otarre points is presently ambiguous. At the Warren Wilson site Otarre points were found in stratigraphic association with and below Savannah River points in the Late Archaic strata (Keel 1976:Table 24), and Keel (1976:231) places them in the Savannah River phase. Moreover, Bass (1977:66, 69) notes that many stemmed points from sealed Stanly strata at the Icehouse Bottom site on the lower little Tennessee River are "indistinguishable" from Otarre and Early Woodland Swannanoa stemmed and Plott short stemmed points, and Cridlebaugh (1977:51) has observed large numbers of these points in Morrow Mountain strata at the Icehouse Bottom and Howard sites. In a developmental sense the Savannah River, Otarre, and Plott/Swannanoa types would appear to be progressively later forms in a broad, straight-stemmed point tradition which underwent gradual reduction in size and increased formal variability over time, but the stratigraphic data from the lower Little Tennessee valley and, to a lesser extent, the Warren Wilson site (Plott and Swannanoa points are stratigraphically above Otarre and Savannah River points at Warren Wilson) suggest very strongly that these generalized point styles were around for several thousand years. Moreover, Oliver (1981b) has recently questioned the validity of the Otarre and Plott categories as types. Obviously, if these types as presently defined are inadequate as temporal indicators, many of the assignments—in this paper and others—of sites to the Terminal Archaic and Early Woodland periods on the basis of the presence of Otarre, Plott, and/or Swannanoa points may be in error, and subsistence and settlement interpretations will be affected. At present both Bass's (1977) and Purrington's (1982) settlement pattern studies are based on the assumption that Otarre points represent the Terminal Archaic period and that Plott and Swannanoa points represent Early Woodland. Therefore, these interpretations should be viewed with appropriate caution. Detailed analyses of formal, technical, and use-wear attributes of these points may result in the identification of chronologically sensitive varieties.

Some of the best evidence in support of the concept of a Terminal Archaic period in the Southern Appalachians comes from the Higgs site in the Ridge and Valley province of east Tennessee (McCollough and Faulkner 1973; McCollough 1973). There Otarre-like points were found in association with a square structure, domesticated sunflower remains, and dates of ca. 900-1000 B.C. (McCollough 1973:64).

The pattern of distribution of Otarre sites in the upper Watauga valley is very much like that of the Savannah River phase with a wide range of habitat types being occupied (Table 3.1). A slight increase in occurrence of Otarre sites on high capability soils in the main valley floodplains over Savannah River sites is not statistically significant. The apparent continuity in settlement patterns from Middle Archaic through Terminal Archaic times in the upper Watauga valley suggests that unlike the Terminal Archaic in eastern Tennessee, horticulture had not become important enough to influence settlement patterns, and cultigens may not even have been present. Given this context, these questions arise:

1. Will further investigation of stratified and single component sites and intensive attribute analysis make it possible to define temporally, culturally, and/or functionally significant attributes and variants of the Otarre type point?
2. Was horticulture present in any of the Terminal Archaic cultures in the Appalachian Summit? If so, was it economically or culturally significant?
3. Is the Otarre point a valid horizon marker for the Terminal Archaic in the Appalachian Summit? What are the diagnostic indicators of this period?

Woodland Period

Swannanoa. The Early Woodland, Swannanoa phase (700-300 B.C.) represents the apparent introduction of ceramics to the Appalachian Summit. [Three sherds from the Macon County Industrial Park site were identified as fibre-tempered by Collins (1977:25), but this identification of a technology that may date to the Late Archaic or Terminal Archaic period has not been verified.] The most common Swannanoa vessels are cord-marked or fabric-impressed simple bowls and conoidal jars. Simple stamping, check stamping, and smoothed plain surfaces are found infrequently and are believed to be relatively late. On rare occasions vessels were decorated with carelessly incised vertical or oblique lines trailing down a short distance from the vessel's rim (Keel 1976:230). Diagnostic points include Swannanoa stemmed, Plott short-stemmed, and Transylvania triangular. The long temporal duration of the general Swannanoa/Plott form was discussed with the Otarre phase. The crude, large triangular Transylvania points should be carefully analyzed to determine if they are, in fact, finished tools and the earliest representatives of a 2000-year-long tradition of triangular projectile points/knives and arrowpoints or if they are preforms of the slightly smaller, stemmed varieties. Other traits associated with this phase include bar gorgets, bone awls, pitted and pebble hammerstones, the use of red and yellow ocher, "net weights," tubular pipes, and continued but less frequent use of soapstone vessels (Keel 1976:230).

In some regions of the Eastern Woodlands, the Early Woodland period is characterized by increasingly sedentary life related at least in part to the introduction or increasing dependence on horticulture and/or intensive harvesting of floodplain commensal plants and, possibly, to the early development of relatively elaborate mortuary practices. In the Appalachian Summit, however, Early Woodland settlement patterns seem to have been essentially a continuation of Archaic precursors. Keel (1976:231) notes that Swannanoa settlements "are present in all microenvironments, indicating a broad adaptation to local resources." Bass (1977:77) indicates that in the Great Smoky Mountains Terminal Archaic/Early Woodland "site distribution is much the same as that in the Middle Archaic period . . . [and] . . . was not centered on the floodplains as in the Late Archaic period." Over 50% of the food-processing sites occurred in the upland zones (Bass 1977:81).

In the analysis of settlement patterns in the upper Watauga valley components identified with a ceramic phase (i.e., Early Woodland and later) have been subdivided into two categories based on the presence or absence of ceramics (Table 3.1; Purrington and Douthit 1977; Purrington 1982). This approach is based on the assumption that the presence of ceramics at a site will tend to reflect a greater number of domestic activities and less mobility than a nonceramic component of a ceramic phase. There is also a strong possibility that the presence of ceramics in assemblages of ceramic phases will reflect the presence of females and, perhaps, whole social units, (i.e., nuclear or extended families), while the absence of ceramics in representative samples of ceramic-phase assemblages will tend to reflect specialized male activities. There are exceptions to this pattern, however. Examples of ceramic vessels being brought on all-male limited activity expeditions are known in the ethnographic record of the Canelos Quichua of the upper Amazon basin (Whitten and Whitten 1978:99); Wesley Cowan (1978b) has suggested that the presence of small light vessels in Kentucky rock shelters represents a similiar practice. Nevertheless, in the southeastern United States male hunting parties are reported to have carried nut meal or parched corn in small pouches rather than heavier and less durable ceramic vessels (Hudson 1976:247).

The absence of ceramics among the remains of ceramic-using cultures does not necessarily indicate that women were absent, but it does suggest that the group represented was relatively mobile and probably involved in a specialized activity or a limited range of activities. On the other hand, the presence of ceramics is more likely to reflect the presence of women, a wider range of activities, and/or a longer period of occupation of the site. It is evident in Tables 3.1 and 3.2 that there are marked differences in the distribution of ceramic and nonceramic sites of the Woodland and Mississippian phases in the upper Watauga valley.

Swannanoa settlement patterns in the upper Watauga valley show a continuation of the Archaic pattern of balanced use of a wide range of habitats with no noticeable increase in utilization of the river bottoms. Unlike Early Woodland societies in much of the Eastern Woodlands, the Swannanoa settlement patterns show little, if any, reliance on horticulture. For example, an increase in size and/or number of floodplain sites would be expected if horticulture and/or intensive harvesting of floodplain commensal plants were more important to this culture than to preceding ones. Moreover, though one would expect a horticultural society to have a higher proportion of its ceramic sites in fertile floodplain settings than nonceramic sites, we find, in fact, that a higher percentage of nonceramic Swannanoa sites (25.0%) occur in fertile river bottoms than ceramic Swannanoa sites (17.4%) (Table 3.1). Swannanoa is also the only ceramic phase in the upper Watauga valley that is known to have ceramic components on main valley floodplain soils with severe agricultural limitations such as poor drainage, stoniness, and a high flood potential (Table 3.1). Such sites probably would have been occupied on a seasonal basis and for nonhorticultural purposes.

Swannanoa is also the only post-Archaic phase in the upper Watauga valley in which ceramic components are known commonly to occur in ridgetop and upland valley settings (Table 3.1). One interpretation of this pattern is that these people may have moved (seasonally?) from one catchment area to another as complete social units (e.g. small extended family band segments) and that both male- and female-related activities were carried out at ceramic sites in the uplands and the valleys. On the other hand, the nonceramic Swannanoa sites may represent specialized, male-oriented activities such as hunting and butchering and other short-term pursuits. These limited activity sites may have been extensions from primary and secondary base settlements represented by the ceramic sites.

The pattern of distribution of ceramics representing Middle Woodland and later phases in the upper Watauga valley is quite different. With one exception, ceramics of post-Swannanoa phases have not been found in either the upland valleys or on the ridgetops. Therefore, it would appear that post-Swannanoa base settlements were largely confined to the main valleys with only specialized task groups venturing onto the upland and higher elevation habitats.

One settlement model that may be constructed from these data is one in which the catchment area of any specific Early Woodland site was substantially smaller than the site catchments of later, more sedentary groups, whereas the geographical range of individual Early Woodland family units/social groups may have been considerably larger. In short, small, mobile Early Woodland family groups moved frequently within an extensive territory in order to take advantage of seasonal and environmental variability in food and other resources. The inferred greater mobility and smaller size of these social units suggest that Early Woodland social organization in the upper Watauga valley may have been much simpler than that of later groups.

The size and distribution of Swannanoa sites in the upper Watauga valley suggests that there was great continuity in settlement patterns and quite possibly in adaptive strategies and social organization from the Archaic into the Early Woodland period. However, there appears to be one major change—Swannanoa culture shows a two- to threefold increase in occupation of rockshelters (Table 3.1). Invariably these Swannanoa components yield ceramics, which again may indicate the presence of small family units.

The spatial distribution of ceramics in the various localities of the Appalachian Summit may provide some of the best evidence for variability within the region. For example, in contrast to the upper Watauga valley, ceramics ranging from Middle Woodland to Late Mississippian times have been found in a wide range of environmental settings, including uplands, in many localities in southwestern North Carolina (Joffre Coe personal communication 1980; Holden 1966; Keel 1976; Moore 1980; Purrington 1981a, b).

The Early Woodland cultures of the Appalachian Summit appear to have deviated from a trend found over much of the Eastern Woodlands in which there was increasing emphasis on floodplain habitats and, in some regions, the emergence of horticulture beginning as early as the Late Archaic period. These changes in subsistence and settlement patterns were part of a positive feedback process (cf. Flannery 1968:68) which led to increasingly sedentary life, larger and more stable social units, and greater complexity in social structure. The settlement pattern data from the Great Smoky Mountains and the Watauga River valley discussed above suggest that these events had not yet taken place in the Early Woodland cultures of the Appalachian Summit. In fact, in the Great Smokies the Late Archaic trend toward increasing use of the floodplains seems to have been reversed in Early Woodland times with a reversion to a more mobile and generalized Middle Archaic pattern. This suggests that preferred lithic resources (quartzite) rather than arable soil or riverine resources may have been a (the) major factor responsible for the valley bottom orientation of the Great Smoky Savannah River people. In light of these distinctive cultural processes in the Appalachian Summit several questions came to mind:

1. Why did the apparent reversion to a more extensive settlement system take place in the Great Smoky Mountains during Early Woodland times?
2. Why did the Late Archaic and Early Woodland adaptive strategies and settlement systems apparently remain generalized in the upper Watauga valley?
3. Why did the Early Woodland cultures of the Appalachian Summit lag behind some other Early Woodland cultures such as Adena in the Ohio valley and Poverty Point in the lower Mississippi valley in adoption of horticulture and in cultural complexity?
4. What is the significance of increased use of rockshelters by Swannanoa people in the upper Watauga valley?

Pigeon. Diagnostic characteristics of the Middle Woodland, Pigeon phase (300 B.C.-A.D. 200) include ceramics that have crushed-quartz temper, compact paste, and a well smoothed to burnished interior with an iridescent sheen produced by rubbing with a steatite pebble (Keel 1976:256-260). Vessel forms of this Pigeon series include conical jars, open hemispherical bowls, and shouldered jars featuring slightly flaring rims and flat bases with four relatively large conical or wedge-shaped feet. Surfaces are predominantly checked stamped or well-smoothed; simple stamped brushed, and complicated stamped surfaces occur infrequently. Limestone-tempered sherds of eastern Tennessee's Candy Creek series are often found in small numbers in Pigeon components. Diagnostic points include the large, generally concave-based Garden Creek (Keel 1976:130-131) or Camp Creek triangular (Kneberg 1956:17-18); the long, narrow Copena triangular (Cambron and Hulse 1969:26); and the shallow side-notched Pigeon point (Keel 1976:127-129). No pure Pigeon components have been reported to date.

Like many Middle Woodland cultures of the Southeast, the Pigeon phase is best known through its ceramics (Keel 1976:226). However, the geographical distribution of Pigeon remains and the types of lithic raw materials they utilized give us some suggestions into the nature of their way of life.

In the Great Smoky Mountains Middle Woodland (Pigeon and Connestee) settlement patterns show an increasing emphasis on the floodplain area with 59.8% of the food processing sites located there. Bass (1977:81) suggests that this pattern may reflect "horticultural or harvest collecting activity." However, he also notes that nearly 40% of food processing sites (his base camps) occur above the valley zone, primarily on "benches" and in coves, and hunting sites are most commonly found in the upland zone. This pattern suggests "that there is still an intensive use of several biogeographic zones" (Bass 1977:81). Keel (1976:226, 229) has observed the same general pattern in Pigeon and Connestee phase sites in the Little Tennessee, Pigeon, and French Broad valleys.

In the upper Watauga valley the distribution of Pigeon sites shows continued utilization of a broad range of habitats but with two significant shifts in settlement patterns: 1) a 10% increase in occurrence of ceramic and nonceramic components in fertile floodplain sites (Table 3.1 and 3.2) and 2) the greatly reduced frequency of occurrence of ceramic Pigeon components in upland valleys and on the ridgetops at the same time that nonceramic components continue to appear in these settings (Table 3.2). These patterns suggest that a substantial shift in subsistence and social organization may have taken place locally in the Early to Middle Woodland transition. Increased use of the main valley bottoms may be a reflection of increased or even initial dependence on horticulture and/or intensive harvesting. Increased sedentism, frequently associated with the adoption of horticulture, may be reflected in the predominant occurrence of Pigeon ceramics in the main valley bottoms and margins while nonceramic Pigeon sites (perhaps special-use sites, e.g. hunting camps) continue to be found commonly (although in somewhat diminished frequencies) in upland valleys and on ridgetops (Table 3.2). A notable local exception to this pattern is the Wakeman 3 site in Watauga County which is located at a stream head at an elevation of 4,000 feet (Figure 3.10). An extremely dark midden which yielded a relatively large number of Swannanoa, Pigeon, and Candy Creek ceramics was revealed at this small upland site.

The emergence of the Middle Woodland cultures in the Appalachian Summit is also characterized by an apparent increase in outside influences and participation in outside exchange systems. This pattern is reflected in the strong influence of ceramic styles centered in Piedmont Georgia (Keel 1976:229), the presence of small numbers of east Tennessee Candy Creek series ceramics in localities of the Appalachian Summit where native limestone is absent, and in the increased use of nonlocal cherts (Bass 1977:61, 113). However, it is interesting to note that Dickens's (1980) analysis of Woodland ceramic diversity in the Southeast shows the Swannanoa component at the Warren Wilson site with a slightly higher index of ceramic diversity (.36) than the Pigeon component at the Garden Creek Mound No. 2 (.31). Dickens's findings would suggest that there was no significant increase in outside contact with the Pigeon phase. Several research questions are pertinent:

1. What sociocultural processes and adaptive trends led to the introduction of ceramic traits from the Georgia Piedmont? How were such traits introduced?
2. Does the increased utilization of bottomland sites in some localities reflect the introduction or increased dependence on horticulture and/or intensive harvesting?
3. Is there a shift toward increasingly permanent base settlements in the main valleys with special-activity parties venturing out from them? If so, what caused this shift?
4. Is there a shift toward larger and more complex social units or is there merely a reduction in the mobility of small social units?
5. Why does the utilization of nonlocal chert increase?
6. What was the nature of the exchange or procurement systems that brought chert into the Appalachian Summit during this period?
7. What, if any, influence did Adena-Hopewell exchange networks have on the Pigeon phase?

Connestee. The Middle Woodland, Connestee Phase (A.D. 200-600) includes such diagnostic characteristics as Connestee series ceramics which are a thin, sand-tempered ware with brushed, simple stamped, or plain-surfaced conoidal jars or hemispherical vessels, with constricted necks and flaring rims. Flat-based vessels were supported by four small feet. Punctated, notched, and incised lips are common. Keel (1976:219) suggests that there is a gradual transition of projectile point forms during this phase from Pigeon side-notched to Garden Creek triangular to Connestee triangular to Haywood triangular (Figure 3.5). Connestee triangular is a medium-sized relatively well made, isosceles triangular point (Keel 1976:131-132); Haywood triangular is a small to medium-sized, almost equilateral triangular point with a straight or subconcave base (Keel 1976:132-133). Keel (1976:219-220) also associates the South Appalachian pentagonal (Keel 1976:133) and Copena triangular points with this phase, as well as flake scrapers, gravers, relatively small pebble hammerstones, and well made cylindrical hammerstones.

Connestee ceramics show a marked shift from the strong influences from the south which produced the Pigeon series to a less spectacular series which reflects influences from the west and northwest (Keel 1976:221). Dickens has shown that Connestee ceramics have a higher index of variability than any earlier or later series in the region. He suggests that this is a reflection of markedly increased contact with groups outside the region followed by a decline in such contacts in Late Woodland times (Dickens 1980).

There is other evidence to support the interpretation that the degree of outside influence on Connestee artifact assemblages (at least in southwestern North Carolina) is much greater than for earlier Appalachian Summit phases. Outside influences from the southeast (Georgia Piedmont) include a small number of Swift Creek trade vessels, perhaps the concept of the flat-topped platform mound, and possibly the technology of thin-walled, sand-tempered ceramics. Contacts with western groups are evident in the fact that small numbers of limestone-tempered Candy Creek ceramics from eastern Tennessee have been found in Connestee components in the Appalachian Summit while Connestee sherds have been found in varying amounts in the Ridge and Valley province of eastern Tennessee particularly at the Icehouse Bottom site (Chapman and Keel 1979). Perhaps the most significant outside influence on Connestee culture is from the Hopewellian cultures of the central Ohio valley to the north, including a prismatic blade and polyhedral core technology which used east Tennessee cherts, Appalachian quartz crystal, and Flint Ridge, Ohio, chalcedony (Keel 1976:140). Other artifacts which reflect Hopewellian influence include Hopewellian cross-hatched rims, large triangular bifaces (cache blades?), Chillicothe Rocker Stamped ceramics, and Hopewell style anthropomorphic and zoomorphic figurines of local Connestee paste (Keel 1976:118-123, 134-144). Ground and polished celts with pentagonal outlines, tabular gorgets, and platform pipes "are viewed as continued development of earlier forms" (Keel 1976:219), and ground-stone plummets and pendants as well as grooved stones "might be the remains of Connestee culture" (Keel 1976:220).

The bulk of the descriptive information on the Connestee phase comes from Keel's (1976) work at the Garden Creek Mound No. 2 on the Pigeon River in Haywood County. The site includes a flat-topped, platform mound constructed in at least two stages and a 20-by-21 foot structure with individually set posts. No burial mounds have been recorded in the vicinity of Garden Creek (Chapman and Keel 1976:157).

The features at the Garden Creek site strongly suggest relatively long-term habitation, although, as Keel (1976:226) says, "Connestee phase sites seem to be more numerous in the uplands than Pisgah and Qualla phase stations and on floodplain topography they are much smaller in size." As indicated above, Bass (1977:81) noted that Middle Woodland sites in the Great Smoky Mountains (Pigeon and Connestee) showed increased utilization of the floodplains while maintaining a pattern of broad-spectrum use of a diversity of upland and lowland environmental zones. In the upper Watauga valley 71.4% of the sites with Connestee ceramics are in the main valley floodplains, whereas 92.3% of the nonceramic Connestee sites are on the main valley margins or in the upland valleys and ridges (Table 3.2). These patterns suggest the establishment of relatively sedentary, possibly horticultural, settlements in the floodplains with continued and increasingly specialized use of the uplands.

A second major characteristic of Connestee culture was its participation in the network of exchange of ideas, activities, artifacts, and raw materials, frequently referred to as the "Hopewellian Interaction Sphere" (Caldwell 1964). The archaeological remains at Garden Creek Mound No. 2 clearly show evidence from such disparate Hopewellian and Hopewellian-related cultures as those at Tunacunnhee (Jefferies 1976) and Mandeville (Kellar, Kelly, and McMichael 1962) in Georgia; Icehouse Bottom in eastern Tennessee (Chapman 1973); the C & O Mounds in eastern Kentucky (Webb 1942b); and the Scioto Hopewell complex of southern Ohio (Prufer 1964, 1968). The Appalachian Summit was the probable source of valuable Hopewellian raw materials and exchange items including mica, quartz crystals, and possibly copper, steatite, and chlorite schists. Connestee vessels, which Prufer (1968) included in his "Southeastern Series," are found occasionally in Ohio Hopewell and other Hopewellian sites (Chapman and Keel 1979:160).

In summary, the Connestee phase in the Pigeon River watershed is characterized by two important trends—increasing sedentism and expansion of outside contacts which are processes that often lead to increased cultural complexity. While it is apparent that the Connestee people did not achieve the same levels of complexity as the Hopewellian peoples to the north and south with whom they exchanged goods and, perhaps, ideas, some advancement over local cultures is evident. A rather dramatic increase in sociocultural complexity is suggested by Collins (1977) who hypothesized that the Middle Woodland occupants of a site in Macon County in the Little Tennessee-Tuckasegee watershed "lived in chiefdom or rank society." She tested five subsidiary hypotheses with data from the Macon County Industrial Park site in an attempt to verify her general hypothesis. These subsidiary hypotheses with parenthetical indications of whether or not Collins considered them to have been supported by the data included: 1) burial patterns reflect differential status (supported); 2) arts show a professional quality (inconclusive evidence); 3) public monuments exist (supported); 4) granaries or public storehouses exist (no evidence); 5) foreign trade items are present (supported). Three of the five indicators are interpreted as supporting the general hypothesis (Collins 1977:31-33).

However, the data used to support the subsidiary hypotheses can be interpreted in several ways. For example, alignments of post molds found in close proximity to two burials at one end of the site, which yielded predominantly Connestee ceramics, are considered to be evidence of monumental architecture (subsidiary hypothesis 3). However, the contemporaneity of the undefined structure(s) and the burials is not demonstrated, nor can the possibility of burial in the floors of domestic structures be precluded. Moreover, the "foreign trade" items at the site (subsidiary hypothesis 5) are nothing more than nonlocal cherts. Such cherts were also imported to southwestern North Carolina during Early and Middle Archaic times. In addition, these cherts were used to produce utilitarian tools in the Connestee assemblage at the Macon County Industrial Park site.

The best evidence to support Collins' general hypothesis comes from the fact that the two burials exposed at the site clearly show differential treatment (subsidiary hypothesis 1). Burial 1 is an extended individual whose head rested on a large slab of polished mica, whereas Burial 2 consisted of four individuals who had been "crowded in flexed positions into a single grave pit adjacent to Burial 1" (Collins 1977:31). Assuming that the graves are contemporaneous, they strongly suggest differential treatment and, quite possibly, differential ranking, but their contemporaneity has not been demonstrated.

While the evidence for a Connestee chiefdom at the Macon County Industrial Park site is inconclusive at best, data from the Garden Creek Mound No. 2 support a hypothesis that the Connestee component included specialized nonsubsistence activities including craft specialization, import and export of raw materials and finished goods, and incipient centralization of religious and political authority. Supporting data include the presence of multistage platform mounds; imported goods and raw materials listed above; and items whose primary functions were primarily in the social or ideological rather than utilitarian spheres (cf. Binford 1962), for example, clay figurines, gorgets, and platform pipes. Export of Connestee goods is evident in the presence of Connestee series ceramics at sites in Georgia, Kentucky, Ohio, and Tennessee, and, by inference, the extensive distribution of mica and other raw materials from the Appalachian Summit during the Middle Woodland period. Differential treatment of the dead is clearly evident at the Tunacunnhee mound in northwestern Georgia (Jefferies 1976), which was constructed by people who were in direct or indirect contact with the Connestee people. Thus there is strong evidence that Connestee society in portions of southwestern North Carolina was at least at an incipient stage of development of formalized status differences if not differences in rank. Whether such social differentiation was achieved or ascribed is open to question.

Further evidence that the Connestee phase represents a relatively dynamic culture is provided by Dickens (1980) in a comparison of indexes of diversity of ceramic surface finish from Early Woodland through Late Woodland times in the South Appalachian region as defined by Holmes (1903). The indexes of ceramic diversity of seven late Middle Woodland components including Connestee components at the Garden Creek and Tuckasegee sites in North Carolina and the Icehouse Bottom site in Tennessee were found to be much higher than those of earlier or later Woodland periods. Dickens concludes that "relatively detached" societies were brought into contact with many new ideas during the period of extensive Hopewellian interaction, A.D. 200-600, and since ceramic idea pools were more diverse at this time, "it is possible that other ideas—e.g. those concerned with social relationships and ideological concepts—were also in a more dynamic state" (Dickens 1980:34). The expanding information on the Connestee phase has generated a number of research questions:

1. Was the shift from the check stamped and well smoothed vessel surfaces of the Pigeon series to the less impressive (to the archaeologist at least) Connestee wares a reassertion of "the basic conservatism of the mountain folk" (Keel 1976:231) or do Connestee ceramics represent a relatively dynamic tradition as Dickens (1980) asserts?
2. Were the apparent changes in settlement patterns and social organization in Connestee culture related to changes in subsistence? If so, what was the nature of these changes?
3. Did the Connestee culture include craft specialization, centralization of religio-political authority, formalized mortuary ritual, ascribed status ranking, and other characteristics of a chiefdom level of society?
4. Why did the Connestee culture not develop the elaborate mortuary ritual of many contemporaneous Hopewellian groups?
5. What was the nature of the interregional exchange systems in which the Connestee people participated and what was the role of the Connestee people in these systems? Were the Garden Creek and Icehouse Bottom sites major regional exchange centers?
6. Was there a significantly greater degree of Hopewellian influence in southwestern North Carolina than in the northwestern portion of the Appalachian Summit? If so, why?
7. What factors led to the development of a presumably more complex Connestee culture?

Unnamed Late Woodland Phase. At the present time the Late Woodland period (A.D. 600-1000) in the Appalachian Summit is very poorly understood and no phase has been defined. Diagnostic characteristics of this very important period have not yet been determined, but they may include Haywood triangular and Southern Appalachian pentagonal points and possibly isosceles triangular points intermediate in size between Connestee triangular and Pisgah triangular points. Ceramics may simply be a continuation of Connestee wares. Keel (1976:238) suggested that this phase may be characterized by a high frequency of plain and brushed ceramics. These predictions are supported by a date of A.D. 770 ± 85 for small triangular points and predominantly plain-surfaced pottery at the Mason site, Tennessee (Charles H. Faulkner cited in Keel 1976:238).

Keel (1976:239) believes that by A.D. 600 the Connestee phase "had evolved into a transition phase which would develop into the Pisgah phase." No archaeological units have been associated yet with this period, but 18 out of 27 radiocarbon dates cited by Keel (1976:Table 32) as "relative to the Connestee period" are more recent than A.D. 600. The Connestee component at the Garden Creek Mound No. 2 has been radiocarbon dated to prior to A.D. 805 ± 85 (Keel 1976:156, 238). Perhaps there is an earlier Connestee phase with Hopewellian elements and a later variant that in the period of post-Hopewellian retrenchment remained relatively stable until the processes leading to the development of Pisgah culture began. Many fundamental questions regarding this period can be asked:

1. Assuming that the Appalachian Summit was not abandoned or seriously depopulated during the period A.D. 600-1000, what were the general characteristics of the cultures of this period?
2. What artifacts and other cultural characteristics are diagnostic of this phase?
3. What was the nature of the transition from or replacement of the Connestee phase by the Pisgah phase? What causative factors were involved in this transition?
4. Did platform mounds appear in the Appalachian Summit during the Late Woodland period or earlier?

Mississippian Period

Pisgah. The Pisgah phase of the Early Mississippian period (A.D. 1000-1450) has such diagnostic characteristics as small, isosceles Pisgah triangular arrow points; a variety of microtools, gravers, perforators, and drills; flake scrapers; and ground stone celts, pipes, discoidals, and small discs. The shell industry includes gorgets, ear pins, beads, and dippers. Gorgets include, in inferred chronological order, the Lick Creek, Citico, and elongated "mask" styles (Dickens 1976, 1979; Keel 1976:217).

Pisgah series ceramics are characterized by a shouldered vessel with a collared rim, which was generally decorated by rows of elongated punctate impressions. In the southwestern North Carolina mountains about 80% of vessel surfaces exhibit rectilinear complicated stamping (Dickens 1976:174), whereas in the mountains in the northwestern part of the state most Pisgah pottery has fabric-impressed, cord-marked, or smoothed surfaces. The typically micaceous paste of Pisgah ware is generally tempered with fine to coarse sand, but in the upper Watauga valley large chunks of crushed quartz, amphibolite, and/or soapstone are common tempering agents (Figure 3.11; Ayers, Loucks, and Purrington 1980). Loop handles, notched rim strips, lugs, and castellations are frequently present on southwestern vessels, whereas those from the

FIGURE 3.11. Pisgah-style ceramics from the Charles Church rockshelter, Watauga River watershed, Watauga County, North Carolina. Note that this pottery has decorative traits which are typical of the Pisgah series, including a polished rim with parallel lines of elongated punctates, but the body walls are relatively thick, with very coarse grit temper. The vessel surface is open weave fabric-impressed. The upper sherd is a rimsherd; the lower sherds, which may be from the same vessel, are body sherds with interior surfaces up.

northwestern part of the state are much less ornate and less varied. Other ceramic artifacts include pipes, discs, beads, animal head effigies, and miniature or toy vessels (Keel 1976:217).

Pisgah villages were stockaded and the dwellings were square to slightly rectangular—about 5.5 to 7.3 meters along the outer walls—with wall trench vestibule entrances, slightly depressed floors, and four large center posts surrounding a raised clay, central fire basin (Dickens 1976:32-46). A circular pattern of post molds at the Warren Wilson site about 3 meters in diameter, enclosing a shallow sand- and boulder-lined pit and adjacent to a square house, may represent the remains of a conical "hot house" or winter house as described by Bartram for eighteenth-century Cherokee towns (Dickens 1978:119-120; Faulkner 1977, 1978).

Civic/ceremonial structures, which appear to have been restricted to the southwestern part of the Mountain region, included earth lodges and rectangular, flat-topped platform mounds raised in several massive constructions and topped by square or rectangular structures. Burials have been found in the mounds and in house floors. The dead were generally buried in a flexed position in a simple pit or less often in a shaft and chamber grave. Grave goods were rare and usually consisted of items of personal adornment (Keel 1976:218).

The Pisgah phase is probably the most intensively studied archaeological culture of the Appalachian Summit. Pisgah culture is interesting because of both its differences from and continuities with preceding Appalachian Summit cultures. The continuity between Pisgah culture and the succeeding Qualla (late prehistoric to historic Cherokee) phase is sufficiently great to allow a relatively confident characterization of Pisgah as "proto-Cherokee." However, the origins of Pisgah culture are much less clear. Coe (1961), Holden (1966:86), and Keel (1976:214) favor an *in situ* development hypothesis for Cherokee culture because of the large number of elements that Pisgah and earlier cultures have in common. Dickens (1979:12) notes that several dominant Cherokee traits begin to appear in the South Appalachian region early in the period between A.D. 600 and 1000, but this period in the Appalachian Summit must be much better understood before the hypothesis of an indigenous Pisgah origin can be verified.

Despite the fact that Pisgah culture shared a large number of material traits with Connestee culture, there were many significant differences too. Rectilinear complicated stamping is rare in Connestee ceramics (Dickens 1979:13) and the distinctive punctated, collared rims, which characterize Pisgah ceramics, are apparently unknown in the Connestee series although thickened rims and plain neck bands with circular or rectangular punctations occasionally appear on Connestee vessels (cf. Keel 1976:247, 249). Seemingly substantial differences between these phases in subsistence, settlement systems, and demography are apparent too. Hunting, particularly of deer and wild turkey (Wing 1976), and gathering, particularly of hickory nuts, acorns, and probably chestnuts and, to a lesser extent, walnuts, butternuts, and several kinds of fleshy fruits (Yarnell 1976b:217), continued to play a major role in Pisgah subsistence. However, horticulture, including corn, beans, squash and/or pumpkin, and sumpweed, seems to have comprised a much greater percentage of the diet than in earlier phases (Yarnell 1976b:217). In addition to the substantial number of domesticates in Pisgah remains, settlement patterns also suggest an increased dependence on horticulture. Surveys in several drainages in the Appalachian Summit "demonstrate that the preferred locations for village sites during both the Pisgah and Qualla phases were floodplains and adjacent terraces and benches" (Figure 3.12; Dickens 1978:132). In the Great Smoky Mountains "a dramatic shift to floodplain-centered habitation sites is apparent by the restriction of activities (except hunting) almost exclusively to the floodplains of the Valley Zone" (Bass 1977:86). In the upper Watauga valley 100% of the Pisgah sites identified as villages have been found on class 1-A soils (generally natural levees) in the main valley floodplain (Table 3.1; Purrington 1982). One-third of the sites classified as farmsteads (Purrington 1982) were in the main valley floodplain (class 1-A soils) and two thirds were on older terraces and colluvial aprons on the main valley margins (class 1-B and 2-B soils). However, nonceramic Pisgah sites, presumably limited-activity loci, have been found in all seven major environmental zones in the upper Watauga valley (Table 3.1). The presence of Pisgah remains at the Wakeman 2 site at 4,200 feet above sea level shows that specialized Pisgah task forces continued the several-thousand-year-old pattern of utilizing a wide range of environmental zones. The Pisgah components at Wakeman 2 include three concentrations, about 10 meters in diameter each, of chert, chalcedony, and jasper flakes respectively. The chert concentration includes very small tabular nodules of chert with cortex still remaining, and the chert and chalcedony concentrations each include small triangular Pisgah arrowpoints of the same material (Ayers 1976). These small concentrations appear to represent short-term, limited activity occupations possibly by hunting parties or by expeditions with a social/political objective such as trading, raiding, visiting, or decision-making. (The Wakeman sites are a few hundred feet below the Watauga-New River divide.)

Dickens (1976:210) has suggested that Pisgah subsistence was based on roughly equal proportions of hunting, gathering, and horticulture, and this diverse economic base is reflected in the settlement patterns which show continued utilization of a broad range of environmental zones

FIGURE 3.12. The Ward site, a Pisgah phase village in the Watauga River watershed, Watauga County, North Carolina. The arrow denotes the excavation of a portion of a palisade wall of the Pisgah component which is located on a natural levee in the relatively broad floodplain at the confluence of the Watauga River (foreground) and Cove Creek. The best agricultural soils in the region are found in well-drained settings such as this.

(Dickens 1978:132; Keel 1976:281; Purrington 1982). However, Dickens (1979) also suggests that Pisgah culture included a settlement system based on nucleation of communities on fertile soils in broad river valleys and the emergence of a hierarchy of communities. This hierarchy included a small number of widely dispersed, relatively large sites with platform mounds, presumably civic-ceremonial centers, that were surrounded by smaller sites without mounds—presumably villages, hamlets, and farmsteads. The discovery of the Brunk site, a relatively extensive open site with a high density of Pisgah ceramics but no evidence of a mound, in a high upland valley in the northern French Broad watershed of Buncombe County, suggests that a new site type should be added to the reconstructed Pisgah settlement system (Moore 1980).

Pisgah culture appears to be less highly developed in the upper Watauga valley than in the French Broad, Pigeon, and Tuckasegee valleys to the southwest. Pisgah ceramics in the upper Watauga valley are much less varied and ornate than those to the southwest; surface treatments are predominantly a continuation of earlier Woodland techniques including fabric impressing, cord marking, and smoothing rather than complicated stamping; and body sherds are often thick, coarse-tempered, and very similar to Early Woodland Swannanoa sherds (Figure 3.11). Pisgah villages in the upper Watauga valley appear to be smaller than those to the southwest; mounds are apparently absent; and the southwestern pattern of "several groupings of communities, each having allegiances to a mound center" (Dickens 1978:136) seems to be absent in the upper Watauga valley, although the Ward site (Ayers, Loucks, and Purrington 1980), which is relatively large and conveniently located at the confluence of the two major streams along which local Pisgah villages and hamlet/farmsteads were found—the Watauga River and Cove Creek— may have served as a local center for social, political, economic, and/or religious activities (Figure 3.12).

The centralization of civic-ceremonial activities in a mound center, as is found in the south central portion of the Appalachian Summit, is a characteristic generally attributable to chiefdoms. However, Dickens (1976:210-211; 1978:136) believes that Pisgah societies were not chiefdoms in the same sense as the powerful, highly stratified societies of the Etowah and Wilbanks cultures of the Georgia Piedmont (Larson 1971) and the Dallas culture of the eastern Tennessee Ridge and Valley province (Hatch 1975; see Sabol 1978 for an alternative interpretation of status and rank in Dallas culture). The Etowah-Wilbanks and Dallas cultures, which appear to have been the ancestral bases of the historic Cherokee Lower and Overhill towns respectively (Dickens 1979), had large mound centers with skillfully produced and undoubtedly valuable grave goods associated with a very low percentage of the burials, i.e., status burials. Pisgah mortuary items are far less elaborate, and although there are minor status distinctions suggested by the burial associations, "there does not seem to be a specific set of items confined to a small elite group" (Dickens 1976:211). Many research questions are inspired by this complex culture:

1. Where did Pisgah culture originate and what processes led to its development in the Appalachian Summit?
2. What were the major characteristics of Pisgah social organization? Was Pisgah society a chiefdom?
3. Why was Pisgah culture less complex than the neighboring and presumably related Dallas and Etowah-Wilbanks cultures?
4. Why was Pisgah culture in the Tuckasegee, Pigeon, and French Broad valleys apparently more complex than in localities to the northeast such as the upper Watauga valley?
5. Does the presence of palisades indicate warfare between different Pisgah groups, a common characteristic of expanding forest horticulturalists?
6. What was the nature of the relationship between Pisgah culture and other cultures outside the Appalachian Summit?

Qualla. The most recent Native American culture in the Appalachian Summit, the Qualla phase appeared in Late Mississippian times (ca. A.D. 1450) and persisted through the protohistoric period and into historic times up to the removal of the Cherokees in 1838 and 1839. Dickens (1979:12) divides Qualla into early (A.D. 1450 to 1650) and late (A.D. 1650 to 1838) phases. In southwestern North Carolina Madison triangular arrowpoints, which are smaller than Pisgah points and often almost equilateral, predominate in the Qualla phase, and small, thick, serrated triangular arrowpoints are occasionally present. In the upper Watauga valley the latter type is more common (Figure 3.13). Other chipped stone tools include flake scrapers, side-scrapers, small drills, and gunflints (Keel 1976:215). Ground stone items include celts, pipes, chunkey stones, discs (which also have ceramic counterparts), and a few pins with expanded heads (hair or ear pins?), which have both ceramic and shell counterparts (Keel 1976:215).

Qualla series ceramics are characterized by moderate to abundant quantities of grit, partial burnishing of vessel interiors, folded finger-impressed rim fillets, large sloppy curvilinear complicated stamping, and bold incising (Egloff 1967:34-35). In addition to complicated stamping, vessel surfaces are also burnished, plain, check stamped, cord-marked, corncob-impressed, and brushed. Vessel forms include simple bowls, carinated bowls, globular jars with short necks, and large jars with constricted mouths. Appendages are rare (Keel 1976:45).

Qualla structures were rectangular and, somewhat late in the phase, circular as well. Circular hearths with raised clay rims were located centrally

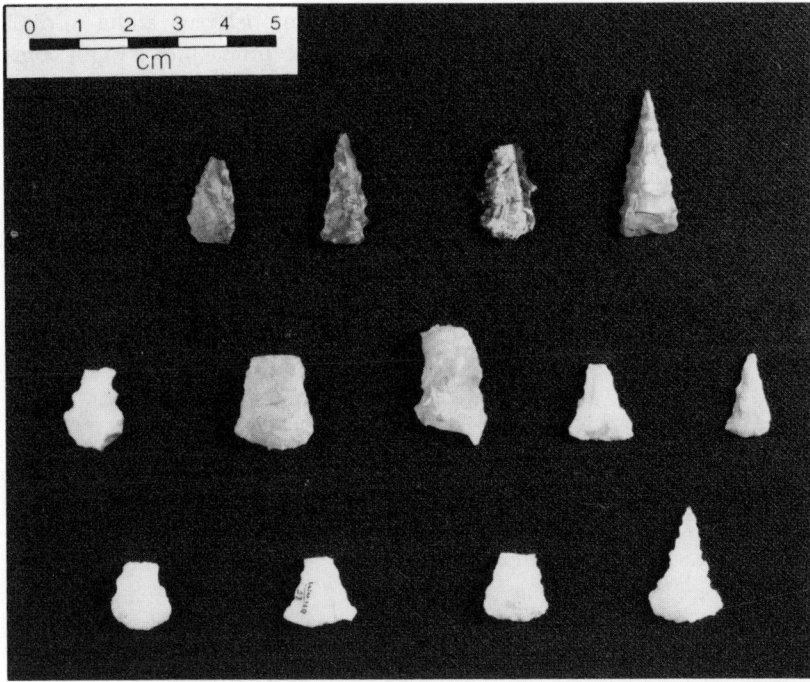

FIGURE 3.13. Thick, narrow, triangular points from late prehistoric assemblages in the Watauga River watershed, Watauga County, North Carolina. The points in the top row are made of chert; the middle row are chalcedony; the bottom row are of white quartz. (Note that many of the points are serrated.)

in these structures (Keel 1976:28-34; Dickens 1978:123). Rectangular platform mounds were constructed in multiple stages, but, unlike the Pisgah mounds, the successive building stages were quite thin (Dickens 1978:124-125). Burials were flexed in simple pit and, less frequently, shaft and chamber graves with few grave goods (Keel 1976:216). European trade goods including glass beads, wine bottles, and metal items appeared toward the end of this phase.

The Qualla phase is the archaeological manifestation of very late prehistoric and early historic Cherokee culture (Dickens 1976, 1979). Continuity between Pisgah and Qualla culture is evident in artifact styles and production techniques, house and mound forms, and undoubtedly many aspects of civic and ceremonial life. However, there are significant differences between the phases not only in diagnostic artifacts but in community structure and regional settlement patterns.

Early Qualla communities appear to have been nucleated like Pisgah villages although it is not known if Qualla sites were stockaded. However, late Qualla sites, such as Townson in the Hiwassee valley, consisted of structures that were loosely grouped or even scattered along a river (Dickens 1978:131). Whereas the densest concentration of Pisgah communities appears to have been in the more spacious intermontane basins, especially the Asheville, Pigeon, and Hendersonville basins, Qualla sites tended to follow a more linear pattern of distribution, "with extensive occupation in some rather narrow stream valleys, such as the Keowee and Little Tennessee valleys" (Dickens 1978:135). Finally, the Qualla phase seems to lack the hierarchical community pattern of the Pisgah culture which consisted of a small number of mound centers surrounded by satellite villages and hamlets. Instead, a much higher proportion of Qualla sites in the southern part of the Appalachian Summit have mounds and some of these sites are quite small and in close proximity to one another. Therefore, Qualla culture appears to have experienced considerable decentralization both within and among communities. It is possible that the probable disappearance of palisaded villages, the dispersal of community dwellings, and civic-ceremonial decentralization were related. This trend toward dispersed communities also occurred in the development of Lamar culture out of the Etowah and Wilbanks cultures in the Georgia Piedmont. Dickens (1978:136) suggests that these changes may have been "primarily related to European or European-induced disruption of the precontact cultural-environmental system." By the early 18th century, individual Cherokee towns were politically autonomous (Gearing 1962:3-5).

A second major change in the Pisgah-Qualla transition is in regional distribution of populations. Permanent populations in the northern and eastern ranges of Pisgah territory including the French Broad valley and points northeast seem to have disappeared in Qualla times, whereas there was a substantial increase in sites to the southwest in the Little Tennessee, Hiwassee, Chatahoochee, Chatooga, and Keowee valleys (Dickens 1978:132-134). Apparently there was a marked shift of the entire Qualla population to the southwest that was accompanied by significant changes in community structure and possibly a simplification or at least a decentralization of the socio-political system.

A population increase is apparent in the Great Smokies during this period (Bass 1977:44-45). On the other hand, in the upper Watauga valley Qualla culture appears to have been attenuated. Recognized Qualla ceramics are rare, and no permanent Qualla communities are known. Nevertheless, small, thick, serrated triangular arrowpoints and Madison points (Figure 3.5, 3.13) are common in the upper Watauga valley, and wood charcoal from a small pit at the Ward site, which also contained charred corn cobs and intruded into a postmold of a Pisgah stockade, has been radiometrically dated at A.D. 1640 (Ayers, Loucks, and Purrington 1980). This evidence strongly suggests that the valley was still occupied, at least on a temporary basis, in late prehistoric and protohistoric times. Nevertheless, late prehistoric-protohistoric settlement patterns in the upper Watauga valley appear to have been quite different from those of the Pisgah people and preceding groups. Late prehistoric-protohistoric sites are found in a relatively narrow range of habitats with 54.5% occurring in the fertile bottoms of the main valleys and 22.7% on the main valley margins (Table 3.1). Rockshelters were frequently occupied on the main valley margins but not in the upland valleys. Use of the uplands in general was limited. The evidence suggests that although large, permanent populations apparently disappeared from the upper Watauga valley during this period, the valley was frequently visited by mobile, limited-activity groups, perhaps hunting, raiding, and/or trading parties. Some permanent populations may have remained in the valley since corn cobs were found in the dated protohistoric feature at the Ward site noted above. If such small, localized populations existed in the upper Watauga valley, they may have continued to use Pisgah ceramics or a still unrecognized variant or type. Further study will be needed to identify the diagnostic characteristics of this as yet poorly defined cultural manifestation in the upper Watauga valley and determine its relationship to Qualla cultures as well as other late prehistoric and protohistoric cultures of the mountains and Piedmont to the north and east.

Several research questions relating to the Qualla phase and the late prehistoric-protohistoric period in the Appalachian Summit can be identified:

1. What are the causes of the southwestward shift of Qualla culture?
2. Does the shift from nucleated to dispersed communities reflect a decline in warfare, changing subsistence, and/or decentralization of socio-political organization? What factors led to this shift?
3. What was the nature of human occupation and use of localities such as the upper Watauga valley and the French Broad valley which were apparently abandoned by large, permanent populations during late prehistoric and protohistoric times?
4. Did the changes that Qualla culture experienced occur primarily as a result of European influence or did they begin prior to European intrusion in the eastern and southern United States?
5. What roles did groups from the central Blue Ridge Mountains and the Virginia and North Carolina Piedmont play in the northern and central Appalachian Summit during late prehistoric and protohistoric times?

CONCLUSIONS

Assessment of Significance in the Appalachian Summit

As was previously discussed, the concept of significance is critical to effective management of cultural resources. The need for the development of criteria for assessing significance in the Appalachian Summit is great.

Currently four major categories of significance are commonly recognized by archaeologists. These include historical, ethnic, public, and scientific significance (Moratto and Kelly 1978). Application of these categories to the assessment of cultural resources enables the researcher and the cultural resource manager to transcend narrow theoretical and geographical perspectives and helps to negate the tendency of non-archaeologists to view cultural resources as "a few arrowheads" or a "handful of flakes." The number of research questions that can be posed when the cultural resources of the Appalachian Summit are viewed in the context of these categories is almost limitless.

In using historical significance as a criterion the archaeologist determines that the site or district is one associated with a specific event or aspect of history or that it provides information about cultural periods in a historic era. For example, many historic Cherokee towns in the Appalachian Summit can be identified and associated with specific historic events such as military campaigns and treaties or with more general aspects of history such as the deerskin trade or the spread of European diseases. Many historic Cherokee and Euro-American sites also contain data that would yield insights on the nature of the American frontier in the colonial period.

Moratto and Kelly (1978:10) define a cultural resource as having ethnic significance if it "holds religious, mythological, spiritual, or other symbolic importance for a discrete group of people." Many sites are of symbolic significance to ethnic groups when they can be associated with specific historical events or periods. In fact, as Moratto and Kelly (1978:11) point out, many ethnic groups such as Native Americans, Afro-Americans, and Hispanic Americans have been excluded from much of written history, and archaeologically derived data are necessary to flesh out the patterns of their history. Such data can also be used to test historical misconceptions and fabrications. In this context the loss of the sites of many important Overhill Cherokee towns in eastern Tennessee to the waters of the Tellico Reservoir is particularly troublesome.

As defined by Moratto and Kelly (1978:12) public significance refers to "those benefits that accrue to a society through the wise stewardship of its archaeological resources." Such benefits include public enjoyment, aesthetic qualities, tourism, and education. Judicious professional development of archaeological resources on and near the Eastern

Cherokee Reservation, such as the Kituwha Mound, could be of aesthetic, recreational, and/or educational benefit to tourists and at the same time could be of economic, educational, and ethnic significance to the Cherokees. Other significant archaeological sites, such as a palisaded Pisgah town, could be similarly developed through the use of grants or private funds.

Archaeological field schools can be of major educational and recreational benefit to the public. Over a decade and a half of research at the Warren Wilson site in Buncombe County and several seasons of research at the Ward site in Watauga County have been supported by summer field schools. Finally, many elementary and secondary school students as well as older residents of the region have collections from a single site or a limited geographical area. A small-scale, nonfunded program was conducted with young collectors in a rural elementary school in Watauga County, North Carolina, from 1976 to 1978 (Purrington 1978b). Students were invited to bring their collections to school. After a presentation on county prehistory and archaeological methods, the lecturer identified artifacts (mostly points) and (when possible—about 70 to 80% of the time) determined site locations of the specimens in the students' collections. Sites were assigned a number and plotted on U.S.G.S. quadrangle maps and site forms were prepared. In many cases uncertain site locations could be verified by follow-up field inspections. This exercise significantly added to the number of recorded sites as well as data on the distribution of diagnostic artifacts in the county. The interest and enthusiasm that many of these young people showed when general methods of correct collecting procedure were explained to them and scientific methods were used to reconstruct human behavior from archaeological remains suggests that they derived significant educational benefits from the experience.

Moratto and Kelly (1978:5) have defined scientific significance as "the potential for using cultural resources to establish reliable facts and generalizations about the past." Sites or districts are scientifically significant when they have the potential to provide answers to specific research questions. Such questions may relate to specific geographical areas and/or periods or they may be free of temporal and spatial limitations.

In their report on the Cache River Project in northeastern Arkansas, House and Schiffer (1975:163) note that "the significance of something depends to a great extent on the context in which it is being viewed . . . [and] . . . archaeological resources acquire scientific or historical significance only as they relate to specific research questions in substantive, technical, methodological, and theoretical contexts." Substantive questions are the kind most frequently asked in the process of assessing archaeological significance. Such questions are concerned with describing or explaining cultural events and processes that occur at a particular time or place. However, House and Schiffer point out that many important research questions would be overlooked (and much data consequently lost) if substantive questions alone were used in the process of assessing significance. Six general categories of scientific questions will be discussed:

Substantive. "Substantive questions are those concerned with describing or explaining cultural events and processes that occur at a particular time or place" (House and Schiffer 1975:163). Several substantive questions were posed at the end of the discussion of each of the Appalachian Summit phases. In addition to these specific questions a number of general questions can be asked of the archaeological remains representative of any phase or period at a site. Such general questions can be phrased as follows:

Could this site provide information that would contribute to the
1. identification of artifact, feature, attribute, or assemblage classes which are diagnostic of a specific culture or period?
2. association of nondiagnostic archaeological remains (artifacts, environmental remains, and features) with specific periods, phases, environmental settings, and/or cultural activities?
3. identification of archaeological remains and sets of such remains that are indicative of and aid in the reconstruction of specific cultural activities, i.e. usage classes or functional types?
4. determination of site use and function?
5. reconstruction of patterns and products of subsistence as well as procurement and use of nonfood resources?
6. reconstruction of size(s) and/or type(s) of social unit(s) represented in the archaeological remains at a site?
7. identification of local and nonlocal artifacts and raw materials in order to reconstruct past exchange and procurement systems?
8. definition of site types based on inferred activities, size and type of social unit, environmental setting, and available resources?
9. reconstruction of past subsistence, resource procurement, settlement, and social systems?
10. comparison of archaeological phenomena from different localities and regions?
11. reconstruction of patterns of sociocultural development including adaptation, stability, and change?

The remaining categories of scientific significance are free of spatial and temporal limitations.

Anthropological. "Here investigators might be expected to contribute to testing general anthropological principles, especially those relating to processes of long-term culture change and ecological adaptation" (Schiffer and House 1977: 253). General anthropological research questions for which the Appalachian Summit data can offer answers include:

1. What variables contribute to continuity and change in strategies of environmental adaptation?
2. What circumstances lead to increased sedentism and greater cultural complexity?
3. Do mountain cultures tend to be conservative, i.e. relatively resistant, to outside influences? Do they tend to maintain a core culture or remain at essentially the same level of sociocultural complexity despite adoption of superficial technological and stylistic innovations? If so, what are the respective roles of environmental and sociocultural variables?
4. How is local variation in adaptive strategies and cultural evolution within an environmentally defined region to be explained?
5. What are the sociocultural dynamics of the introduction of technological and stylistic innovations (e.g. ceramic styles) to a region and the diffusion of these techniques and styles throughout the region?
6. What are the causes and dynamics of abandonment of localities or regions?

Social Scientific. These questions relate more generally to social science but may include specifically anthropological questions (Schiffer and House 1977:253). Many theoretical models and general principles of economics, history, political science, psychology, geography, and sociology, particularly those dealing with dynamics and change, are amenable to testing with archaeological data. General social scientific research questions relevant to the archaeology of the Appalachian Summit region include:

1. What are the dynamics of artifact reuse or recycling (Schiffer and House 1977:253)?
2. What are the effects of modernization, particularly forced modernization, on small-scale, traditional societies (Purrington 1978c)?
3. What are the human effects of population dislocation and immigration?
4. What are the environmental effects (with long-term economic implications) of overpopulation, abandonment, or initial settlement of mountain habitats?
5. What are the mechanisms and dynamics of population control in mountain environments?

6. Is sociocultural disruption inevitable when small-scale, traditional societies are confronted by technologically and organizationally dominant groups (Purrington 1978c)?

Technical. One of the foremost questions confronting archaeologists is how to recover archaeological data so that their maximum potential to yield information can be realized. In addition data recovery techniques must also be developed to take into account the exigencies of limited time, funds, and personnel in the face of rapid destruction of the archaeological resource base. Many technical questions can be as easily investigated on sites in the Appalachian Summit as elsewhere, but some technical questions are particularly relevant to the Appalachian Summit. For example:

1. What are the effects of natural, lumbering-induced, and agriculturally-induced erosion on the archaeological record of upland sites?
2. How have sites in the valleys been affected by flooding, erosion, plowing, and colluvial deposition?
3. What are the most effective techniques of site reconnaissance and data recovery in rugged, overgrown terrain? What are the most cost-effective procedures for shovel testing, leaf clearance, etc.?
4. What are the most effective techniques of site reconnaissance and data recovery on alluvial and colluvial landforms where deeply buried cultural horizons may be present?
5. What kinds of archaeological data can be recovered from collection and analysis of soil samples? From the study of microflora growing on the surface of sites?
6. What analytical techniques, including experimental production, use, and discard of artifacts, will produce culturally and temporally meaningful archaeological data sets?
7. What sampling techniques will provide the most representative pictures of past settlement, subsistence, and resource procurement systems in a region with significant local environmental diversity and variable distribution of sites?

Methodological. The category method refers to the procedures of analysis and ordering of data. Archaeological methods are the pathway to achieving the three major traditional goals of archaeological research: 1) reconstructing culture history, 2) reconstructing past lifeways, and 3) studying cultural processes (Binford 1968:8-16). These reconstructions of presumably "real" cultural phenomena, events, and processes provide the basis for proposing explanations of past cultural behavior and human-environment interaction and the formulation of "laws" of human behavior. Again, many methodological questions could be tested in the

Appalachian Summit. Some questions that are particularly pertinent to the region include:

1. What categories of form, including production technique, style, wear patterns, and other indicators of use, of artifacts and features can be most effectively used in temporal ordering of archaeological sites?
2. What archaeological units including attributes, artifact and feature types, environmental remains, and complexes of such data can be used to identify past human activities at archaeological sites and the respective roles of such sites in past environmental, social, and cultural systems?
3. What data recovery and ordering techniques and methods can be used in the reconstruction of size(s) and type(s) of social units at individual sites?
4. Can a dynamic typology of sites based on cultural-temporal indicators, inferred activities, size and type of social units, environmental setting, and available resources (including site catchment) be developed and the relationships between contemporaneous site types be identified?
5. What are the relative analytical and interpretive values of archaeological assemblages from various topographic and edaphic settings and different contexts of disturbance and non-disturbance (cf. Ward 1980b)? What kinds of information can be derived from assemblages confined to the plow zone; shallow, deflated, and eroded upland sites; and other disturbed contexts (cf. Lewarch and O'Brien 1981; Talmage and Chesler 1977)?
6. How should the relative proportions of research time devoted to investigation of large, stratified floodplain sites versus shallow, semi-disturbed sites be allotted? (See Trinkley 1980b and Woodall 1981 for opposing arguments.)

Theoretical. "The category theory refers to the conceptual framework of a single discipline" (Kluckhohn 1940:43). Because archaeological data consist primarily of material remains and their associations the conceptual framework of the discipline has been most strongly oriented toward culture change and environmental adaptation (cf. Plog 1974; House and Schiffer 1975). Many theoretical questions of concern to archaeologists are fundamentally anthropological questions, and several of these questions have been discussed above. However, because of the unique nature of archaeological data, a number of theoretical constructs specific to the discipline can be developed. In particular a specifically archaeological theory can contribute to a better understanding of the behavioral and environmental processes that create an archaeological record and the meaning of this record in terms of human behavior and human-environment interaction.

Questions of archaeological theory applicable to the Appalachian Summit include:

1. What are the behavioral implications of stylistic variability and change?
2. What cultural processes are responsible for specific patterns of site formation and site distribution?
3. How is the formation of archaeological sites and the preservation of archaeological context affected by natural processes and post-depositional human activities?
4. Do cultural practices and processes such as population growth, infanticide, migration, and resistance to innovations leave a recognizable archaeological record?
5. What characteristics in the form and structure of material assemblages are indicative of sociocultural differences between neighboring, contemporaneous social groups?
6. What does the presence or absence of ceramics in components of a ceramic phase mean in terms of the composition, mobility, and structure of social groups? For example, does the presence of ceramics generally imply that females occupied a site or that a ceramic component represents greater sedentism and/or a broader range of cultural activities than a nonceramic component?
7. What kinds of archaeological data can be used to test hypothetical constructions of levels of sociocultural integration, i.e. band, tribe, chiefdom, or state?
8. How can archaeologists measure the relative diversity of "ideas" in past societies (Dickens 1980:34)?

A General Research Design For The Appalachian Summit Region

As noted above, Raab and Klinger (1977) have stressed the value of assessing archaeological site significance from within the context of explicit, problem-oriented research designs, particularly those that are regional in scope. As early as 1964, Binford (1964b) stated that cultural systems could be most effectively studied through the development and application of regional research designs, and within the past decade archaeological research has been increasingly systematized as more and more of these strategies have been developed. Goodyear, Raab, and Klinger (1978:161) define a research design as:

an explicit plan for solving a problem or set of problems. It is a plan that must contain theoretical goals in the form of a specific problem or hypothesis, relevant analytic variables, and specification of data that will allow empirical testing. To be complete, the design must lay out the methods and techniques for acquiring and analyzing the data, and predict the expected outcomes of the analysis.

General research designs of the kind developed by Mathis (1979) for North Carolina's statewide archaeological survey are critical for both archaeological research and effective cultural resource management. The larger the analytical unit under consideration, the more general the research design should be. Regional research designs, therefore, should provide a general framework of technique, method, and theory that will be a foundation for the development and application of more specific strategies to smaller geographical units such as drainage basins.

In order to meet current needs research designs also should be usable as management tools. On the basis of such research designs it should be possible to assess significance and identify management priorities. Explicit, problem-oriented, regional/local research designs should significantly aid the archaeologists in preserving or salvaging the most significant components of their inevitably and rapidly disappearing data base.

Explicit, problem-oriented research designs have not yet been developed for the Appalachian Summit region. Such research designs, whether project-specific, local, subregional (e.g. watersheds), or regional in scope, should be based on the following goals.

The fundamental goals of archaeology in the Appalachian Summit include:

1. Reconstruct culture histories, particularly local chronological sequences.
2. Reconstruct past lifeways in their environmental contexts including environmental, social, and cultural systems.
3. Identify cultural processes including cultural stability and change and the interrelationships between humans and their environment.
4. Develop models to explain cultural processes.
5. Use the Appalachian Summit archaeological data to evaluate general theories of human behavior.
6. Use the Appalachian Summit data to experiment with and test archaeological techniques, methods, and theory.
7. Develop a set of management strategies for the study area including models to predict the probability of site presence and absence and sets of criteria for assessing site significance.

In order to meet these goals the region's past environmental, social, and cultural systems and their interrelationships must be understood as fully as the data will allow. Therefore it is critical that a representative picture of the full range of human activities be obtained. It should be determined which natural environmental zones and which resources potentially available for human use were utilized and which were not. Finally archaeological research should be conducted in the context of the known archaeology and potentially available resources in neighboring regions.

Archaeological research and management strategies should, therefore, be based on the need to obtain representative samples of all potentially habitable landforms and site types (cf. Ward 1980b:8). This approach is critical to effective cultural resource management for it means that when small, shallow upland sites are underrepresented in the known local or regional data base their potential to contribute to our understanding of the past is high. Therefore, it is justifiable to assess a representative sample of them as significant and as deserving of systematic investigation and federal protection as large, stratified floodplain sites (cf. King 1975; Talmage and Chesler et al. 1977).

Surveys that emphasize a regional, systematic approach of this kind will facilitate the development of site typologies. Once such typologies have begun to emerge it should be possible to understand more fully local sociocultural systems and adaptive strategies, to develop predictive models of site presence or absence for early stage planning of construction projects, and to establish priorities of individual site significance within each class of sites of a particular type.

Any research design should be based on a set of research questions, and its implementation should generate new questions. As Dixon (1977:279), Lynott (1980), and others have warned, research questions and research designs should not bind us to inflexible criteria of significance but should, instead, be dynamic. A number of research questions for the Appalachian Summit have been posed, but they represent only the tip of the proverbial iceberg. It is to be hoped they will provide a dynamic framework for the study and management of the cultural resources of one of the most beautiful and scientifically intriguing regions in the nation.

4

Through a Glass Darkly: An Archaeological View of North Carolina's More Distant Past

Joffre L. Coe

INTRODUCTION

The phrase, "nothing much is known about North Carolina archaeology," has become an overworked cliche in recent archaeological reports. The inference is that if nothing much is really known, the writer then cannot be expected to know much either. Since this statement has appeared in a number of recent studies submitted as professional appraisal of various aspects of North Carolina archaeology, a random check was made to determine the extent of its use. This review revealed over thirty instances where the "nothing much is known" syndrome was used to qualify or apologize for the conclusions. Of course, there are many things we do not know and probably will never know about the past, but by any relative standard a great deal is really known today about North Carolina archaeology. The basic outline for prehistoric cultural development has been established throughout the state, and details of discrete units are being compounded with increasing frequency. A bibliography (Phelps 1974) on North Carolina archaeology was published in 1974 that contained 120 entries. A more recent publication (Hargrove 1980) identifying reports on file in the office of the Archaeology Branch contained 661 items. Three professional monographs and two more popular books are available on North Carolina archaeology. One of these (Coe 1964) has been reprinted four times with a sale of over 25,000 copies. Dissertations on archaeology at the University of North Carolina at Chapel Hill alone exceed 20,000 pages. Current research at many of our institutions is rapidly increasing our knowledge and understanding of the lives of our early inhabitants. For these reasons it is hard to understand a statement published as recently as 1979, which claims: "North Carolina is still archaeologically *Terra incognita* (Newkirk 1979:50). Rather, I submit, the problem lies closer to *Persona ignoramus*.

When one climbs a hill along a steadily rising path, there is a tendency to concentrate only on the path ahead. Progress seems slow and one cannot see very far ahead. If, however, the climber stops and turns around to see whence he came, a vast panorama opens up before him, and he can know that he has made progress. In a sense this is true of our archaeological effort. As we work day by day trying to find and recover the scant evidence of the past, it is easy to feel that through the years man and nature have conspired to conceal or destroy the sources of our data. Compared with what we would like to know, we do, indeed, know very little. It is at this point that we need to stop, turn around, and view the progress that has been made.

Archaeologists must classify everything and arrange their data according to periods. The previous speakers have arranged things to their liking, and I will take the privilege of doing the same. First, I would like to discuss briefly what I will call a "Search for Identity." In this case, I am referring to the identity of the people who were responsible for the prehistoric remains found in North Carolina. Were they ancestors of the historic Indians, or were they some lost race of mysterious origin? The second period I will call "Foundation Building," and I will begin it with the organization of the Archaeological Society of North Carolina in 1933. For nearly forty years there has been a steady, systematic, but often lonely, effort to lay a foundation upon which others might build. Then, there is the present period that I think can be appropriately called "Explanation and Frustration."

SEARCH FOR IDENTITY

The last two decades of the nineteenth century have been called "Archaeology's Enchanted Hour" by Edward Carpenter, who in 1950 wrote:

> Though their techniques were naive and faulty by contemporary standards, though their sequences were more on inference than empirical data, archaeologists made an unequalled contribution; they helped destroy the concept of degeneration and reinstated man in the developmental series. With eloquent optimism, they argued that archaeology proved the idea of progress, which promised to mankind an ever-improving secular future as a necessity of nature itself (Carpenter 1950:13).

In simpler terms archaeology proved the myth of the mound builders to be just that—a myth. There was no evidence for the fall of man. There was no evidence for a lost race of civilized men preceding the Indians. But myths die hard, and North Carolina reputedly gave supporting data to both sides.

In the 1880s Mann S. Valentine of Richmond, Virginia, became interested in Indians and together with his sons began collecting everything available. What they did not find themselves, they bought from whoever would supply them. In time their interest turned to western North Carolina, and A. J. Osborne of Haywood County became their collecting agent. Osborne was very successful in his collecting efforts. He bought specimens from the local farmers, and he dug into various mounds for additional materials. On the slopes of Mt. Pisgah in Haywood County he began to find in his excavations a large variety of carved-stone objects, which included may figures of animals and people. The style and subjects did not appear to be Indian. Some of the carvings were in the form of a hippopotamus, a camel, a rhinocerous (Figure 4.1), and other nonnative animals. If these were not the work of Indians, then of whom? The logical explanation for the time would be "a lost race of civilized mound builders." The Pisgah or Haywood finds became famous, not only in America, but in Europe as well. An article appeared in the Journal of the Anthropological Institute of Great Britain and Ireland in June, 1882 (Thomas 1894:346). Another article appeared in the New York *World* on August 17, 1882. In this latter article the author stated: "If Mr. Valentine has formulated any theory in regard to the objects I am not aware of it, but theories abundant have been advanced by others who have examined them." Valentine also went to Washington to let the Smithsonian Institution have its day. The reception there was predictable, and the following is his own account of this experience:

> Before placing them [artifacts] before the archaeologists of Europe Mr. Valentine was determined that his friend Prof. S. F. Baird should see them. At the appointed time this gentleman was not in his office but the curator Dr. Charles Rau was present in the building and they were placed on a table for his inspection. Unfortunately for science and truth, Dr. Rau is like many one sided investigators in this age whose preconceived opinions shut out all except that which will minister to his own views. A man so wedded to the idea of Dr. Rau's infallibility in matters of American Archaeology that he can in a moment dispose of a question by a simple remark, "Frauds, I know them to be, for nothing like them has ever been found in this country..." Dr. Rau has about as much intellectual right on his side to stand at the door of the Smithsonian Institution and say to the visitors 'don't bring in specimens which will disprove my theory' as a man would have to say lets set fire to the British Museum and destroy the Elgin Marbles because I don't understand them (Valentine 1883:8-11).

In defense of Valentine, I should add that when his agent began to find carvings showing people with feather headdresses, riding horses, and carrying guns, he washed his hands of the whole affair. The coup de grace was delivered by one of Dr. Rau's associates, J. W. Emmert, who went to Haywood County and "had the same parties who stated they had made some articles for Mr. Valentine make quite a number of similar articles for the Bureau" (Thomas 1894:347). This success on the part of the Smithsonian, unfortunately, cost North Carolina its most ardent and capable student of archaeology. Prior to the Pisgah affair the work of the Valentines showed more insight than would have been expected for the period. Valentine saved animal bones so that diet might be studied. He preserved

FIGURE 4.1. One of the many Pisgah Fakes purchased by the Valentines in the 1880's.

soil samples for analysis in hope that they would shed light on specific activities. Most of all, he seemed to understand that the mounds were structures and should be excavated in such a way as to show the basic details of construction. After his humiliation over the fakes at Pisgah, he withdrew from archaeology altogether and devoted his later years to the finer arts in his museum at Richmond.

At about the same time that Valentine was collecting his evidence for a Pisgah civilization, Cyrus Thomas of the Smithsonian sent one of his agents, J. P. Rogan, to Caldwell County, North Carolina. In the Happy Valley at the headwaters of the Yadkin River he excavated several sites. Two of the sites were on the land of the Reverend T. F. Nelson, and they have become known as the Nelson Triangle and the Nelson Circle because the Indians were alleged to have excavated a triangular pit in one area and a circular pit in the other area before covering them with earth. A contemporary newspaper account described the work as follows:

> On Tuesday and Wednesday of last week they opened a mound . . . 27 skeletons were found . . . a chief was lying at the bottom, face downward with out stretched arms . . . his face rested in a shell . . . the whole concave surfaces of which was filled with hieroglyphics . . . a glass bead and three pieces of iron . . . were found (Richmond Dispatch 1883).

This association with European objects was what Thomas was looking for—proof that mound building continued into the historic period and that the builders of the early mounds were only the ancestors of the later Indians. Although we now know these sites to be the remains of the historic Catawba Indians, they were Cherokee to Cyrus Thomas. In a three-part article entitled "The Cherokee in Pre-Colombian Times," which was published in *Science* in 1890, Thomas devoted most of Part II to describing the Caldwell County sites. He concluded:

> It is evident, from the mode of burial and the articles found, that these works cannot be attributed to white men of post-Colombian times. Can they be attributed to the Indians found inhabiting this region at the time of the advent of the whites? If the evidence justifies this conclusion, we may then attribute them without hesitation to the Cherokees (Thomas 1890:325).

His statement was not exactly convincing. On the margin of Valentine's personal copy of this article was inscribed this note: "This is an imaginative design, no such regularity is found to exist—else all our care in uncovering skeletons goes for naught." Perhaps this was a case of Thomas's being right for the wrong reasons. While we applaud his efforts in behalf of North American archaeology, we wish he had handled his data with more integrity. He had many men working in the field digging "mounds," but few of them had any knowledge or experience in what they were doing. They sent Thomas reports and specimens, and he used the information that suited his purpose. Unfortunately, the reports were usually inaccurate and, at least in the case of the North Carolina material, fabricated more than observed. With most of his writing there is no way of knowing what the original context of the material may have been.

It may be of some interest that on March 23, 1883, Thomas wrote Rogan at Lenoir, North Carolina, and in a five-page letter gave him complete instructions for excavating the mounds. He was very specific with statements such as, "Watch carefully the dirt thrown out for little implements, pieces of pottery, or anything artificial," or "as soon as you strike anything that does not come out easily, get down into the opening and dig around it as carefully as possible." On the other hand he had some insight as to relative age and instructed Rogan to watch out for "intrusive burials made long after the mound was first formed."

After the Thomas-Valentine controversy archaeological interest in North Carolina declined. The first thirty years of the twentieth century saw only sporadic forays into the state by outside investigators. Professor Charles Peabody vacationed in Cumberland County with his granddaughter and dug a mound near Hope Mills to provide entertainment. Fred Turbyfill went pot-hunting in the western counties for the Heye Foundation. William Henry Holmes looked at some pottery from the Yadkin River, and Warren King Moorehead dug a portion of a small rockshelter in Swain County. In 1933 one might have truly said, "nothing much is known about North Carolina archaeology."

FOUNDATION BUILDING

The first annual meeting of the Archaeological Society of North Carolina was held in the home of Burnham S. Colburn at Biltmore Forest near Asheville on October 7, 1933. The two principal speakers were Dr. John R. Swanton of the Bureau of American Ethnology and Dr. Neil M. Judd of the United States National Museum (Figure 4.2). Dr. Swanton talked about the Indians of the Southeast, their language, and some aspects of their culture. Dr. Judd spoke about "financial difficulty, the difficulty of getting attendance at meetings, the difficulty of coordinating the numerous activities in the field of Indian study" (Johnson 1934:4). Specifically, he stressed the importance of making an archaeological survey of the state and the necessity of reeducating the public on the question of the commercial value of Indian relics.

The following spring meeting of the society was held in Raleigh on April 28, 1934. The speakers included the Reverend Douglas L. Rights of Winston-Salem, Professor Sanford Winston of Raleigh, Professors Wallace E. Caldwell and R. D. W. Connor of Chapel Hill, and a young Turk from Greensboro named Coe. The main part of the program dealt with the place of Indians in history, including the problem of the identity of the "Robeson County Indians." Coe's talk, on the other hand, was intended to lay the basis for "Planning an Archaeological Survey of North Carolina." He emphasized the following points: "a survey is the logical first step in the archaeological study of any region"; "a complete archaeological survey cannot be made within a few weeks or months"; and, finally, "the most important problem is preparing and adopting a standard form" (Coe 1934:11). Nearly a half-century later we are still talking about the need for archaeological survey and the need for developing the ultimate form.

At the society's second annual meeting, held in Charlotte on October 6, 1934, the program consisted of talks about the "Indian Occupation of the Charlotte Area"; "A Cherokee Story" told in Cherokee; a demonstration of "Indian Sign Talk" (Boy Scout style); and the "Next Step in our Archaeological Survey." In discussing these next steps, Coe reported that a form had been designed and that the survey committee wished to include information about the artifacts as well as the site location. In concluding he stated that "little has been said about how we are going to get these forms filled in" (Coe 1935:21) and that it would be up to the society members to make the survey a success. Unfortunately, very few society members ever bothered to use these nicely printed forms.

In the fall of 1934 Coe tried to set an example by surveying as much of Transylvania County as possible on foot. Within a year thirty-two sites were recorded, and approximately 2,000 specimens were collected. In May, 1935, the Archaeological Society of Brevard College published a bulletin, which contained six short articles, all on the topic, "The Value of Archaeology to the Advancement of Mankind." The authors were Fay-Cooper Cole, University of Chicago; T. M. N. Lewis, University of Ten-

FIGURE 4.2. The attendance at the first meeting of the Archaeological Society of North Carolina included Dr. John R. Swanton (back row, second from the right) and Dr. Neil M. Judd (second row, first from the left). The meeting was held at the home of Burnham S. Colburn (first row, third from the left) in Biltmore Forest.

nessee; N. C. Nelson, American Museum of Natural History; Frank H. H. Roberts, Jr., Smithsonian Institution; John R. Swanton, Smithsonian Institution; and Clark Wissler, American Museum of Natural History. The comments varied from cliches like "the task of archaeology is to make the past live again" (Cole 1935:7) to a frank "the finest thing about archaeology is that it serves no utilitarian purpose!" (Wissler 1935:13). Nevertheless what was in everyone's mind, even at this time, was a concern with the application of archaeological data to *culturological* problems. This was the year that the Society for American Archaeology was organized and also the year that the society published its first issue of *American Antiquity*.

The first relief programs involved with archaeology began in 1933. In December the Smithsonian Institution received authorization for eleven projects under the first of several relief agencies, the CWA (Civil Works Administration). Within two weeks the Smithsonian had employed 1,500 workers and thus began the largest relic hunt in North American history.

One of the first eleven projects was the Peachtree Mound near Murphy, North Carolina (Figure 4.3). This site was selected primarily because of the high level of unemployment in the area and because John R. Swanton thought this might be the town of Guasili, which Spanish explorer Her-

FIGURE 4.3. Excavations in progress in 1934 at the Peachtree Mound, near Murphy, North Carolina (top). The work force at the Peachtree excavations consisted of 104 men supplied by the Civil Works Administration (bottom).

nando DeSoto visited in 1540. Work began on December 21, 1933, and ended April 1, 1934. Two supervisors and 104 men were assigned to the project. The archaeologist in charge was Jesse D. Jennings, then a graduate student at the University of Chicago, and in true Chicagoan fashion he and his legion of men chomped through the mound like a hungry beaver cutting through a log.

Peachtree is also of interest to us because it was one of the mounds tested by Valentine. This fact was noted by Jennings in a footnote: "Ten burials were reported to have been removed by the Valentine brothers of Richmond in 1885 from the top of the secondary mound. Since no fragmentary human bones were found in the fill of their excavation, this statement may be erroneous (Setzler and Jennings 1941:17). In another footnote he stated: "John Macomb, an old settler, says that when he first saw the mound there were four large posts at corners of a 20-foot square, on top of the mound" (Setzler and Jennings 1941:19).

Actually, this early work had begun in 1880, not 1885. The digging was done by R. D. McComb, the father of Jennings's informant, not the Valentine brothers. Valentine did keep close track of the work by correspondence and sent McComb questionnaires about points that were unclear. In all, some seventy pages of notes and drawings survive, and they indicate that in some ways McComb had a better understanding of the nature of the site than did Jennings, in spite of his advantage of fifty years of additional knowledge. Nevertheless, the Peachtree report (Setzler and Jennings 1941) was the first major publication of a systematic excavation of an archaeological site in North Carolina. Even though time and knowledge have changed our perspective, many of Jennings's observations are still valid.

In 1935 Coe went to the University of North Carolina at Chapel Hill as a student, and for better or for worse he and his faculty supporters began the North Carolina archaeological program. In the spring of 1936 the first excavation was made at a village site in Randolph County. This site was thought to have been the one called Keyauwee, which John Lawson visited in 1701. The excavation was funded by donations made to the Archaeological Society of North Carolina. The society members provided the labor. The North Carolina State Museum provided equipment, and the university provided space and transportation. The total cost of the project was $143.50.

The first work at Town Creek began in 1937 as a Works Projects Administration (WPA) project sponsored by the University of North Carolina (Figure 4.4). In 1938 work was continued with National Youth Administration (NYA) workers, and from 1939 until the beginning of World War II excavations at Town Creek were part of a statewide WPA project, also sponsored by the university at Chapel Hill (Figure 4.5). After World

War II and until 1955 work at Town Creek was funded by the State Parks System. From 1955 to the present it has been a state historic site under the jurisdiction of the Division of Archives and History. In spite of the variety of administrative sponsors, the University of North Carolina at Chapel Hill has provided continuity of research since the beginning of the program. A systematic analysis of the total data received from this site has just begun. When complete, the work at Town Creek should stand as a major landmark in Southeastern archaeology.

There is no need to detail all of the projects in which we had an interest between 1935 and 1970. Those projects have been covered, in part, in the preceding talks. I would like to emphasize, however, that the archaeological program at Chapel Hill has always been problem oriented. Sites were not selected at random or because they were convenient.

The first phase of our research was directed toward the identification of the Piedmont Siouan tribes through the application of the direct historical approach. This research began in 1936 with our work at Keyauwee and continued in 1938 with work on the Roanoke River. In 1940 the Occaneechi village at Hillsborough was excavated, and work is continuing today at Saura Town on the Dan River.

The second phase was directed toward finding stratified, short-term occupation sites in the alluvial floodplains. Where found, these sites contained the most conclusive evidence for time-space context of discrete cultural units. The early work at the Doerschuk site in 1948 and at the Hardaway site in the 1950s was very rewarding and provided us with our first clear insight into the nature and diversity of the Archaic cultures of the Piedmont. Further work in the Roanoke, the Yadkin, the Catawba, and the Tennessee drainage of western North Carolina have reinforced those early observations. At all stages of its development the floodplain had a stable surface upon which plants grew and animals and man lived. With the passage of time some parts of the floodplain eroded and other parts were buried under more recent deposits. In the first case all evidence is lost. In the second case all surviving evidence is sealed in and protected from further disturbance. The trick is to find with archaeologists' puny squares in the broad expanse of floodplains just where man might have lived in the past and where that evidence is still preserved. In our work we have been lucky.

Our third and current phase of research was called "the ecological and cultural base of the Cherokee Nation." This rather ambitious program began in 1965 as a three-year National Science Foundation project and is still active fifteen years later. The intent was simple enough—define Cherokee culture at the contact period and see whence it came. Toward this goal a thorough survey was made of the area, and four sites were extensively excavated. In Haywood County, near the Pisgah fraud area, two

FIGURE 4.4 The first season of excavation at the Town Creek Indian Mound (Frutchey Mound) in 1937, financed by the Works Projects Administration (WPA) (top). The program was jointly sponsored by the University of North Carolina, the State Museum, the Department of Conservation and Development, and the Historical Commission. By the end of the 1937 season, enough had been learned about the Town Creek site to warrant planning for an extended research program. The excavations revealed the entrance to a premound, earth-covered town house (two parallel trenches, lower right) (bottom).

FIGURE 4.5. Work continued at Town Creek with the help of WPA and NYA funding until the spring of 1942 (top). Since World War II all work at the site has been accomplished with state funds, first under the administration of the State Parks System, then under the direction of the Division of Archives and History. The research during this period continued to be supervised by the University of North Carolina. Excavations in the plaza area of the Town Creek site, 1963 (bottom).

town house mounds were excavated (Figure 4.6). In Macon County near Franklin a third town house and plaza area were completely excavated. In Buncombe County near Swannanoa a multicomponent village on the campus of Warren Wilson College is still being excavated.

EXPLANATION AND FRUSTRATION

The decade just past has seen many changes. Over thirty professionally trained archaeologists are now working in the state. Emphasis has shifted from problem-oriented research to environmental impact surveys or "cultural resource management." The one point that the three previous papers agree upon is that contract archaeology has had, and will continue to have, a dominating influence on archaeology. Phelps views this trend as disastrous, while Purrington sees it as a necessary goal. Whether or not academic and contract archaeology make compatible bed partners is really not the point; they will have to learn to live together throughout the foreseeable future.

It seems to me that Phelps succeeded very well in presenting a cultural-historical model of Coastal Plain prehistory. I found little that I would change or question. There are, however, a few points of information that may be of interest. The "probable burial mound near Salter Path on Bogue Banks" was actually a sand dune into which pit burials intruded. Although the "mound" was a natural feature, the burials appeared to be Middle Woodland in content, a situation not unlike the Glacial Kame burials of Ohio. A second comment deals with the burial mounds of the Cape Fear. Burial mounds tend to imply Middle Woodland and somehow a Hopewell connection. In this case I believe these mounds are much later and are in effect inverted ossuaries rather than tomb structures. Near Wilmington, South tested the MacFayden Mound in 1962, and recently we excavated a pit ossuary nearby on the north side of the Cape Fear River. The physical type and the cultural remains of these two sites were the same—Oak Island. According to Phelps's cultural sequence chart, the Oak Island period covered a time span of some 700 years, from about A.D. 1000 to historic contact.

A final comment deals with fiber-tempered pottery. I have always held the opinion that early fiber-tempered pottery was insignificant north of the Cape Fear River. I am still not convinced that it is significant. In discussing fiber temper, it is necessary to distinguish between stray inclusions of vegetable fibers and the deliberate tempering with fiber. We also need to know if the pottery is from the same time frame. Most of the sherds that I have seen appear to me to be later—a situation somewhat similar to steatite-tempered wares to the north. In any event it is an interesting problem to explore.

FIGURE 4.6. The last major program of the Research Laboratories of Anthropology of the University of North Carolina was directed toward the prehistory of the Cherokee. The program began with a National Science Foundation grant in 1965 and continued for over a decade. Excavation of a complex town house mound structure at the Garden Creek site, near Canton, September 1966 (top). Completion of the mound excavation in the fall of 1968 revealed two semi-subterranean, earth-covered lodges beneath the mound fill (bottom). The mound fill had served as the foundation for later town houses.

Dr. Ward's paper has dealt more with the problems of interpretation than attempting to summarize the already well-known sequence. In this effort he discusses three areas that are of interest to me. The first area deals with explanation. In this connection I would like to say that archaeology explains nothing. Archaeologists do all of the explaining, and therein lies the frustration. Archaeology can only recover the physical manifestation of an act. It can never recover the meaning of the act. Meanings, values, and beliefs are not necessarily inherent in any act or form. The archaeologist must infer meaning or give explanation to the act. The problem that we see too often is a form of myopic determinism that assigns one and only one explanation to an observed phenomenon when several alternative explanations might fit the situation just as well.

A second point made in Ward's paper deals with type. Like him, I object to the use of the term "intuitive types." I am not sure just what that means. No one that I know has that ability. Archaeological types are arrived at through hard work. Attributes are analyzed, hypotheses are tested, and the distribution of specimens are evaluated in the light of their occurrence in time and space. It does not matter whether you use a pencil or a card with holes in it. It is the concept that is important.

A final comment should be made concerning site evaluation. Both Phelps and Ward have stated that most of the recent contract work has contributed little to our knowledge of North Carolina archaeology. This assertion is probably true for various reasons. When one reads a series of reports that consistently describe the cultural association as "no material," "one rock," "one flake," or "some pottery," there is a tendency to lose confidence in the ability of the observer to report anything. When one reads at the same time names assigned to sites such as "Lucky Thirteen," "30-ought-6," "Lost Flake," and "Joke Site," this negative impression is confirmed. Is it this kind of undergraduate humor that is going to let us "see the peoples of the past and their archaeological remains as parts of environmental, social, and cultural systems"? I think not. All too often inadequately trained and poorly supervised students are sent to do professional work. The fault lies not with the student but rather with those of us who let them attempt work for which they are not adequately prepared.

Dr. Purrington's detailed review of the archaeology of the mountain region comes close to a synthesis even though he prefers to call that premature. The majority of his text was devoted to summarizing the various archaeological periods already known for the region. His strong and pervading interest, however, was a concern with explanation and interpretation. In each section he posed from three to seven "research questions" for a total of seventy. Still other questions were asked in the descriptive part of the text. Altogether, there were a lot of questions asked, but unfortunately not many could be answered with the data available. I received the impression that if one could just ask the right questions, then the answers should be forthcoming. This reminds me a little of Groucho Marx—say the right word and a duck will drop from the ceiling. There is no magic in archaeology. The right formula, the right word, the right question may be helpful to the investigator, but the goal should be total recovery of all possible data, not that of setting limits before you begin.

There are several other more specific items that should be mentioned. In discussing the Swannanoa phase, Purrington states, "Swannanoa is the only post-Archaic phase whose ceramic components are known to occur in ridgetop and upland valley settings." This statement, unfortunately, is the result of inadequate information. We have now found all ceramic styles in all major topographic areas of their region. Swannanoa was not unique.

Dr. Purrington also appears to have been misinformed when he says that "small sites and upland sites have been largely ignored." At least in our work we have tried to search all possible areas for evidence of habitation. We have located sites on the ridges, in the uplands, and places where no sane Indian should ever have gone. It is nonsense, however, to think that one can learn as much from small sites with poor context as one can learn from large sites with good context. There is a considerable difference in the nature of the cultural remains that may be found in an outhouse and those that are present in the dining room. Again, it is counterproductive to limit one's choices. All sites, small or large, are significant as part of the overall pattern that we are trying to understand.

In summary Purrington feels that, "In the not-too-distant future it should be possible to develop and test hypothetical explanations for cultural phenomenon and processes and apply them to the development of general laws of human behavior." This idealistic goal is unlikely to succeed in archaeology before it is reached in the study of the living. Can a handful of stone flakes and tools 8,000 years old really explain "the nature of *social* [emphasis added] interaction between resident and outside groups and between local resident populations"?

> We know in part, and we prophesy in part.
> But when that which is perfect is come, then
>   that which is in part shall be done away.
> When I was a child, I spoke as a child, I
>   understood as a child, I thought as a child;
>   but when I became a man, I put away childish
>   things.
> For now we see through a glass, darkly;
>   but then face to face.
>
>   1 Corinthians xiii:9-12

As we observe our rites of passage, I feel that North Carolina archaeology has successfully passed the trials of puberty, but until it develops higher standards and greater discipline, it cannot meet the challenge of maturity. We can never see the total reality of the past face to face, but we can, in time, see through the glass more clearly.

REFERENCES CITED

Adovasio. J. M., J. D. Gunn, J. Donahue, and R. Stuckenrath
1978 Meadowcroft Rockshelter, 1977: an overview. *American Antiquity* 43:632-651.

American Anthropological Association
1981 Cultural resource management: crisis in the '80s? *Anthropology Newsletter*.

Anderson, David G.
1975 Inferences from distribution studies of prehistoric artifacts in the Coastal Plain of South Carolina. *Southeastern Archaeological Conference Bulletin* 18:180-194.

Ashe, W. W.
1897 Forests of North Carolina. *North Carolina Geological Survey Bulletin* 6:141-224.

Ayers, Harvard G.
1976 The occupation of ridgetop sites in the Blue Ridge Mountains by Savannah River Archaic peoples. Paper presented at the 33rd annual Southeastern Archaeological Conference, Tuscaloosa, Alabama.

Ayers, Harvard G., L. J. Loucks, and B. L. Purrington
1980 Excavations at the Ward site, a Pisgah village in western North Carolina. Paper presented at the 37th Southeastern Archaeological Conference, New Orleans.

Baker, Charles M.
1979 An intensive archaeological reconnaissance on the Qualla reservation, Cherokee (Swain and Jackson counties), North Carolina. Ms. on file, Archaeology Laboratory, Department of Sociology and Anthropology, Western Carolina University.

Barnette, Karen L.
1978 *Woodland subsistence-settlement patterns in the Great Bend area, Yadkin River valley, North Carolina*. Master's thesis, Department of Anthropology, Wake Forest University.

Bass, Quentin R., II
1977 *Prehistoric settlement and subsistence patterns in the Great Smoky Mountains*. Master's thesis, Department of Anthropology, University of Tennessee.

Bellis, Vincent, M. P. O'Connor, and S. R. Riggs
1975 Estuarine shoreline erosion in the Albemarle-Pamlico region of North Carolina. *University of North Carolina Sea Grant Publication* SG-75-29. Raleigh.

Binford, Lewis R.
1962 Archaeology as anthropology. *American Antiquity* 28:217-225.

1964a *Archaeological and ethnohistorical investigation of cultural diversity and progressive development among aboriginal cultures of coastal Virginia and North Carolina*. Ph.D. diss., Department of Anthropology, University of Michigan.

1964b A consideration of archaeological research design. *American Antiquity* 31:203-210.

1968 Archeological perspectives. In *New perspectives in archeology*, edited by S. R. Binford and L. R. Binford, pp. 5-32. Aldine, Chicago.

Bollinger, Catherine E. (Compiler)
1982 Addendum II: A guide to research papers in the archaeology of North Carolina on file with the Archaeology Branch of the North Carolina Division of Archives and History. *North Carolina Archaeological Council Publication* 17.

Boyce, Douglas W.
1976 1976 archaeological surface survey, scenic highway corridor, Mount Rogers National Recreation Area. Report to the United States Forest Service, Jefferson National Forest, Roanoke, Virginia.

References

　1978　Iroquoian tribes of the Virginia-North Carolina Coastal Plain. In *Handbook of North American Indians*, Vol. 15 (Northeast), edited by B. G. Trigger, pp. 282-289. Smithsonian Institution.

Braun, E. Lucy
　1950　*Deciduous forests of eastern North America*. Philadelphia: Blakiston.

Broyles, Bettye J.
　1971　Second preliminary report: the St. Albans site, Kanawha County, West Virginia, 1964-1968. *West Virginia Geological and Economic Survey Report of Archaeological Investigations* 3.

Caldwell, Joseph R.
　1958　Trend and tradition in the prehistory of the eastern United States. *American Anthropological Association, Memoir* 88.

　1964　Interaction spheres in prehistory. In Hopewellian Studies, edited by J. R. Caldwell and R. L. Hall, pp. 133-143. *Illinois State Museum, Scientific Papers* No. 12.

Caldwell, Joseph R., and A. J. Waring, Jr.
　1939　Pottery type descriptions. *Southeastern Archaeological Conference Newsletter* 1(5):4-12.

Cambron, James W., and D. C. Hulse
　1969　*Handbook of Alabama archaeology, part 1, point types*. Archaeological Research Association of Alabama, Inc., Birmingham.

Carpenter, Edmund S.
　1950　Archaeology's enchanted hour. *Pennsylvania Archaeologist* 20(1-2).

Chapman, Jefferson
　1973　The Icehouse Bottom site, 40Mr23. *University of Tennessee, Department of Anthropology, Report of Investigations* 13.

　1975　The Rose Island site and the bifurcate point tradition. *University of Tennessee, Department of Anthropology, Report of Investigations* 14.

　1977　Archaic period research in the lower Little Tennessee River valley—1975: Icehouse Bottom, Harrison Branch, Thirty Acre Island, Calloway Island. *University of Tennessee, Department of Anthropology, Report of Investigations* 18.

Chapman, Jefferson, and B. C. Keel
　1979　Candy-Creek-Connestee components in eastern Tennessee and western North Carolina and their relationship with Adena-Hopewell. In *Hopewell archaeology: the Chillicothe Conference*, edited by David S. Brose and N'omi Greber, pp. 157-171. The Kent State University Press, Kent, Ohio.

Chomko, Stephen A., and G. Crawford
　1978　Plant husbandry in prehistoric eastern North America: new evidence for its development. *American Antiquity* 43(3):405-408.

Clarke, David L.
　1977　Spatial information in archeology. In *Spatial archeology*, edited by David L. Clarke, pp. 1-28. Academic Press, New York.

Clark, Michael G.
　1979　Problems in correlation of the Appalachian Quaternary record: examples and future research possibilities south of the glacial border. *Proceedings of the Second Annual Conference on the Quaternary History of the Southeastern United States* 1;5.

Coe, Joffre L.
　1934　Planning an archaeological survey of North Carolina. *Bulletin of the Archaeological Society of North Carolina* 1 (2).

1935   Next steps in our archaeological survey. *Bulletin of the Archaeological Society of North Carolina* (1).

1952   The cultural sequence of the Carolina piedmont. In *Archaeology of the eastern United States*, edited by James B. Griffin, pp. 301-311. University of Chicago Press, Chicago.

1961   Cherokee archaeology. In Symposium on Cherokee and Iroquois culture, edited by John Gulick. *Smithsonian Institution, Bureau of American Ethnology, Bulletin* 180:53-60.

1964   The formative cultures of the Carolina piedmont. *Transactions of the American Philosophical Society*, n.s., 54(5).

Coe, Joffre L., and E. Lewis
  1952   Dan River series statement. *Prehistoric pottery of the Eastern United States*, edited by James B. Griffin. Museum of Anthropology, University of Michigan.

Coe, Joffre L., and H. T. Ward
  1976   Final report: an archaeological evaluation of the Falls of the Neuse reservoir. Ms. on file, Research Laboratories of Anthropology, University of North Carolina, Chapel Hill.

Coe, Joffre L., H. T. Ward, M. Graham, L. Navey, S. H. Hogue, and J. H. Wilson, Jr.
  1982   *Archaeological and paleo-osteological investigations at the Cold Morning site, New Hanover County, North Carolina.* Report prepared for the Interagency Archeological Services (Atlanta) by the Research Laboratories of Anthropology, University of North Carolina, Chapel Hill.

Cole, Fay-Cooper
  1935   The value of archaeology to the advancement of mankind. *Bulletin of the Archaeological Society of Brevard College* 1:7.

Collins, Susan M.
  1977   A prehistoric community at the Macon County Industrial Park site. *North Carolina Archaeological Council Publication* 2.

Corbitt, David L. (editor)
  1953   *Explorations, descriptions and attempted settlements of Carolina, 1584-1590.* State Department of Archives and History, Raleigh.

Cowan, C. Wesley
  1978a   Seasonal nutritional stress in a Late Woodland population: suggestions from some eastern Kentucky coprolites. *Tennessee Anthropologist* 3(2):117-128.

  1978b   Prehistoric adaptation to the Cumberland Plateau: a view from the western periphery. Paper presented at the 35th annual Southeastern Archaeological Conference, Knoxville, Tennessee.

Crawford, R. G. H.
  1966   *An archeological survey of Lenoir County, North Carolina.* Master's thesis, Department of Anthropology, University of Florida.

Cridlebaugh, Patricia A.
  1977   *An analysis of the Morrow Mountain components at the Icehouse Bottom site and a reassessment of the Morrow Mountain complex.* Master's thesis, Department of Anthropology, University of Tennessee.

Custer, Jay F.
  1979   Settlement-subsistence systems in the Blue Ridge and Great Valley sections of Virginia: a comparison. Paper presented at the 9th Middle Atlantic Archaeological Conference, Rehoboth Beach, Delaware.

Davis, John C.
  1973   *Statistical and data analysis in geology.* Wiley, New York.

References

Deetz, James
    1968   Cultural patterning of behavior as reflected by archaeological materials. In *Settlement archaeology*, edited by K. C. Chang, pp. 31-43. National Press Books, Palo Alto.

Delcourt, Paul A., and H. R. Delcourt
    1979   Late Pleistocene and Holocene distributional history of the deciduous forest in the southeastern United States. *Veroffentlichungen des Geobotanischen Institutes der ETH, Stiftung Rubel* (Zurich) 68:79-107.

Dickens, Roy S., Jr.
    1970   *The Pisgah culture and its place in the prehistory of the southern Appalachians.* Ph.D. diss., Department of Anthropology, University of North Carolina, Chapel Hill. University Microfilms, Ann Arbor.

    1976   *Cherokee prehistory: the Pisgah phase in the Appalachian Summit region.* University of Tennessee Press, Knoxville.

    1978   Mississippian settlement patterns in the Appalachian Summit area: the Pisgah and Qualla phases. In *Mississippian Settlement Patterns*, edited by Bruce D. Smith, pp. 115-139. Academic Press, New York.

    1979   The origins and development of Cherokee culture. In *The Cherokee Indian nation: a troubled history*, edited by Duane H. King, pp. 3-32. University of Tennessee Press, Knoxville.

    1980   Ceramic diversity as an indicator of cultural dynamics in the Woodland period. *Tennessee Anthropologist* 5:34-36.

Dixon, Keith A.
    1977   Applications of archaeological resources: broadening the basis of significance. In *Conservation archaeology: a guide for cultural resource management studies*, edited by M. B. Schiffer and G. J. Gumerman, pp. 277-290. Academic Press, New York.

Dragoo, Don W.
    1973   Wells Creek—an Early Man site in Stewart County, Tennessee. *Archaeology of Eastern North America* 1:1-56.

Dunnell, Robert C.
    1972   The prehistory of Fishtrap, Kentucky. *Yale University, Publications in Anthropology* 75.

    1979   Trends in current Americanist archaeology. *American Journal of Archaeology* 83:437-449.

Egloff, Brian J.
    1967   *An analysis of ceramics from Cherokee towns.* Master's thesis, Department of Anthropology, University of North Carolina, Chapel Hill.

Egloff, Keith T.
    1971   *Methods and problems of mound exploration in the Southern Appalachian area.* Master's thesis, Department of Anthropology, University of North Carolina, Chapel Hill.

Evans, Clifford
    1955   A ceramic study of Virginia archaeology. *Bureau of American Ethnology Bulletin* 160. Smithsonian Institution.

Fairbanks, Charles H.
    1942   The taxonomic position of Stalling's Island, Georgia. *American Antiquity* 7(3):223-231.

Faulkner, Charles H.
    1977   The winter house: an early southeast tradition. *Midcontinental Journal of Archaeology* 2:141-159.

1978   Origin and evolution of the Cherokee winter house. *Journal of Cherokee Studies* 3:87-93.

Faulkner, Charles H., and Major C. R. McCollough
1977   Fourth report of the Normandy Archaeological project: 1973 excavations on the Hicks I (40CF62), Eoff I (40CF32) and Eoff III (40CF107) sites. *Department of Anthropology, University of Tennessee, Report of Investigations* 19.

Feest, Christian F.
1978   North Carolina Algonquians. In *Handbook of North American Indians*, Vol. 15 (Northeast), edited by B. G. Trigger, pp. 271-281. Smithsonian Institution.

Fenneman, Nevin M.
1938   *Physiography of the Eastern United States.* New York: McGraw Hill.

Ferguson, Leland G.
1971   *South Appalachian Mississippian.* Ph.D. diss., Department of Anthropology, University of North Carolina, Chapel Hill.

1974   Prehistoric mica mines in the southern Appalachian. *South Carolina Antiquities* 6:1-7.

Fitting, James E.
1978   Regional cultural development, 300 B.C. to A.D. 1000. In *Handbook of North American Indians*, Vol. 15 (Northeast), edited by B. G. Trigger, pp. 44-57. Smithsonian Institution.

Flannery, Kent V.
1968   Archeological systems theory and early Mesoamerica. In *Anthropological archeology in the Americas*, edited by B. J. Meggers, pp. 67-87. The Anthropological Society of Washington, Washington, D.C.

Foss, Robert W.
1977   *Man and mountain: an archaeological overview of the Shenandoah National Park.* Master's thesis, Department of Anthropology, University of Virginia.

1980   Geographic variation in prehistoric settlement of the Blue Ridge. Paper presented at the 10th Middle Atlantic Archaeological Conference, Dover, Delaware.

Funk, Robert E.
1978   Post-Pleistocene adaptations. In *Handbook of North American Indians*, Vol. 15 (Northeast), edited by B. G. Trigger, pp. 16-27. Smithsonian Institution.

Gardner, William M.
1974   (editor) *The Flint Run Paleo-Indian complex: a preliminary report, 1971-73 seasons.* Archeology Laboratory, Department of Anthropology, The Catholic University of America, Washington, D.C. *Occasional Publication*, No. 1.

1979   Paleo-Indian settlement patterns and site distribution in the Middle Atlantic. Ms. on file, Department of Anthropology, Catholic University.

Gardner, William M., and R. A. Verrey
1979   Typology and chronology of fluted points from the Flint Run area. *Pennsylvania Archaeologist* 19(1):13-46.

Garrow, Patrick H.
1978   Archaeological, botanical, and wildlife survey: proposed greater Washington 201 facilities plan, Washington, North Carolina. Ms. on file, Soil Systems, Inc., Atlanta.

Garrow, Patrick H., and G. M. Watson
1978   A cultural resource investigation of the Mattamuskeet National Wildlife Refuge, Hyde County, North Carolina. Ms. on file, Soil Systems, Inc., Atlanta.

Gearing, Fred O.
1962   Priests and warriors: social structures for Cherokee politics in the eighteenth century. *American Anthropological Association, Memoir*, 93.

References

Goad, Sharon I.
  1976 Copper and the Southeastern Indians. *Early Georgia* 4:48-67.

Goddard, Ives
  1978 Eastern Algonquian languages. In *Handbook of North American Indians*, Vol. 15 (Northeast), edited by B. G. Trigger, pp. 70-79. Smithsonian Institution.

Goodyear, Albert C.
  1974 The Brand site: a techno-functional study of a Dalton site in northeast Arkansas. *Arkansas Archaeological Survey Research Series* 7.

Goodyear, Albert C., L. M. Raab, and T. C. Klinger
  1978 The status of archaeological research design in cultural resource management. *American Antiquity* 43(2):159-173.

Graham, Russell W.
  1980 Final report on paleontological and archaeological excavations and surface surveys at Mastodon State Park—1980. Ms. on file, Illinois State Museum, Springfield.

Griffin, James B.
  1952 (editor) *Archaeology of eastern United States*. University of Chicago Press, Chicago.

  1967 Eastern North American archaeology: a summary. *Science* 156:175-191.

Haag, William G.
  1958 The archeology of Coastal North Carolina. *Louisiana State University Coastal Studies Series* 2.

Hall, Dolores A.
  1979 Previous archaeological research and prehistory. In North Carolina statewide archaeological survey: an introduction and application to three highway projects in Hertford, Wilkes, and Ashe counties, assembled by M. A. Mathis, pp. 65-70. *North Carolina Archaeological Publication* 11.

Hamel, Paul B., and M. U. Chiltoskey
  1975 *Cherokee plants and their uses: a 400 year history*. Herald Publishing Company, Sylva, North Carolina.

Hargrove, Thomas H. (compiler)
  1980 A guide to research papers in the archaeology of North Carolina on file with the Archaeology Branch of the North Carolina Division of Archives and History. *North Carolina Archaeological Council Publication* 13.

  1981 Addendum I: a guide to research papers in the archaeology of North Carolina on file with the Archaeology Branch of the North Carolina Division of Archives and History. *North Carolina Archaeological Council Publication* 14.

Harrington, J. C.
  1962 Search for the cittie of Raleigh. *National Park Service Archaeological Research Series* 6.

Harrington, M. R.
  1922 Cherokee and earlier remains on upper Tennessee River. *Indian Notes and Monographs*.

Hatch, James W.
  1975 Social dimensions of Dallas burials. *Southeastern Archaeological Conference, Bulletin* 18:132-138.

Haynes, Gary
  1976 Review of (Keel) *Cherokee archaeology a study of the Appalachian Summit*. *Archeological Society of Virginia, Quarterly Bulletin* 31:99-100.

Heye, G. G., F. W. Hodge, and G. H. Pepper
  1918 The Nacoochee mound in Georgia. *Contributions from the Heye Museum of the American Indian, Heye Foundation* 2(1).

References

Hoffman, Michael A., and R. W. Foss
  1980 Blue Ridge prehistory: a general perspective. *Archaeological Society of Virginia, Quarterly Bulletin* 34:185-210.

Hoffman, Michael A., R. W. Foss, J. Van Atta, and R. W. Vernon
  1979 Patterns in time: human adaptations to the Blue Ridge from 7000 B.C. to 1930 A.D. Report to the United States National Park Service, Philadelphia.

Holden, Patricia P.
  1966 *An archaeological survey of Transylvania County, North Carolina.* Master's thesis, Department of Anthropology, University of North Carolina, Chapel Hill.

Holland, C. G.
  1970 An archaeological survey of southwest Virginia. *Smithsonian Contributions to Anthropology* 12. Smithsonian Institution Press, Washington, D.C.

Holland, C. G., S. E. Pennell, and R. O. Allen
  1981 Geographical distribution of soapstone artifacts from twenty-one aboriginal quarries in the eastern United States. *Quarterly Bulletin, Archeological Society of Virginia* 35:200-208.

Holmes, J. A.
  1883 Indian mounds of the Cape Fear. Reprinted in *Southern Indian Studies* 18.

Holmes, William D.
  1903 Aboriginal pottery of the eastern United States. *Bureau of American Ethnology, Smithsonian Institution, Twentieth Annual Report, 1898-99*, pp. 1-237.

Houck, D. F.
  1956 *Floodplain flora of the Deep River triassic basin.* Master's thesis, Botany Department, University of North Carolina, Chapel Hill.

House, John H., and D. L. Ballenger
  1976 An archeological survey of the Interstate 77 Route in the South Carolina Piedmont. *Institute of Archeology and Anthropology, University of South Carolina, Research Manuscript Series* 104.

House, John H., and M. B. Schiffer
  1975 Significance of the archeological resources of the Cache River basin. In the Cache River Archeological Project: an experiment in contract archeology, assembled by M. B. Schiffer and J. H. House. *Arkansas Archeological Survey Research Series* 8:163-186.

House, John H., and R. Wogaman
  1978 Windy Ridge: a prehistoric site in the inter-riverine Piedmont in South Carolina. *Institute of Archeology and Anthropology, the University of South Carolina, Anthropological Studies* 3.

Hudson, Charles
  1976 *The Southeastern Indians.* University of Tennessee Press: Knoxville.

Jefferies, Richard W.
  1976 The Tunacunnhee site: evidence of Hopewell interaction in northwest Georgia. *Anthropological Papers of the University of Georgia* 1.

Johnson, Guy B.
  1934 A report of the Asheville meeting. *Bulletin of the Archaeological Society of North Carolina* 1.

Keel, Bennie C.
  1970 Excavation at the Red Springs Mound RB4, Robeson County. *Southern Indian Studies* 22:17-22.

  1972 *Woodland phases of the Appalachian Summit area.* Ph.D. diss., Washington State University.

References

    1976   *Cherokee archaeology: a study of the Appalachian Summit.* University of Tennessee Press, Knoxville.

Kellar, James H., A. R. Kelly, and E. V. McMichael
    1962   The Mandeville site in southwestern Georgia. *American Antiquity* 27:336-355.

King, Philip B.
    1968   Geology of the Great Smoky Mountains Park, Tennessee and North Carolina. *U. S. Geological Survey, Professional Paper* 587.

King, Tom
    1976   Archeological property nominations. *11593* 1:7-9.

Kluckhohn, Clyde
    1940   Conceptual structure in Middle American studies. In *The Maya and their neighbors*, edited by C. L. Hay, et. al., pp. 41-51. D. Appleton-Century: New York. (Reprinted by the University of Utah Press.)

Kneberg, Madeline D.
    1956   Some important projectile point types found in the Tennessee area. *Tennessee Archaeologist* 12:17-28.

Kroeber, A. L.
    1939   Cultural and natural areas of native North America. *University of California Publications in American Archaeology and Ethnology* 38.

Larson, Lewis H., Jr.
    1971   Archaeological implications of social stratification at the Etowah site, Georgia. In Approaches to the social dimensions of mortuary practices, edited by James A Brown. *Society for American Archaeology, Memoirs*, No. 25:38-67.

Lawson, John
    1967   *A new voyage to Carolina*, edited by Hugh Lefler. University of North Carolina Press, Chapel Hill.

Lee, William D.
    1955   The soils of North Carolina: their formation, identification, and use. *North Carolina Agricultural Experiment Station Technical Bulletin* 115, Raleigh.

Leighty, W. J., S. O. Perkins, C. W. Croom, and W. A. Davis
    1958   *Soil survey of Watauga County, North Carolina.* U. S. Department of Agriculture, Soil Conservation Service, Washington, D.C.

Lewarch, Dennis E., and M. J. O'Brien
    1981   The expanding role of surface assemblages in archaeological research. In *Advances in archaeological method and theory*, edited by M. B. Schiffer, 4:297-342. Academic Press, New York.

Lewis, Thomas M. N., and M. K. Lewis
    1961   *Eva, an Archaic site.* University of Tennessee Press, Knoxville.

Linzey, Alicia U., and D. W. Linzey
    1971   *Mammals of the Great Smoky Mountains National Park.* University of Tennessee Press, Knoxville.

Loftfield, Thomas C.
    1976   A briefe and true report . . . : an archaeological interpretation of the southern North Carolina Coast. Ph.D. diss., Department of Anthropology, University of North Carolina, Chapel Hill.

    1979a A prehistoric archaeological study of the X-3 highway corridor between Wilmington and Benson, North Carolina. Report on file, Coastal Zone Resources Division, Ocean Data Systems, Inc., Wilmington.

    1979b Excavations at 31On33, a late Woodland seasonal village. Ms. on file, University of North Carolina, Wilmington.

Lorant, Stefan
  1965   *The New World.* Duell, Sloan and Pearce, New York.

Loucks, L. Jill
  1981   On the New River: ups and downs of archaeology in the mountains. Paper presented at the 38th Southeastern Archaeological Conference, Asheville, North Carolina.

  1982   The fact or fiction of prehistoric and historic highland adaptation in the New River Valley, North Carolina. In Collected papers on the archaeology of North Carolina, ed. by J. B. Mountjoy, pp. 1-27. *North Carolina Archaeological Council Publication* 19.

Lynott, Mark J.
  1980   The dynamics of significance: an example from Central Texas. *American Antiquity* 45(1):117-120.

MacCord, Howard A., Jr.
  1966   The McLean Mound, Cumberland County, North Carolina. *Southern Indian Studies* 18:3-45.

Manson, Carl
  1948   Marcey Creek site: an early manifestation in the Potomac Valley. *American Antiquity* 13(3):223-227.

Mathis, Mark A.
  1979   (assembler) North Carolina statewide archaeological survey: an introduction and application to three highway projects in Hertford, Wilkes, and Ashe counties. *North Carolina Archaeological Council Publication* 11.

  1981   Investigations in the New River Valley of northwestern North Carolina: preliminary observations. Paper presented at the 38th Southeastern Archaeological Conference, Asheville, North Carolina.

McCollough, Major C. R.
  1973   Supplemental chronology for the Higgs site (40LO45), with an assessment of Terminal Archaic living and structure floors. *Tennessee Archaeologist* 29:63-68.

McCollough, Major C. R., and C. H. Faulkner
  1973   Excavation of the Higgs and Doughty sites, I-75 salvage archaeology. *Tennessee Archaeological Society, Miscellaneous Paper* 12.

McCormick, Olin F. III
  1970   *Archaeological resources of the New Hope reservoir area, North Carolina.* Master's thesis, Department of Anthropology, University of North Carolina, Chapel Hill.

McNett, Charles W., Jr., S. B. Marshall, and E. E. McDowell
  1975   Second season of the Upper Delaware Valley Early Man Project. Report prepared for the National Geographic Society and National Science Foundation, Department of Anthropology, The American University, Washington, D.C.

Michalek, Daniel D.
  1969   *Fan-like features and related periglacial phenomena of the southern Blue Ridge.* Ph.D. diss., Department of Geology, University of North Carolina, Chapel Hill. University microfilms.

Mook, Maurice A.
  1944   Algonkian ethnohistory of the Carolina Sound. *Journal of the Washington Academy of Sciences* 34(6-7).

Moore, David G.
  1980   The Brunk site—an upland Pisgah site. *Southeastern Archaeological Conference Bulletin* 23:9-10.

References

Moratto, Michael J., and R. E. Kelly
    1978   Optimizing strategies for evaluating archaeological significance. In *Advances in archaeological method and theory*, edited by M. B. Schiffer. Academic Press, New York.

Newkirk, Judith A.
    1978   *The Parker site: a Woodland site in Davidson County, North Carolina*. Master's thesis, Department of Anthropology, Wake Forest University.

    1979   An archaeological and historic site survey of Chatham County and Poplar Point Recreation Areas and Crosswinds Boat Ramp and Access Road, B. Everett Jordan Dam and Lake, North Carolina. Ms. on file, Commonwealth Associates Inc., Jackson, Michigan.

North Carolina Division of Archives and History
    1978   *Environmental assessments of historical and archaeological resources*. Archaeology and Historic Preservation Section, Raleigh.

Oaks, Robert Q., and N. K. Coch
    1963   Pleistocene sea levels, southeastern Virginia. *Science* 140:979-983.

Oliver, Billy L.
    1980   The Piedmont Archaic: reflections and perspectives. Paper presented at the 37th annual Southeastern Archaeological Conference, New Orleans.

    1981a   The point, the pendulum, and perception: extracting meaning from the cold stones of reality. Paper presented at the 38th annual meeting of the Southeastern Archaeological Conference, Asheville, North Carolina.

    1981b   *The Piedmont Tradition: refinement of the Savannah River Stemmed point type*. Master's thesis, Department of Anthropology, University of North Carolina, Chapel Hill.

Painter, Floyd
    1977   The Currituck site, Currituck County, North Carolina. *Eastern States Archaeological Federation Bulletin* 35-36:19.

Paschal, Herbert R.
    1953   *The Tuscarora Indians in North Carolina*. Master's thesis, Department of History, University of North Carolina, Chapel Hill.

Peabody, Charles
    1910   The exploration of mounds in North Carolina. *American Anthropologist* 7(3):425-433.

Peele, W. J.
    1907   The proposed Raleigh memorial institute. *Publications of the North Carolina Historical Commission* 1:283-291.

Perkins, S. O., and W. Gettys
    1947   *Soil Survey of Swain County, North Carolina*. U. S. Department of Agriculture, Washington, D.C.

Perkinson, Phil H.
    1971   North Carolina fluted projectile points—survey report number one. *Southern Indian Studies* 23:3-40.

    1973   North Carolina fluted projectile points—survey report number two. *Southern Indian Studies* 25:3-60.

Perry, Myra J.
    1974   *Food use of "wild" plants by Cherokee Indians*. Master's thesis, Department of Home Economics, University of Tennessee.

Peterson, Nicolas
    1976   The natural and cultural areas of aboriginal Australia. In Tribes and boundaries in Australia, edited by Nicolas Peterson. *Australian Institute of Aboriginal Studies, Social Anthropology Series* 10.

Phelps, Davis S.
  1964   *The final phases of the Eastern Archaic.* Ph.D. diss., Department of Anthropology, Tulane University.

  1968   Thom's Creek ceramics in the Central Savannah River locality. *Florida Anthropologist* 21(1):17-30.

  1974   (editor) Anthropological bibliography of North Carolina. *North Carolina Archaeological Council Publication* 1.

  1975a Test excavations at the Parker Site (31Ed29) at Speed, Edgecombe County, North Carolina. In Archaeological surveys of four watersheds in the North Carolina Coastal Plain, pp. 57-105. *North Carolina Archaeological Council Publication* 16 (1981).

  1975b Archaeological survey of the Stoney Creek watershed, Wayne County, North Carolina. In Archaeological surveys of four watersheds in the North Carolina Coastal Plain, pp. 106-137. *North Carolina Archaeological Council Publication* 16 (1981).

  1976a Archaeological survey of the Swift Creek Watershed. In An environmental assessment and impact analysis for the Swift Creek watershed, Pitt, Beaufort, and Craven counties, North Carolina. Wm. F. Freeman Associates, High Point, N.C.

  1976b An archaeological survey of the Thoroughfare Swamp basin, Wayne County, North Carolina. Ms. on file, Archaeology Laboratory, East Carolina University.

  1977a Recent archaeological research in Northeastern North Carolina. *Eastern States Archaeological Federation Bulletin* 35-36:19-20.

  1977b An archaeological-historical study of the proposed waste treatment facility, Greenville, North Carolina. Ms. on file, Archaeology Laboratory, East Carolina University.

  1977c An archaeological survey of the eastern shore of Roanoke Island from Shallowbag Bay to Wanchese Harbor. In Archaeological studies in the Northern Coastal Zone of North Carolina, pp. 49-71. *North Carolina Archaeological Council Publication* 6 (1978).

  1978   Archaeological studies in the Northern Coastal Zone of North Carolina. *North Carolina Archaeological Council Publication* 6.

  1980a Archaeological salvage of the Thorpe Site and other investigations along the U.S. 64 bypass, Rocky Mount, North Carolina. *East Carolina University Archaeological Research Report* 1.

  1980b Carolina Algonkian ossuaries. Paper presented at the 37th annual meeting of the Southeastern Archaeological Conference, New Orleans.

  1981a Prehistoric and historic archaeological survey of Merchants Millpond State Park, Gates County, North Carolina. Ms. on file, Archaeology Laboratory, East Carolina University.

  1981b The archaeology of Colington Island. *East Carolina University Archaeology Research Report* 3.

  1981c Archaeological surveys of four watersheds in the North Carolina Coastal Plain. *North Carolina Archaeological Council Publication* 16.

Piper, Harry M.
  1977   *Prehistoric settlement-subsistence patterns in the Mount Rogers National Recreation Area, Virginia.* Master's thesis, Department of Anthropology, University of South Florida.

Piper, Harry M., and J. G. Piper
  1977   1977 test excavations in the corridor of the proposed scenic highway in the Mount Rogers National Recreation Area, Virginia. Report to the U. S. Department of Agriculture, Forest Service, Jefferson National Forest, Roanoke.

References

Piper, Jacquelyn G.
    1977   An interpretation of Mount Rogers National Recreation Area culture history. Master's thesis, Department of Anthropology, University of South Florida.

Plog, Fred T.
    1974   The study of prehistoric change. Academic Press, New York.

Prufer, Olaf H.
    1964   The Hopewell complex of Ohio. In Hopewellian studies, edited by J. R. Caldwell and R. L. Hall. Illinois State Museum Scientific Papers 12:35-84.

    1968   Ohio Hopewell ceramics—an analysis of extant collections. Museum of Anthropology, University of Michigan, Anthropological Papers 33.

Purrington, Burton L.
    1976   Early man and environments in the southern Appalachians. Paper presented at the 33rd Southeastern Archaeological Conference, Tuscaloosa, Alabama.

    1978a   Archeological investigations at the Slipoff Branch site, a Morrow Mountain culture campsite in Swain County, North Carolina. North Carolina Archaeological Council Publication 15 (1981).

    1978b   Archeology in the rural Appalachian classroom. Paper presented at the first Appalachian Studies Conference, Berea, Kentucky.

    1978c   Prehistoric and modern Appalachia: archeological models and contemporary social policy. Paper presented at the 1978 annual meeting of the Southern Anthropological Society, Lexington, Kentucky.

    1980   An archeological survey of the proposed Yancey County Recreational Park, Yancey County, North Carolina. Ms. on file, Center for Archaeological Research, Southwest Missouri State University, Springfield.

    1981a   The Misery Mountain Survey: an intensive archaeological survey and assessment of archaeological resources in tracts N-647, N-647a, and N-647b, in the proposed Duke Power Company land exchange, Nantahala National Forest, Transylvania County, North Carolina: 1978. Report to the North Carolina Department of Cultural Resources, Raleigh, and the U.S. Forest Service, Asheville, North Carolina.

    1981b   The Cox Exchange Survey: An intensive archaeological survey and assessment of archaeological resources in tracts F-605d, F-605e, and P-66 in the Walter E. Cox land exchange, Pisgah National Forest, Madison and Buncombe counties, North Carolina: 1977. Report to the North Carolina Department of Cultural Resources, Raleigh, and the U.S. Forest Service, Asheville, North Carolina.

    1982   Continuity and change in late prehistoric settlement patterns in an Appalachian North Carolina locality: some preliminary interpretations. Tennessee Anthropologist 7:51-61.

Purrington, Burton L., and M. L. Douthit
    1976   Soils and site distribution in the upper Watauga valley, North Carolina: a preliminary report. Paper presented at the 6th Middle Atlantic Archaeology Conference, Front Royal, Virginia.

    1977   Changing patterns of habitat utilization in a southern Appalachian locality. Paper presented at the 42nd annual meeting of the Society for American Archaeology, New Orleans.

Quinn, David B. (editor)
    1955   The Roanoke voyages, 1584-1590. Hakluyt Society, London.

Raab, L. Mark, and T. C. Klinger
    1977   A critical appraisal of "significance" in contract archeology. American Antiquity 42(4):629-634.

Richmond Dispatch
- 1883　Indian mounds. Lenoir Topic. Specific date unknown; clipping on file with the Research Laboratories of Anthropology, University of North Carolina, Chapel Hill.

Riggs, Stanley, and M. P. O'Connor
- 1975　Evolutionary succession of drowned Coastal Plain-barbuilt estuaries. Paper presented at the annual meeting of the Geological Society of America, Salt Lake City.

Ritchie, William
- 1959　The Stony Brook site and its relation to archaic and transitional cultures on Long Island. *New York State Museum and Science Service Bulletin* 372.

Robertson, Linda B., and B. P. Robertson
- 1978　The New River Survey: a preliminary report. *North Carolina Archaeological Council Publication* 8.

Roper, Donna C.
- 1978　Settlement-subsistence systems in the Truman Reservoir area. Paper presented at the 43rd annual meeting of the Society for American Archaeology, Tucson.
- 1979a　The method and theory of site catchment analysis: a review. In *Advances in Archaeological Method and Theory* (Vol. 2), edited by M. B. Schiffer, pp. 120-136. Academic Press, New York.
- 1979b　The Woodland period in the Ozarks: the concept, its history, and its place in prehistory. Paper presented at the 37th Plains Conference, University of Tennessee Press, Knoxville.

Runquist, Jeanette
- 1979　Analysis of the flora and faunal remains from proto-historic North Carolina Cherokee Indian sites. Ph.D. diss., Department of Zoology, North Carolina State University, Raleigh.

Sabol, John G., Jr.
- 1978　Trade and development of local status and rank in Dallas society. *Tennessee Anthropologist* 3:14-30.

Salmon, Merrilee H.
- 1976　"Deductive" versus "inductive" archaeology. *American Antiquity* 41(3):376-380.

Schiffer, Michael B.
- 1976　*Behavioral archaeology*. Academic Press, New York.

Schiffer, Michael B., and George J. Gumerman (editors)
- 1977　*Conservation archaeology: a guide for cultural resource management studies*. Academic Press, New York.

Schiffer, Michael B., and John H. House
- 1977　An approach to assessing site significance. In *Conservation archaeology: a guide for cultural resource management studies*, edited by M. B. Schiffer and G. J. Gumerman, pp. 249-257. Academic Press, New York.

Schmits, Larry J.
- 1978　The Coffey site: environment and cultural adaptation at a prairie Plains Archaic site. *Midcontinental Journal of Archaeology* 3:69-195.

Sears, William H.
- 1954　A Late Archaic horizon on the Atlantic Coastal Plain. *Southern Indian Studies* 6:28-36.

Sears, William H., and J. B. Griffin
- 1950　Fiber-tempered pottery of the Southeast. In *Prehistoric pottery of the eastern United States*. Museum of Anthropology, University of Michigan.

References

Setzler, Frank M., and Jesse D. Jennings
    1941   Peachtree mound and village site, Cherokee County, North Carolina. *Bureau of American Ethnology, Smithsonian Institution, Bulletin* 131.

Sharpe, Bill
    1954   *A new geography of North Carolina*. Raleigh: Sharpe Publishing Co.

Sharrock, Floyd W., and Donald K. Grayson
    1979   "Significance" in contract archaeology. *American Antiquity* 44(2):327-328.

Shelford, Victor
    1963   *The ecology of North America*. University of Illinois Press, Urbana.

Smith, Gerald P.
    1971   *Protohistoric sociopolitical organization of the Nottoway in the Chesapeake Bay-Carolina Sounds region*. Ph.D. diss., Department of Anthropology, University of Missouri.

Snow, Dean R.
    1978   Late prehistory of the East Coast. In *Handbook of North American Indians*, Vol. 15 (Northeast), edited by B. G. Trigger, pp. 357-361. Smithsonian Institution.

South, Stanley
    1966   Exploratory excavation of the McFayden Mound, Brunswick County, N.C. *Southern Indian Studies* 18:59-61.

    1976   An archaeological survey of southeastern North Carolina. *University of South Carolina Institute of Archaeology and Anthropology Notebook* 8.

South, Stanley, and R. J. Widmer
    1976   Archeological sampling survey at Fort Johnson, South Carolina. *University of South Carolina Institute of Archaeology and Anthropology Notebook* 93.

Speck, Frank
    1916   Remnants of the Machapunga Indians in North Carolina. *American Anthropologist* 18(2):271-272.

Stephenson, Robert L., and A. L. Ferguson
    1963   The Accokeek Creek site: a Middle Atlantic seaboard culture sequence. *Museum of Anthropology, University of Michigan Anthropological Papers* 20.

Stoltman, James B.
    1966   New radiocarbon dates for Southeastern fiber-tempered pottery. *American Antiquity* 31(6):872-874.

Stuckey, J. L.
    1965   *North Carolina: its geology and mineral resources*. North Carolina Department of Conservation and Development, Raleigh.

Stupka, Arthur
    1964   *Trees, shrubs and woody vines of Great Smoky Mountains National Park*. U.S. Dept. of the Interior.

Swanton, John R.
    1946   The Indians of the southeastern United States. *Bureau of American Ethnology Bulletin* 137.

    1952   The Indian Tribes of North America. *Bureau of American Ethnology Bulletin* 145.

Talmage, Valerie, and O. Chesler
    1977   *The importance of small, surface, and disturbed sites as sources of significant archaeological data*. Office of Archeology and Historic Preservation, National Park Service, Washington, D.C.

Tant, Phillip L., H. J. Byrd, and R. E. Horton
    1974   *General soil map of North Carolina*. Soil Conservation Service, Raleigh.

Thomas, Cyrus
  1883 Personal communication to John P. Rogan, March 23, 1883. Letter on file with the Research Laboratories of Anthropology, University of North Carolina at Chapel Hill.
  1887 Work in mound exploration of the Bureau of American Ethnology. *Bureau of American Ethnology, Smithsonian Institution, Bulletin* 4.
  1890 The Cherokees in Pre-Columbian times, part II. *Science* XV(382).
  1891 Catalogue of prehistoric works east of the Rocky Mountains. *Bureau of American Ethnology, Smithsonian Institution, Bulletin* 12.
  1894 Report on the mound explorations of the Bureau of American Ethnology. *Bureau of American Ethnology, Smithsonian Institution, 12th Annual Report.*

Thomas, David Hurst
  1978 The awful truth about statistics in archeology. *American Antiquity* 43(2):231-244.
  1979 *Archaeology.* Holt, Rinehart and Winston, New York.

Thornbury, William D.
  1965 *Regional geomorphology of the United States.* Wiley, New York.

Trimble, Stanley W.
  1974 *Man-induced soil erosion on the southern Piedmont 1700-1970.* Soil Conservation Society of America. Ankeny, Iowa.

Trigger, Bruce G. (editor)
  1978 *Handbook of North American Indians,* Vol. 15 (Northeast). Smithsonian Institution.

Trinkley, Michael
  1977 Science with a small s. *Southeastern Archaeological Conference Newsletter* 19:7-10.
  1980a A typology of Thom's Creek pottery for the South Carolina coast. *South Carolina Antiquities* 12(1):1-35.
  1980b Survey methodology: perspective from the Carolina Piedmont. *Southeastern Archaeological Conference Bulletin* 22:139-141.

Tuck, James A.
  1974 Early Archaic horizons in eastern North America. *Archaeology of Eastern North America* 2:72.80.
  1978 Regional cultural development, 3000-300 B.C. In *Handbook of North American Indians,* Vol. 15 (Northeast), edited by B. G. Trigger, pp. 28-43. Smithsonian Institution.

Ubelaker, Douglas H.
  1974 Reconstruction of demographic profiles from ossuary skeletal samples. *Smithsonian Contributions to Anthropology* 18.

University of North Carolina Archaeological Consortium
  1980a Late Woodland Coastal ceramics. *UNCAC Newsletter* 1(2):3-5.
  1980b A correlation of Coastal Plain ceramics. *UNCAC Newsletter* 1(3).

Valentine, Mann S.
  1883 Manuscript X-1, pp. 1-11. Ms. on file with the Research laboratories of Anthropology, University of North Carolina at Chapel Hill.

Ward, H. Trawick
  1980a *The spatial analysis of the plow zone artifact distributions from two village sites in North Carolina.* Ph.D. diss., Department of Anthropology, University of North Carolina, Chapel Hill.

1980b Trend surfaces and the delineation of disturbed and *in situ* site structure: two examples from North Carolina. *Southeastern Archaeological Conference Bulletin* 23:4-8.

Ware, Donna M.
1973 Floristic survey of the Thompson River watershed. *Castanea* 38:349-378.

Watanabe, Hitoshi
1972 The Ainu. In *Hunters and gatherers today*, edited by M. G. Bicchieri, pp. 448-484. Holt, Rinehart and Winston, New York.

Watson, Patty Jo, S. A. LeBlanc, and C. Redman
1971 *Explanation in archeology: an explicitly scientific approach*. Columbia University Press: New York.

Webb, William S.
1942 The C and O mounds at Plaintsville, sites Jo-2 and Jo-9, Johnson County, Kentucky. *University of Kentucky Reports in Anthropology* 5(4).

Webb, W. S., and D. L. DeJarnette
1942 An archaeological survey of the Pickwick basin in the adjacent portions of the states of Alabama, Mississippi, and Tennessee. *Smithsonian Institution, Bureau of American Ethnology Bulletin* 129.

Weichman, Michael S.
n.d. Drainage basins as archaeological research units. Ms. on file, Historic Preservation Program, Missouri Department of Natural Resources, Jefferson City, Missouri.

White, Max E.
1972 The Evans Gap site: a Late Archaic site in Jackson County, North Carolina. Paper presented at the 29th annual Southeastern Archaeological Conference, Macon, Georgia.

1976 Exo-zone adaptations and utilizations in the southern Appalachians: the ethnohistoric and prehistoric evidence. Paper presented at the 1976 annual meeting of the Southern Anthropological Society, Atlanta.

Whitehead, Donald R.
1972 Developmental and environmental history of the Dismal Swamp. *Ecological Monographs* 42:301-315.

1973 Late-Wisconsin vegetational changes in unglaciated eastern North America. *Quaternary Research* 3:621-631.

Whittaker, R. H.
1956 Vegetation of the Great Smoky Mountains. *Ecological Monographs* 26:1-80.

Whitten, Dorothea, and N. E. Whitten, Jr.
1978 Ceramics of the Canelos Quichua. *Natural History* 87:90-99.

Wilde-Ramsing, Mark
1978 A report on the New Hanover Archaeological Survey: a CETA project. Ms. on file, Archaeology Branch, North Carolina Division of Archives and History.

Wilkins, Gary R.
1978 Prehistoric mountaintop occupations of southern West Virginia. *Archaeology of Eastern North America* 6:13-40.

Willey, Gordon R.
1966 *An introduction to American archaeology*, Vol. 1 (North and Middle America). Prentice-Hall, Inc., Englewood Cliffs.

Willey, Gordon R., and P. Phillips
1962 *Method and theory in American archaeology*. University of Chicago Press (Phoenix edition), Chicago.

Willey, Grodon R., and J. A. Sabloff
  1974 *A history of American archaeology*. W. H. Freeman and Company, San Francisco.

Williams, Stephen
  1965 (editor) The Paleo-Indian era: Proceedings of the 20th Southeastern Archaeological Conference. *Southeastern Archaeological Conference Bulletin* 2.
  1968 The Waring papers. *Papers of the Peabody Museum of Archaeology and Ethnology* 8.

Williams, Talcott
  1896 The surroundings and site of Raleigh's colony. *Annual Report of the American Historical Association*, pp. 47-61. Washington, D.C.

Wilson, Jack H.
  1977 Feature fill, plant utilization, and disposal among the historic Sara Indians. Master's thesis, Department of Anthropology, University of North Carolina, Chapel Hill.
  1976 Final report: 1974 excavations within the New Hope reservoir. Ms. on file, Research Laboratories of Anthropology, University of North Carolina, Chapel Hill.

Wing, Elizabeth S.
  1976 Faunal remains from the Warren Wilson site. In *Cherokee prehistory: the Pisgah phase in the Appalachian Summit region*, by Roy S. Dickens, Jr., pp. 224-229. University of Tennessee Press, Knoxville.

Wissler, Clark
  1935 The value of archaeology to the advancement of mankind. *Bulletin of the Archaeological Society of Brevard College* 1:13.

Witthoft, John
  1977 Cherokee Indian use of potherbs. *Journal of Cherokee Studies* 2(3):250-255.

Woodall, J. Ned
  1976 An archeological reconnaissance of the Great Alamance Creek water supply project region. *Museum of Man, Wake Forest University, Publications in Archeology* 4.
  1979 Archeological investigations in the Great Alamance Creek water supply project area: phase II test excavations and site evaluation. Ms. on file, Archeology Laboratories, Museum of Man, Wake Forest University.
  1981 Survey methodology: a different perspective from the Carolina Piedmont. *Southeastern Archaeological Conference Newsletter* 23:6-9.

Wormington, H. M.
  1957 *Ancient man in North America*. Denver Museum of Natural History, Denver.

Yarnell, Richard A.
  1976a Early plant husbandry in eastern North America. In *Cultural change and continuity*, edited by Charles E. Cleland, pp. 265-273. Academic Press, New York.
  1976b Plant remains from the Warren Wilson site. In *Cherokee prehistory: the Pisgah phase in the Appalachian Summit region*, by Roy S. Dickens, Jr., pp. 217-224. University of Tennessee Press, Knoxville.

Zawacki, April A., and G. Hausfater
  1969 Early vegetation of the lower Illinois Valley. *Illinois State Museum, Reports of Investigations* 17.

INDEX

A

Adena culture, 135, 137
Adena-Hopewell culture. *See* Adena culture
Afro-Americans, 152
Agriculture. *See also* Food and food preparation; Soil and soil types
  in Coastal Plain, 5-6, 20, 32, 35, 40, 46, 50, 173
  in Mountain region, 85, 93, 95, 127, 129, 131, 132, 133, 134, 136, 137, 139, 145, 147, 148, 150, 151, 156, 157, 163
  in other states, 66, 135
  in Piedmont, 55, 56, 65, 69, 72, 73, 74, 76, 77, 78, 79
Alabama, 67
Albemarle Sound, 4, 50
Alder Branch (N.C.), 7
Algonkian-speaking peoples, 8, 9, 10, 15, 16, 17, 22, 36, 37, 39, 40, 43, 46, 48, 49, 50
Algonkian (Carolina) phase, 17
Alleghany County, N.C., 100
Amateur archaeologists, 18, 21, 64, 77. *See also* Pot-hunters
Amazon River, 133
American Antiquity, 167
American Museum of Natural History, 167
Amphibians. *See* Fauna
Animals. *See* Fauna
Anson County, N.C., 54, 70, 72
Anthropology, 83, 102, 154-55, 157, 163
Appalachian Mountains, 59, 83, 84, 89, 90, 99, 130, 131, 137, 138, 141, 142, 144. *See also* Mountain region
Appalachian State University, 100
Appalachian Summit. *See* Mountain region
Archaeological Society of Brevard College, 166
Archaeological Society of North Carolina, 57, 58, 162, 165-67, 169
Archaeology. *See also specific archaeologists, sites, and topics*
  and agriculture, 5
  and anthropology, 102
  and bureaucracy, 60, 85
  and cultural resource management, *see* Cultural resource management
  and environment and environmental impact studies, 2, 6, 11, 12-13, 14, 18, 20, 49, 50, 51, 54, 173
  and history, 1, 8, 9, 11, 36, 85, 86, 102, 152, 153, 155, 170, 171, 173

  categories of significance used in, 152-60
  contract, 6, 173, 175
  funding of research in, 80, 100, 153, 156, 166, 169
  in N.C., *see* North Carolina: archaeology of and archaeological study in
  methodology of and trends in, 1, 2, 6, 7, 8, 9-10, 11-12, 13, 49, 53, 59-60, 71, 72, 77-81, 85-87, 88, 100, 102-3, 152-77
  training in, 43, 49, 153, 175
  types of, 60
Archaeology Branch, North Carolina Division of Archives and History, 14, 86, 100, 108, 161
Archaic period
  and Paleo-Indian period, 22, 25
  ceramics from, 10, 26, 28, 29, 32, 66, 67, 70, 131
  in Coastal Plain, 10, 16, 17, 18, 19, 20, 22-26, 29, 32, 47, 50
  in Mountain region, 10, 105, 110-31, 132, 133, 134, 135, 140, 176
  in other states, 64
  in Piedmont, 10, 61, 62, 65-70, 71, 72, 76, 101, 170
  projectile points from, 21, 23, 30, 66, 70, 109, 121
Arkansas, 13, 110, 153
Armor. *See* Weapons and armor
Art, 8, 26, 42, 138, 139, 140, 144, 163, 164
Ashe County, N.C., 100, 106, 108
Asheville, N.C., 89, 92, 108, 150, 166
Astoria site (31Mt16) (N.C.), 33
Atlantic Ocean, 2, 4, 5, 9, 21, 24, 28, 32, 33, 39, 40, 42, 43, 44, 48, 54, 89, 145
Atlatls. *See* Weapons and armor
Awls. *See* Tools
Axes. *See* Tools
Ayers, Harvard, 100, 103

B

Badin
  ceramics, 31, 61
  projectile points, 62, 77
Baird, S. F., 163
Baker, Charles Michael, 100, 101
Balsam Range, 108
Barlowe, Arthur, 40
Bartram, _____, 144
Baum site (Currituck County village site) (31Ck9) (N.C.), 33, 37, 39, 40, 41, 42
Beaches. *See* Atlantic Ocean

195

Beads, 38, 39, 42, 44, 45, 46, 47, 50, 142, 149, 164
Beaufort County, N.C., 18
Bertie County, N.C., 18, 40, 43
Big Sandy projectile points, 110, 112, 113, 114, 118, 120
Biltmore Forest, 165, 167
Birds. See Fauna
Blue Ridge escarpment, 53, 54, 55, 92
Blue Ridge Mountains and Blue Ridge physiographic province, 83, 84, 89, 100, 101, 111, 151. See also Mountain region
Boats, 25
Bodie Island, 9
Bogs. See Marshes, swamps, and bogs
Bogue Banks, 35, 173
Bogue Inlet, 39
Bone pins, 26, 39, 42, 44, 45
Boreal forests. See Forests
Borrow pits, 74
Botany. See Ethnobotany; Flora
Branchville ceramics, 44
Brevard College, 166
Broad River, 54, 55, 96, 97, 111
Brunk site (N.C.), 111, 147
Brunswick County, N.C., 26
Brunswick Town State Historic Site, N.C., 10
Buffalo. See Fauna
Buggs Island Reservoir, 171
Buncombe County, N.C., 98, 108, 147, 153, 173
Bureau of American Ethnology, Smithsonian Institution, 98, 166
Burial Mound period (Willey), 16
Burials, burial mounds, and cremations
 and artifacts, 41, 42, 46
 and projectile points, 26
 and Willey, 16
 in Coastal Plain, 7-8, 10, 11, 26, 27, 33, 34, 35, 40-43, 44, 46, 47, 49, 51, 173
 in Mountain region, 98, 107, 126, 132, 138, 139, 140, 141, 142, 144, 147-48, 149, 165, 169
 in North America, 7
 in Ohio, 173
 in Piedmont, 67, 74, 77, 78
Bynum Taylor site (N.C.), 126

C

Cache River Project (Ark.), 153
Caldwell, Wallace E., 166
Caldwell County, N.C., 164, 165
Canada, 36
C & O Mounds site (Ky.), 139

Camp Creek
 ceramics, 135, 136-37, 138
 projectile points, 135
Canelos Quichua people, 133
Caney River, 96, 97, 212
Canton, N.C., 89, 174
Cape Fear
 ceramics, 35
 phase, 17, 32, 35, 36, 173
Cape Fear River, 4, 17, 28, 37, 54, 55, 173
Cape Fear Indians, 47
Cape Hatteras National Seashore, 9
Cape Lookout, 4, 39, 48
Caraway
 ceramics, 39, 63
 phase/complex, 57
 projectile points, 62
Carolina Bays, 4
Carolina Slate Belt, 54
Carpenter, Edward, 162
Carteret ceramics, 35
Carteret County, N.C., 18, 39, 42, 48, 49
Cashie
 ceramics, 37, 39, 43-44
 phase, 17, 36, 43, 44, 45, 46, 47, 50
Cashie River, 43
Catawba College, 70
Catawba Indians, 164
Catawba River, 54, 55, 96, 97, 170
Celts. See Tools
Cemeteries. See Burials, burial mounds, and cremations
Ceramics, 7, 9, 10, 11, 16, 24-39 passim, 43-44, 48, 49, 61, 62, 63, 66, 67, 70, 71, 72, 76, 77, 99, 115, 116, 118, 119, 131-44 passim, 147, 148, 150, 158, 173 See also specific ceramic types
Ceremonials. See Religion and ceremonials
Chapman, Jefferson, 69-70
Charles Church rockshelter (N.C.), 143
Charlotte, N.C., 166
Chatahoochee River, 150
Chatham County, N.C., 54, 78
Chatooga River, 96, 97, 150
Cherokee Archaeological Project, 99
Cherokee County, N.C., 98, 108
Cherokee Indians, 15, 59, 83, 84, 88, 93, 99, 102, 144, 147, 148, 149, 150, 152-53, 164, 165, 166, 170-72, 174
Chert. See Stones and minerals
Chesapeake Bay, 48
Chillicothe ceramics, 138
Chowan (N.C.) locality, 26
Chowanoke Indians, 43
Chowan River, 4, 11, 27, 31, 32, 37, 40, 43

Index

Chowan River (Hallowell) site (31Co5) (N.C.), 37, 40, 41, 42
Citico gorgets, 142
Civil Works Administration (CWA), 167, 168
Clarksville projectile points, 39, 44, 62
Clements phase/complex, 32, 63
Cleveland County, N.C., 54
Climate
  of Coastal Plain, 2, 5, 23, 24
  of Mountain region, 89, 92, 93, 94, 95, 96, 108, 109
  of Piedmont, 54, 56
Clovis
  phase
    in Coastal Plain, 17, 18, 19
    in Mountain region, 106
  projectile points, 18, 19, 20, 23, 63, 64, 106, 107, 108
Coastal Plain: physiography, economy, cultures, and archaeology of, 1-51, 53, 90, 97, 98, 173. *See also* Inner Coastal Plain; North Coastal region; South Coastal region; Tidewater region; *and specific sites and topics*
Coast and coastline. *See* Atlantic Ocean; Coastal Plain
Code of Federal Regulations, 85-86
Coe, Joffre
  and Archaeological Society of North Carolina, 165-66
  and ceramics, 173
  and Cherokees, 99, 170-72
  and Connestee site, 98
  and Coastal Plain, 8
  and Doerschuk site, 170
  and Guilford County, 57
  and Hardaway site, 111, 170
  and H. MacCord, 11
  and Mountain region, 8, 83, 87-88, 98, 100, 101, 103, 170
  and N.C. archaeology, 8
  and Piedmont, 8, 10, 22, 57, 58-59, 61, 66, 70, 71, 72, 101, 111, 124, 170
  and projectile points, 23
  article by, 161-77
Colburn, Burnham S., 165, 167
Cole, Faye-Cooper, 166
Colington
  ceramics, 36, 37, 38, 44
  phase, 17, 36, 37, 38, 39, 40, 41, 42, 43, 46, 47, 48, 49, 50
Colington Island, 4, 9, 32, 33, 40
Collins, Susan, 100
Colonization. *See* England; Europe
Computers, 71, 72
Conch shells. *See* Fish and fishing

Coniferous forests. *See* Forests
Connestee
  ceramics, 116, 119, 137, 138, 139, 140, 141, 142, 144
  phase, 104, 136, 137-141, 142, 144
  projectile points, 104, 116, 119, 137, 142
Connestee (Puette) site (31Tr1) (N.C.), 98, 111
Connor, R. D. W., 166
Contact period. *See* England; Europe
Continental Shelf, 21, 90
Contract archaeology, 6, 173, 175
Cooking. *See* Food and food preparation
Copena projectile points, 135, 137
Corn. *See* Agriculture; Food and food preparation
Counties (N.C.), 3, 14, 53. *See also specific counties*
Cove Creek, 91, 146, 147
Coweeta Creek site (N.C.), 88, 111
Craven County, N.C., 18, 49
Cremations. *See* Burials, burial mounds, and cremations
CRM. *See* Cultural resource management
Croatan Sound, 40
Crops. *See* Agriculture; Food and food preparation
Cultigens. *See* Agriculture
Cultivation. *See* Agriculture
Cultural resource management (CRM), 1, 12-13, 14, 49, 59-60, 77, 78, 79, 80, 85, 86, 89, 103, 152, 159, 160, 173
Cultures. *See specific cultures, sites and topics*
Cumberland-Allegheny Plateau, 111
Cumberland County, N.C., 7, 165
Cumberland Plateau, 129
Cumberland projectile points, 18, 108
Currituck County, N.C., 31, 33, 40
Currituck County village site. *See* Baum site
Currituck peninsula, 9
CWA, 167, 168

D

Dallas culture, 147, 148
Dalton-Hardaway. *See* Hardaway-Dalton
Dalton projectile points, 18, 19, 106, 109, 110
Dams, 10
Dan River, 54, 55, 57, 59, 68, 70, 78, 170
Dan River ceramics, 63, 76
Deciduous trees. *See* Forests
Deep Creek
  ceramics, 29, 30, 31, 32, 33
  phase, 17, 18

Deep River, 54, 55, 68
Deer. See Fauna
Demography, 102, 145
Deptford ceramics, 28, 30, 31
DeSoto, Hernando, 167-69
Diet. See Food and food preparation
Diseases and medicines, 93, 152
Dismal Swamp, 5, 21, 35
Doerschuk site (N.C.), 55, 59, 67, 70, 101, 170
Donnaha site (N.C.), 55, 70, 72
Dorwin, John, 100
Drawings. See Art
Duck River, 101
Dunes. See Sand and sand dunes
Duplin County, N.C., 7
Durham County, N.C., 57

E

East Carolina University, 12, 21, 26, 43
Eastern Cherokee Reservation, 152-53
Eastern United States, 15, 18, 63, 64, 68, 89, 92, 98, 101, 102, 107, 109, 151. See also Eastern Woodlands culture
Eastern Woodlands culture, 15, 107, 110, 132, 133, 134. See also Middle Atlantic Subarea; Southeast Subarea
Ecology, 66, 68, 155, 170
Edgecombe County, N.C., 18
Ellison Mountain, 128
Emmert, J. W., 163
England and English exploration-colonization, 7, 8, 9, 20, 40, 46, 56, 57, 152, 170, 173
Eno River, 55, 57
Environmental archaeology, 2, 6, 11, 14, 18, 20, 49, 50, 51, 173
Environments. See specific regions and sites
Erosion, 4, 5, 6, 7, 20, 44, 56, 57, 77, 85, 156, 170
Estuaries. See Atlantic Ocean; and specific estuaries
Ethnobotany, 65, 66, 76
Ethnography, 8, 15, 16, 36, 135, 152, 153
Ethnohistory, 8, 9, 10, 11, 14, 15, 36, 37, 39, 47. See also History
Etowah culture, 147, 148, 150
Europe and European exploration-colonization, 16, 36, 43, 68, 76, 95, 149, 150, 151, 152, 163, 164, 170, 173
Evans Gap site (N.C.), 129
Exploration. See England; Europe

F

Fall line, 3, 5, 23, 37, 43, 55

Families, 40, 46, 47, 124, 132, 133, 134
Farming. See Agriculture
Fauna, 5, 22, 23, 24, 33, 40, 44, 46, 47, 54, 56, 64, 65, 66, 67, 68, 69, 73, 76, 83, 93, 94, 95, 101, 107, 108, 120, 124, 138, 145, 152, 163, 170
Federal government. See United States government
Fish and fishing, 5, 6, 7-8, 33, 36, 38, 39, 40, 44, 45, 46, 47, 50, 67, 68, 95, 107, 129. See also Food and food preparation
Fishtrap locality (Ky.), 129
Flint Ridge (Ohio), 138
Floods and floodplains, 4, 5, 20, 24, 25, 46, 56, 66, 68, 69, 78, 93, 95, 113, 120, 121, 126, 127, 129, 131, 132, 133, 134, 135, 136, 138, 139, 145, 146, 156, 157, 160, 170
Flora, 4, 6, 23, 24, 40, 54, 64, 65, 66, 67, 68, 69, 83, 92, 93, 94, 95, 156, 170
Florida, 48
Flowers. See Flora
Food and food preparation, 5, 22, 23, 24, 25, 26, 32, 33, 36, 40, 44, 46, 47, 48, 50, 53, 56, 61-77 passim, 88, 93, 94-95, 96, 102, 103, 107, 109-10, 113, 120-36 passim, 139, 144-45, 151, 154. See also Agriculture; Fish and fishing
Forests, 4, 5, 20, 22, 23, 40, 44, 47, 56, 63, 66, 68, 83, 85, 92, 93, 94, 109, 145, 148, 150, 156
Fortifications, 43, 46, 144, 146, 148, 149, 150, 153
Fort Raleigh and Fort Raleigh National Historic Site, N.C., 7, 9, 11, 37
Fowl. See Fauna
Franklin, N.C., 173
Freeman site (31Hf19) (N.C.), 32, 35
French Broad River, 96, 97, 108, 111, 113, 136, 147, 148, 150, 151
Frutchey Mound site. See Town Creek site
Fruits. See Flora; Food and food preparation
Funding of archaeological research, 80, 100, 153, 156, 166, 169

G

Game. See Fauna
Garbage, trash, and refuse, 23, 24, 33, 46, 74, 75, 76, 77, 78
Garden Creek Mound No. 2 site (31Hw2) (N.C.), 88, 98, 111, 125, 137, 138, 139, 140, 141, 142, 174
Garden Creek projectile points, 104, 135, 137

Index

Gardens. *See* Agriculture
Gaston ceramics, 44, 63
Gaston County, N.C., 54
Gaston Reservoir (N.C.), 71
Gaston site (N.C.), 23, 29, 59, 67, 70
Gates County, N.C., 18, 43
Gathering. *See* Agriculture; Food and food preparation
Geier, Clarence, 101
Genetics, 6
Geology, 2, 4, 39, 53, 54, 89-92, 153. *See also* Stones and minerals
Georgia, 28, 31, 35, 63, 67, 83, 136, 137, 138, 139, 140, 147, 150
Glacial Kame burials (Ohio), 173
Glaciers and glacial periods, 2, 5, 92, 108, 173
Gloucester site (31Cr14) (N.C.), 37, 40, 42
Gorgets. *See* Weapons and armor
Grain. *See* Agriculture; Food and food preparation
Grandfather Mountain, 129
Grants. *See* Funding of archaeological research
Granville County, N.C., 54
Graves. *See* Burials, burial mounds, and cremations
Great Bend (Yadkin River), 72
Great Smoky Mountains and Great Smoky Mountains National Park, 89, 100, 103, 111, 112, 113, 120, 121, 122, 124, 125, 126, 127, 129, 132, 135, 136, 139, 145, 150, *See also* Mountain region
Greene County, N.C., 26
Greensboro, N.C., 166
Griffin, James B., 18
Guasili (town), 167
Guilford County, N.C., 57
Guilford
  phase/complex
    in Coastal Plain, 17
    in Mountain region, 105, 108, 124-25
    in Piedmont, 61, 66
  projectile points, 23, 62, 77, 105, 108, 114, 118, 124, 125
Gulf of Mexico, 89
Gypsy projectile points, 29, 30, 31, 62

H

Haag, William, 9, 10, 11, 33, 35, 37
Halifax
  phase, 17
  projectile points, 23, 62
Hallowell site. *See* Chowan River site
Hampton Roads, 39
Handbook of the American Indians, 1

Hand site (N.C.), 44
Hanover ceramics, 32, 35
Happy Valley, 164
Hardaway-Dalton
  phase
    in Coastal Plain, 17
    in Mountain region, 106, 109-10
  projectile points, 18, 19, 23, 62, 63
Hardaway
  phase, 17, 64
  projectile points, 18, 19, 23, 62, 63, 64, 65, 109, 110, 114, 118
Hardaway site (N.C.), 19, 23, 55, 59, 61, 63, 64, 101, 170
Harrington, J. C., 9
Harvesting. *See* Agriculture; Food and food preparation
Hatteras Island, 9, 40
Hatteras Island site (31Dr38) (N.C.), 37, 40-42
Haw River, 54, 55, 56, 64, 68
Haywood County, N.C., 98, 138, 162, 163, 170
Haywood projectile points, 104, 137, 142
H-D method, 79, 100
Hempelian logic, 79
Hendersonville, N.C., 89, 150
Hertford County, N.C., 18
Heye, George G., 98. *See also* Museum of the American Indian
Heye Foundation, 165
Hides. *See* Hunting
Higgs site (Tenn.), 131
Highways. *See* Roads
Hillsboro projectile points, 62
Hillsborough, N.C., 56, 57, 171
Hillsborough ceramics, 63
Historic period
  in coastal plain, 17, 25, 173
  in Mountain region, 83, 88, 95, 99, 148, 164
  in Piedmont, 56, 57, 63, 70, 71, 73
  of Cherokees, 99
  of Tuscarora, 9
History. *See also* Ethnohistory; *and specific topics*
  and anthropology, 83
  and archaeology, 1, 8, 9, 11, 36, 85, 86, 102, 152, 153, 155, 170, 171, 173
  and culture, 1, 2, 6, 12, 13, 15, 69, 88, 101, 173
  and Trigger, 15
Hiwassee River, 96, 97, 98, 111, 149, 150
Hodges (John) site (31Wt184) (N.C.), 104
Hoes. *See* Tools
Holmes, J. A., 7, 11
Holmes, William Henry, 165
Holocene epoch, 2, 24

Index

Holston River, 111
Hope Mills, N.C., 7, 165
Hopewellian culture, 18, 138, 139, 141, 142, 173
"Hopewellian Interaction Sphere," 139
Horticulture. See Agriculture; Flora
Houses and structures, 73-74, 80, 144, 148-149, 150, 171, 173, 174
Howard site (N.C.), 111, 130
Hunting. See also Food and food preparation
  by Paleo-Indians, 21, 107
  in Coastal Plain, 33, 40, 43, 46, 47
  in Dismal Swamp, 21
  in Mountain region, 107, 109, 110, 122, 124, 126, 127, 135, 136, 145, 151
  in Piedmont, 64, 65, 66, 67, 68, 69, 72, 73, 76
  in southeastern U.S., 133
Hypothetico-deductive (H-D) method, 79, 100

I

Icehouse Bottom site (Tenn.), 111, 130, 138, 139, 141
Igneous rocks. See Geology
Indians, 56, 98, 162, 163, 164, 165, 166, 176. See also specific tribes and topics
Inhumations. See Burials, burial mounds, and cremations
Inner Coastal Plain: physiography, economy, cultures, and archaeology of, 2, 3, 4-5, 17, 20, 24-25, 32, 33, 36, 37, 43, 46, 48. See also Coastal Plain; and specific sites and topics
Interior Plateau province, 89
Interments. See Burials, burial mounds, and cremations
Interstate 77 project, 101
Iroquoian-speaking peoples, 15, 36, 37, 40, 43, 84. See also Meherrin Indians, Nottoway Indians
Islands, 4, 40

J

Jackson County, N.C., 129
James River, 39, 47
Jennings, Jesse D., 169
Johnson, Guy B., 57
Johnson, Harold T., 98
Jordan Revervoir (N.C.), 64, 70, 73
Jordan's Landing site (31Br7) (N.C.), 37, 43, 44-46, 47
Judd, Neil M., 166, 167

K

Kanawha projectile points, 105, 120
Kentucky, 66, 67, 129, 133, 139, 140
Keowee River, 150
Kessel projectile points, 106, 110, 113, 114, 118
Keyauwee site (N.C.), 55, 57, 58, 169, 170
Kings Mountain range, 54
Kirk
  phase/complex
    in Coastal Plain, 17, 25, 66
    in Mountain region, 106, 110-20
    in Piedmont, 61, 66
  projectile points, 23, 62, 65, 106, 110, 112, 113, 114, 118, 120
Kitty Hawk Bay site (N.C.), 39
Kituwha Mound, 153

L

Lake Gaston, 55
Lamar culture, 150
Lawson, John, 56, 57, 169
LeCroy
  phase, 105, 120-21, 122
  projectile points, 105, 120, 121
Ledbetter projectile points, 105, 125
Lenoir County, N.C., 11, 165
Lewis, T. M. N., 166
Lick Creek gorgets, 142
Lime and limestone. See Stones and minerals
Linguistics, 8, 15, 16, 36, 37, 166
Lithic materials. See Geology; Stones and minerals
Lithosols. See Soil and soil types
Little Tennessee River, 96, 97, 101, 108, 111, 113, 120, 121, 123, 130, 136, 139, 150
Lost Colony, 7, 9
Loucks, L. Jill, 100
Lower Saura Town site (N.C.), 57, 170

M

McComb, R. D., 169
MacCord, Howard, 11
MacCorkle projectile points, 120
MacFayden Mound site (N.C.), 173
Machapunga, 8
McLean Mound (N.C.), 11
Macomb, John, 169
Macon County, N.C., 92, 100, 139, 173
Macon County Industrial Park site (N.C.), 100, 131, 139, 140

Madison County, N.C., 106, 108
Madison projectile points, 104, 148, 150
Maize. *See* Agriculture; Food and food preparation
Mammals. *See* Fauna
Mandeville site (Ga.), 139
Marcey Creek ceramics, 9, 28, 29
Marginella shell beads. *See* beads
Marine sediments. *See* Atlantic Ocean
Marshes. *See* Swamps, marshes, and bogs
Maryland, 32
Masks, 39, 42
Mason site (Tenn.), 142
Mastodons. *See* Fauna
Meadowcraft Rockshelter site (Pa.), 107
Medicine. *See* Diseases and medicines
Meherrin Indians, 11, 17, 36, 37, 43, 44
Meherrin phase, 17
Meherrin River, 43
Middens. *See* Garbage, trash, and refuse
Middle Atlantic Subarea of Eastern Woodlands culture, 3, 15, 16, 26, 28-29, 31, 39, 48. *See also* Eastern Woodlands culture
Miller, Peter, 100
Milling stones. *See* Food and food preparation
Minerals. *See* Geology; Stones and minerals
Misery Mountain site (N.C.), 111, 112
Mississippian period, 104, 133, 134, 147-51
Mississippian Tradition, 16
Mississippi River, 135
Missouri, 66, 107
Mitchell Branch site (N.C.), 110, 111, 112
Mockley ceramics, 32, 36
Mollusks. *See* Fish and fishing; Food and food preparation
Montgomery County, N.C., 54
Mook, Maurice, 8-9
Moorehead, Warren King, 165
Morrow Mountain
  phase/complex
    in Coastal Plain, 17, 25
    in Mountain region, 105, 113, 120, 121, 122-24, 125, 130
    in Piedmont, 61, 66
  projectile points, 23, 62, 105, 114, 118, 122, 123
Mortuaries. *See* Burials, burial mounds, and cremations
"Mound Builders," 7, 98, 162, 163
Mounds, burial. *See* Burials, burial mounds, and cremations
Mountain (Appalachian Summit) region: physiography, economy, cultures, and archaeology of, 3, 4, 8, 15, 22, 50, 83-160, 170, 175-76. *See also specific mountains, mountain ranges, sites, and topics*
Mount Pisgah, 163
Mount Pleasant
  ceramics, 30, 32, 33, 35
  phase, 17, 30, 32, 34
Mount Rogers (Va.), 92, 100, 111, 112
Mount Rogers National Recreation Area (Va.), 100
Murphy, N.C., 89, 167, 168
Museum of the American Indian, 98. *See also* Heye, George G.
Mussels. *See* Fish and fishing; Food and food preparation

N

Nash County, N.C., 18
National Park Service, 9
National Register of Historic Places, 2, 12, 14, 49, 50, 78, 85-86
National Science Foundation, 170, 174
National Youth Administration (NYA), 169, 172
Nelson, N.C., 167
Nelson, T. F., 164
Nelson Circle (N.C.), 164
Nelson Triangle (N.C.), 164
Neuse Reservoir, 70
Neuse River, 4, 9, 11, 16, 25, 26, 27, 28, 31, 35, 37, 39, 43, 54, 55
New Bern, N.C., 39
New Hanover, N.C., 49
New Hope Creek, 57
New River
  ceramics, 31, 32
  phase, 17
New River, 89, 96, 100, 108, 113, 125, 145
New World, 107
New York, 9
Nolichucky River, 96, 97, 111, 112
Norfolk, Va., 39
Normandy Reservoir (Tenn.), 101
North Albemarle (N.C.), locality, 26
North America, 1, 7, 8, 84, 165, 167
North Carolina. *See also specific regions, cities, sites, and topics; and entries immediately following*
  and Piedmont, 54
  archaeology of and archaeological study in, 1, 8, 11-12, 13, 14, 15, 21, 51, 57, 59, 61, 87, 88, 98, 100, 113, 158, 159, 160, 161-77
  counties of, 3, 14, 53
  economic, political, and social divisions of, 54

physiography of, 54
soils in, 46
North Carolina Archaeological Society, 57, 58, 162, 165-67, 169
North Carolina Department of Conservation and Development, 171
North Carolina Division of Archives and History, 12, 14, 86, 87, 100, 170, 172
North Carolina Historical Commission, 171
North Carolina Parks System, 170, 172
North Carolina State Museum, 169, 171
North Central Escarpment, 96, 97
North Coastal region: physiography, economy, cultures, and archaeology of, 3, 5, 9, 11, 15, 16, 17, 26, 28, 29, 31, 32, 33, 36. *See also* Coastal Plain; *and specific sites and topics*
Northeastern culture area (Trigger), 15, 16
Northeastern United States, 15, 18, 19, 25, 28, 56
Northeast Escarpment, 96, 97
"Northern Tradition" (Cadlwell), 29
Nottoway Indians, 11, 36, 37, 43, 44
Nottaway River, 43
Nuts: *See* Food and food preparation; Forests
NYA, 169, 172

O

Oak Island
ceramics, 48, 49
phase, 17, 47-48, 49, 173
Occaneechi site (31Or11) (N.C.), 55, 56, 57, 78, 170
Ochre, 26
Office of Naval Research, 9
Ohio, 139, 140, 173
Ohio River, 10, 89, 135, 138
Onslow County, N.C., 31, 48
Orange County, N.C., 56, 57
Organic soils. *See* Soil and soil types
Osborne, Mr. and Mrs. A.J., 98, 162-63
Ossuaries. *See* Burials, burial mounds, and cremations
Otarre
phase, 104, 130-31
projectile points, 104, 115, 118, 130, 131, 132
Outer Banks, 4, 22, 40
Oysters. *See* Fish and fishing
Ozark Highland, 93, 101

P

Paleo-Indian period
and Archaic period, 22, 25
in Coastal Plain, 16, 17, 18-22, 23, 24, 50
in eastern U.S., 10
in Mountain region, 10, 106, 107-10
in Piedmont, 10, 61, 62, 63-65, 66
projectile points, 18-19, 20, 21, 23, 107, 109
Paleozoic epoch, 54
Palisades. *See* Fortifications
Palmer
phase/complex, 17, 61
projectile points, 19, 21, 23, 62, 63, 65, 106, 110, 111, 112, 113, 114, 118, 120
Pamlico River, 9
Pamlico Sound, 4, 9
Pamlico Terrace, 2
Panther masks, 39, 42
Parker site (N.C.), 29, 70, 72, 73
Peabody, Charles, 7, 11, 165
Peachtree Mound site (N.C.), 98, 111, 167, 168-69
Pee Dee
ceramics, 63
culture, 15
Pee Dee River, 16, 28, 31, 68
Pennsylvania, 107
Phelps, David Sutton, 1, 61, 173, 175
Piedmont: physiography, economy, cultures, and archaeology of, 3, 4, 8, 10, 13, 15, 16, 18, 19, 22, 32, 35, 48, 50, 53-81, 84, 89, 90, 95, 97, 98, 111, 121, 122, 124, 136, 137, 138, 147, 150, 151, 170. *See also specific sites and topics*
Piedmont Plateau province, 89
Pigeon
ceramics, 115, 119, 135, 136, 137, 138, 141, 143, 144, 147
phase, 104, 135-37, 139
projectile points, 104, 115, 119, 135, 137, 145
Pigeon River, 96, 97, 98, 111, 136, 138, 139, 147, 148, 150
Pisgah
ceramics, 116, 119, 143, 144, 147
phase, 99, 104, 138, 142-48, 149, 150, 151
projectile points, 104, 114, 116, 119, 142, 145, 148
Pisgah Fakes, 164, 170
Pitt County, N.C., 18
Plants. *See* Agriculture; Flora; Food and food preparation
Pleistocene epoch, 2, 5, 24, 50, 54, 64, 65, 92, 107
Plott projectile points, 104, 130, 131, 132
Pocosins. *See* Swamps, marshes, and bogs

Index

Political organization and leaders, 39, 42, 43, 51, 54, 64, 139, 140, 141, 145, 147, 148, 150, 151, 155, 158, 164
Pollen cores, 5, 35
Pothunters, 63, 77, 78, 85, 101, 165. *See also* Amateur archaeologists
Pottery. *See* Ceramics
Poverty Point, 135
Pre-Paleo-Indian period, 107
Priests. *See* Religion and ceremonials
Private sector archaeology, 13, 18, 108
Projectile points, 18, 19, 20, 21, 23, 26, 29, 30, 31, 33, 38, 39, 44, 62, 63, 64, 65, 66, 70, 72, 77, 101-37 passim, 142, 145, 148, 149, 150. *See also specific types of projectile points*
Protohistoric period, 10, 11, 16, 37, 114-17, 148, 151
Puette site. *See* Connestee site
Punctuate ceramics, 28
Purrington, Burton L., 83, 100, 101, 103, 173, 175-76

Q

Quad projectile points, 18
Qualla
  ceramics, 148, 150
  phase, 99, 104, 116, 119, 138, 144, 145, 148-51
Quarry sites. *See* Stones and minerals

R

Radiocarbon dating, 10, 16, 18, 29, 32, 33, 35, 39, 44, 48, 61, 63, 64, 126, 142
Raleigh, Sir Walter, 7
Raleigh, N.C., 166
Randolph County, N.C., 54, 57, 169
Rau, Charles, 163
Regional archaeology in N.C., 8, 11-12, 13, 14, 51, 87, 88, 113, 158, 159, 160. *See also specific regions*
Relic collectors. *See* Pothunters
Religion and ceremonials, 39, 42, 44, 46, 93, 140, 141, 144, 147, 149, 150, 152, 164
Reptiles. *See* Fauna
Research Laboratories of Anthropology, University of North Carolina, 63, 70, 73, 78, 88, 98, 174
Reservations, Indian, 43
Richmond, Va., 98, 162, 164, 169
Rich Mountain and Rich Mountain Gap site (N.C.), 127, 128
Ridge and Valley province, 84, 89, 90, 92, 95, 101, 108, 111, 112, 113, 120, 121, 122, 125, 129, 131, 138, 147

Rights, Douglas L., 57, 166
River basin salvage projects, 101
Rivers. *See specific regions and rivers*
Roads, 6, 20, 100, 101
Roanoke
  ceramics, 36
  projectile points, 29, 31, 33, 38, 39, 44
Roanoke Island, 4, 7, 8, 9, 33, 40
Roanoke Rapids (N.C.) reservoir, 10
Ronaoke River, 10, 22, 27, 33, 43, 44, 50, 57, 67, 170
Roberts, Frank H. H., Jr., 167
Robeson County, N.C., 7
"Robeson County Indians," 166
Rockhouse (N.C.), 92
Rocks. *See* Geology; Stones and minerals
Rockshelters. *See* Houses and structures
Rocky River, 55
Rogan, J. P., 164, 165
Rogers, Anne, 100
Rush Point (Colington Island), 32

S

St. Albans projectile points, 105, 120
St. Albans site (W. Va.), 101, 111
Salter Path, 173
Sampson County, N.C., 7
Sand and sand dunes, 2, 4, 5, 7, 22, 35, 37, 40, 44, 173
Sangamon Interglacial sea, 2
Saponi site (N.C.), 57
Saura Indians, 70
Sauratown Mountains, 54
Saura Town sites. *See* Lower Saura Town site; Upper Saura Town site
Savannah River
  phase
    in coastal Plain, 10, 17, 25-26, 29
    in Mountain region, 105, 125-30, 131, 135
    in Piedmont, 61, 66, 70, 71
  projectile points, 23, 26, 29, 62, 70, 105, 115, 118, 125, 126, 129, 130
Savannah River, 16, 23, 29, 31
Scioto Hopewell complex (Ohio), 139
Scarpers. *See* Tools
Sea level. *See* Atlantic Ocean
Shamans. *See* Religion and ceremonials
Shellfish. *See* Fish and fishing
Shell middens. *See* Garbage, trash, and refuse
Shelters. *See* Houses and structures
Shenandoah National Park, 100
Shenandoah Valley, 107
Sherds. *See* Ceramics
Shipyard Landing site (31Br1) (N.C.), 37, 40

Siouan-speaking peoples, 10, 15-16, 37, 47, 48, 49, 57, 73
Skeletons. *See* Burials, burial mounds, and cremations
Slate. *See* Geology; Stones and minerals
Slipoff Branch site (N.C.), 111, 122, 123, 124
Smithsonian Institution, 98, 163, 164, 166, 167
Social life, 6, 25, 32-33, 36, 39, 43, 46, 51, 54, 64, 86, 88, 94, 96, 99, 100, 102, 103, 120-60 passim
Society for American Archaeology, 166
Soil and soil types, 4, 6, 20, 44, 46, 56, 57, 70, 93, 95, 129, 131, 135, 145, 146, 147, 156, 164. *See also* Agriculture
Sounds. *See* Atlantic Ocean; and *specific sounds*
South, Stanley, 10, 11, 173
South Carolina, 10, 15, 16, 26, 28, 35, 83, 101
South Central Escarpment, 96, 97
South Coastal region: physiography, economy, cultures, and archaeology of, 3, 5, 7, 11, 15, 16, 17, 26, 28, 31, 35, 36, 47, 48, 51. *See also* Coastal Plain; *and specific sites and topics*
Southeastern United States, 8, 15, 16, 18, 26, 27, 28, 31, 57, 61, 80, 88, 92, 99, 110-33 passim, 136, 137, 166, 170
Southeast Escarpment, 96, 97, 112, 113
Southeast Subarea of Eastern Woodlands culture, 3, 15, 16, 27. *See also* Eastern Woodlands culture
Southern Appalachian Mountains. *See* Appalachian Mountains
Southern United states, 151
Spain, 167
Stallings
  ceramics, 26, 27, 28, 29, 31
  phase, 17
Stanly
  phase
    in Coastal Plain, 17
    in Mountain region, 105, 121-22, 130
    in Piedmont, 61, 66
  projectile points, 23, 62, 105, 121
Stockades. *See* Fortifications
Stokes County, N.C., 54, 70
Stones and minerals, 6, 20-22, 39, 44, 54, 65, 66, 69, 74, 76, 86, 89-92, 93, 95, 99, 100, 107, 108, 109, 110, 134, 135, 136, 137, 138, 139, 140, 143, 145, 148, 149, 151, 165, *See also* Geology; Projectile points
Stoney Creek ceramics, 29
Storage pits, 74, 75, 76, 77
Streams. *See specific regions and streams*

Structures. *See* Houses and structures
Sturgeon Head ceramics, 44
Susbistence. *See* Agriculture; Food and food preparation; Hunting
Suffolk Scarp, 2
Surry County, N.C., 54
Susquehannah phase, 25
Swain County, N.C., 123, 165
Swamps, marshes, and bogs, 4, 5, 22, 40, 56, 68
Swannanoa
  ceramics, 115, 118, 132, 133, 134, 136, 147
  phase, 104, 113, 125, 130, 131-35, 137
  projectile points, 62, 104, 115, 118, 130, 131, 132
Swannanoa, N.C., 173
Swanton, John R., 8, 83, 166, 167
Swidden agriculture. *See* Agriculture
Swift Creek vessels, 138
Swift Creek watershed, 24
Symposiums, 39, 101

T

Talbot Terrace, 2
Tar River, 4, 20, 26, 27, 29, 37, 46, 47, 54, 55
Tellico Reservoir (Tenn.), 101, 113, 152
Temple Mound period (Willey), 16
Temples. *See* Religion and ceremonials
Tennessee, 63, 64, 66, 67, 83, 92, 100, 101, 107, 111, 112, 113, 125, 129, 130, 131, 135, 136, 138, 139, 140, 141, 142, 147, 152, 166-67
Tennessee River, 89, 98, 110, 170
31An19 site. *See* Trestle site
31Br1 site. *See* Shipyard Landing site
31Br7 site. *See* Jordan's Landing site
31Cb4 site. *See* Turner site
31Ch8 site, 64
31Ch29 site, 64, 73
31Ck9 site. *See* Baum site
31Co5 site. *See* Chowan River site
31Cr14 site. *See* Gloucester site
31Dr35 site. *See* Tillet site
31Dr38 site. *See* Hatteras Island site
31Hf19 site. *See* Freeman site
31Hw2 site. *See* Garden Creek Mound No. 2 site
31Mt16 site. *See* Astoria site
31Ns3 site, 37
31Ns3b site. *See* Thorpe site
31On33 site. *See* Uniflite site
31Or11 site. *See* Occaneechi site.
31Pt3 site, 19-20
31Rk12 site, 78
31Sk1 site. *See* Upper Saura Town site

Index

31Tr1 site. *See* Connestee site
31Wt105 site, 104
31Wt149 site, 106
31Wt175 site. *See* Wakeman 2 site
31Wt184 site. *See* Hodges site
Thomas, Cyrus, 7, 98, 164, 165
Thompson River, 112
Thom's Creek ceramics, 26, 27, 28, 30, 31
Thoroughfare Swamp, 25
Thorpe site (31Ns3b) (N.C.), 29, 32, 44, 46
Thunderbird site (Va.), 19
Tides. *See* Atlantic Ocean
Tidewater region: physiography, economy, cultures, and archaeology of, 2, 3, 4, 5, 9, 17, 24, 32, 33, 36, 39, 48, 84. *See also* Coastal Plain; *and specific sites and topics*
Tillet site (31Dr35) (N.C.), 32, 33, 39
Toe River, 37, 96, 97, 110, 112
Tolley, George, 101
Tools, 21, 23, 26, 33, 38, 39, 44, 46, 54, 57, 63, 65, 66, 67, 72, 73, 93, 110, 111, 112, 122, 124, 125, 126-27, 129, 132, 137, 138, 140, 142, 148
Topography. *See specific regions*
Town Creek site, Town Creek Temple Mound (Frutchey Mound), and Town Creek Indian Mound State Park and State Historic Site (N.C.), 55, 57, 58, 59, 169-70, 171, 172
Townsend ceramics, 36
Townson site (N.C.), 88, 111, 149-50
Toxaway River, 96, 97
Trade, 37, 39, 44, 50, 51, 56, 68, 129, 139, 140, 141, 145, 149, 151
Transylvania County, N.C., 98, 102, 112, 166
Transylvania projectile points, 104, 132
Trash. *See* Garbage, trash, and refuse
Travel, 25, 54, 96
Trees. *See* Forests
Trestle site (31An19) (N.C.), 72
Trigger, Bruce G., 15
Tuckasegee River, 96, 97, 109, 122, 123, 129, 139, 147, 148
Tuckasegee site (N.C.), 88, 111, 125, 141
Tunacunnhee site (Ga.), 139, 140
Turbyfill, Fred, 165
Turner site (31Cb4) (N.C.), 26
Tuscarora Indians, 9, 17, 36, 37, 43, 46, 50
Tuscarora phase, 17
Tuscarora War, 9, 43

U

Uniflite site (31On33) (N.C.), 37, 48

Universities, 8, 11, 13, 14, 49, 60, 87, 161. *See also specific universities*
University of Chicago, 166, 169
University of North Carolina at Chapel Hill, 8, 10, 35, 63, 70, 73, 78, 83, 88, 98, 100, 161, 169, 170, 171, 172, 174
University of North Carolina at Wilmington, 12
University of North Carolina system, 11
University of Tennessee, 166-67
United States, 10, 13, 56, 85, 86. *See also specific regions and states*
United States Army Corps of Engineers, 64
United States Geological Survey, 153
United States government, 12, 85, 86, 87, 100, 160. *See also specific government agencies*
United States National Museum, 166
United States Navy, 9
Upper Saura Town site (31Sk1) (N.C.), 55, 59, 60, 73, 74, 75, 76, 170
Uwharrie
ceramics, 63
phase/complex, 57, 61, 63, 71, 72, 73
projectile points, 62
Uwharrie Mountains, 62

V

Valentine, Mann S., and brother, 162, 163-64, 165, 169
Valentine Museum, 98, 164
Valley province. *See* Ridge and Valley province
Valley River, 96, 97
Vanceboro, N.C., 35
Vandalism. *See* Pothunters
Vegetation. *See* Flora
Vessels. *See* Ceramics
Villages, 35, 40, 42, 43, 44, 46, 51, 70, 73, 78, 144, 145, 147, 150, 169, 173
Vincent ceramics, 61
Vinette ceramics, 29
Virginia, 5, 9, 11, 15, 16, 19, 29, 32, 37, 39, 43, 48, 63, 83, 84, 92, 98, 100, 107, 151, 162, 164, 169
Virginia Electric and Power Company, 10

W

Waccamaw Indians, 37, 47
Waccamaw phase, 17
Wake County, N.C., 7
Wake Forest University, 70
Wakeman sites (N.C.), 111, 128, 145
Wakeman 2 site (31Wt175) (N.C.), 91, 127, 128, 129, 145

Wakeman 3 site (N.C.), 128, 136
Wakeman 4 site (N.C.), 128
Wanchese site (N.C.), 40
Ward, H. Trawick, 53, 175
Ward site (N.C.), 111, 146, 147, 150, 151, 153
Warren Wilson College, 173
Warren Wilson site (N.C.), 70-71, 88, 111, 125, 130, 137, 144, 153
Wars and warfare, 148, 151, 152. *See also* Weapons and armor
Watauga County, N.C., 91, 104, 108, 126, 127, 128, 136, 143, 146, 149, 153
Watauga River, 88, 91, 96, 97, 100,101, 103, 110-51 passim
Watercolors. *See* Art
Waterfowl. *See* Fauna
Water supply, 25, 95
Wayne County, N.C., 25
Weapons and armor, 23, 26, 33, 35, 39, 66, 125, 132, 138, 140, 142. *See also* Projectile points
Wells Creek Crater site (Tenn.), 107
Western Carolina University, 100
"Western Intrusive horizon," 23
Western United States, 64
West Virginia, 64, 101, 111, 120
White, John, 8, 42
White Court site (N.C.), 39
White Oak ceramics, 48
White Oak River, 48
Whitewater River, 96, 97
Wilbanks culture, 147, 148, 150
Wildlife. *See* Fauna
Wilkes County, N.C., 100
Willey, Gordon R., 16, 18
Williams, Talcott, 7
Williamson site (N.C.), 21

Windy Ridge site (S.C.), 101
Winston, Sanford, 166
Winston-Salem, N.C., 166
Wisconsin glacial period, 5, 108
Wissler, Clark, 167
Woodland period
  and Algonkians, 22
  burials during, 173
  ceramics from, 10, 28, 29, 48, 61, 70, 98, 131, 132, 134, 135, 137, 141, 147
  in Coastal Plain, 16, 17, 18, 20, 22, 24, 25, 27-49, 50, 173
  in Kentucky, 129
  in Mountain region, 98, 104, 113, 125, 130, 131-42
  in Piedmont, 10, 48, 61-63, 66, 69, 70-76, 78
  in southeastern U.S., 136, 137
  late unnamed phase of, 142
  projectile points from, 121. *See also* specific types and phase names
Woodlands culture. *See* Eastern Woodlands culture
Woods. *See* Forests
Works Projects Administration (WPA), 98, 169, 171, 172
World War II, 9, 58, 98, 169, 172
WPA, 98, 169, 171, 172
Wyanoke Indians, 11

Y

Yadkin
  ceramics, 61, 72
  projectile points, 62, 72
Yadkin River, 54, 55, 57, 67, 70, 71, 72, 96, 97, 164, 165, 170
Yancey County, N.C., 110, 112